Praise for *Life Lessons from the Amazon*

"*Fascinating insights i...*"
Ross Edgley, extr...

"*A book with the ...*"
Helen Skelton, adv... ...presenter

"*Brave, strong and determined female adventurers.*"
Paul Chekema, leader of Masakenari

"*A remarkable journey.*"
Ed Stafford, explorer and the first person
to walk the length of the Amazon River

"*A wonderful read, exhilarating from start to finish. Pip shares
her unique knowledge of this jungle frontier and takes us
on a journey of discovery through some of the harshest
terrain on earth. An incredible adventure.*"
Levison Wood, explorer, writer and photographer

"*A tough jungle expedition by an even tougher team.*
Life Lessons from the Amazon *is their story told
with humour, humility and honesty.*"
Ben Fogle, broadcaster, writer and adventurer

"*An absolute page-turner in which Pip shares her
fascinating inner journey including doubt, struggles and
overcoming challenges. A brilliantly candid and
thought-provoking escape to the wild.*"
Reza Pakravan, explorer, filmmaker and writer

"*Stewart is a wonderful travelling companion. Not only
does she take us through the physical and mental highs and
lows of adventure travel, she tackles head-on the ethics
and morals of modern-day travel, addressing privilege,
over-tourism and sustainability: an absolute joy.*"
Monisha Rajesh, journalist and travel writer

LIFE LESSONS FROM THE AMAZON

A Guide to Life From One
Epic Jungle Adventure

PIP STEWART

summersdale

LIFE LESSONS FROM THE AMAZON

An Hachette UK Company
www.hachette.co.uk

Summersdale Publishers Ltd
Part of Octopus Publishing Group Limited
Carmelite House
50 Victoria Embankment
LONDON
EC4Y 0DZ
UK

www.summersdale.com

Printed and bound by CPI Group (UK) Ltd, Croydon, CR0 4YY

ISBN: 978-1-78783-980-9

See page 334 for trademark details

For the people of Masakenari: Kîrwanhê.
Thank you for making this expedition possible.

Contents

Author's Note   8
Route Map   12

Part One:
Life in the Jungle
Direction   14
Patience   29
Appreciation   42
Commitment   55
Belonging   66
Problems   85
Growth   96
Storytelling   111
Mystery   124
Map of the Essequibo's
Tributaries   133
Resilience   134

Part Two:
Life on the River
Kindness   148

Slowness   162
Instinct   176
Conflict   191
Limits   213
Connection   224
Rest   235
Happiness   244
Sustainability   254
Hope   266
Gratitude   281
Love   294
Death and Life   306

Kit List   326
Acknowledgements   329
About the Author   333

Author's Note

As you navigate your own journey through life, I do hope this book may be of assistance. However, it may not be, so it's probably best to be clear about that from the get-go. What follows are reflections born from near-death experiences; literal blood, sweat and tears – and a flesh-eating parasite thrown in for good measure. Experience has been my greatest teacher and I hope to share some of the lessons I've learned. However, take these words with a pinch of salt; they are not a "quick fix" to achieve happiness, nor would I want them to be. Life is beautifully messy and striving for something other than that will always be like paddling upstream.

I am not sure the term "explorer" has much credence in modern life. However, I think a desire to explore lurks deep within some of us – that alluring pull to understand what exists beyond our horizons. It's partly why I found myself embarking on a life-changing river journey, joining a multinational team and attempting a world-first source-to-sea kayak expedition. The siren song of adventure would lead us up mountains and through dense jungle, before depositing us at the mouth of an ocean. The river offered us a chance to deepen our understanding of ourselves and the world around us; our journey would be an exploration of life.

I'd ventured into the wilderness before. However, this expedition would be the most remote I'd ever been on, and my teammates and I would spend nearly three months in the rainforest in one of the most isolated and unexplored parts of the planet. The "world-first" bit wasn't what appealed; I was drawn to the opportunity to escape in this hyperconnected world. A chance to go off-grid, at least for a while. To return to a more natural way of living. To explore what really matters in life – learnings I'd love to share with you. Perhaps, ironically, much of what we discovered could have been learned from home, but then that's part of the point of this book: daily life is echoed in the extreme, and vice versa.

I often think people are either running from something, or toward something. In my case, if I'm honest, I was running from the feeling that, somehow, I wasn't making the most of my life. A fear of not fully living. In this busy, fast-paced world it's easy to feel overwhelmed – I know I do. Fear propels me, and it's why I found myself flying out to paddle the 1,014 kilometres of Guyana's Essequibo River. I hope the following pages will offer insights for anyone who has ever felt the same and help on your own journey through life – ideally without a flesh-eating parasite in tow.

We knew this journey was going to be difficult and potentially life-threatening. What I hadn't anticipated was how being hunted by caimans or having a jaguar prowl through our camp would make me reconsider how I use technology. I could never have imagined that a hummingbird would change my perspective on criticism and happiness or that an ant would tutor me in appreciation. As such, our expedition went far beyond a physical one. It often became a mental exercise in how to become more loving and accepting, as well as in how to handle fear, self-doubt and extreme distress.

These are all learnings I still use today, and they're the basis for this book. Where needed, a few names and details have been changed to protect people's identities. Each chapter starts with a reflection that came up for us during the expedition – a "life lesson". I've then shared the stories that led me to those thoughts, so that, when you need to, you can flick to the start of the chapter that most resonates – whether it's about being able to handle more than you think you can (even if it doesn't always feel like that) or about how to deal with the crazy thoughts your brain comes up with at 3 a.m.

It's also key to acknowledge that adventure travel is a privilege that many of us have access to purely through an accident of birth. This is why the author fee from this book is going to be shared between the community of Masakenari – without whom this trip and these words would not have been possible – and the Drugs for Neglected Diseases *initiative* (DND*i*), which works tirelessly to find cures for illnesses that impact some of the world's poorest and most remote communities.

Ultimately, we are all trying to find our way in the world. You're the only person who knows what the best life for you looks like: find what works. Discard the rest. I am not a trained therapist, medical practitioner, psychologist or soothsayer. I am a hypocritical idealist who has made many cock-ups and taken wrong turns in life, and is likely to do so again. I am working on having the humility to acknowledge when I'm wrong and the courage to improve. This book is written from my perspective, and with that comes my inability to see my own blind spots. Apologies in advance. However, for all our individual quirks and self-doubt, I truly believe everyone can teach you something. This book may not change your life, but I do hope it helps you along the path you choose to tread...

Pip x

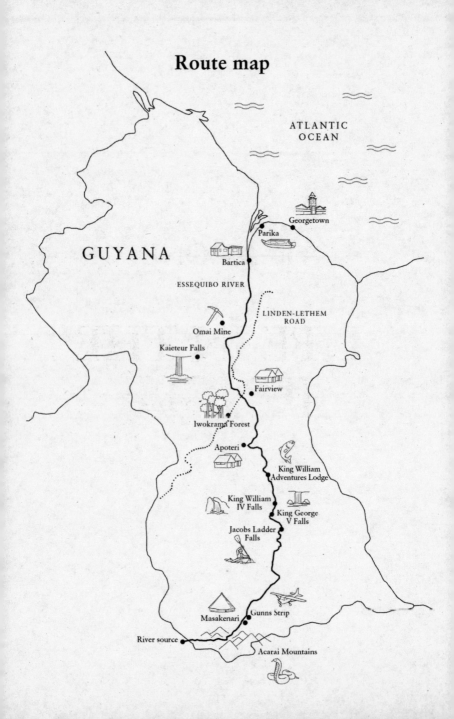

PART ONE

LIFE IN THE JUNGLE

Direction

(noun): a course along which someone or something moves.

How do you shape the most fulfilling life possible? It's a question I've pondered a lot over the last few years. If you're unsure about where you're trying to get to or what you want out of life, it's a question that can feel massively overwhelming. Perhaps I've spent too long around rivers, but the clay found in them has helped me to develop a weird visual to deal with a lack of direction: I think of life as pottery.

We all start with a lump of clay and – regardless of how much we have, its consistency or type – we all have the ability to shape something out of it. Whenever I feel out of my depth about where I'm going or what I'm doing, I always try to remind myself: *Don't worry! I'm still shaping my pot; I just don't know what it's going to look like yet.* We might not be sure what the artistic direction of our masterpiece will be, but the key is in showing up to the potter's wheel and giving it a whirl. If we get our hands dirty and attempt to shape the clay in some way, then at least we have created something. The jungle showed me that even if you have a plan in life, you need to be flexible. However much you try, your pot might look squiffy, have a wonky handle or end up a different shape than you expected. Embrace these things as part of your story, and don't let them throw you.

Thorough preparation is a good way to arm yourself against a change of plan, and will stand you in good stead whether your goal is to kayak down a river or deliver a presentation at work. First, figure out everything you might need for the undertaking, practise the skills you require, ask for help from those with more experience and check that your plan makes sense. Think about your physical and mental prep; what's your backup if it all goes wrong? Work through these scenarios in your brain and then factor in the unexpected. If you do so, you're less likely to get flustered when something does threaten to change the shape of your pot – which will probably happen, because that's life.

Changing direction in life – whether this is taking up something new, starting or ending relationships, moving, or having an honest conversation – is scary. For many of us it's bravery in action, as we must acknowledge our fears and the stress they bring. In some ways our fear acts as a barometer, showing us the size of our challenge and how much we have to do to reach our goal. But, if you do decide you want it, how do you push through that feeling?

There might not be an answer other than to just accept it. I took the fear with me to the jungle. I kept my hands, however shaky, on the potter's wheel. Yet, for all the angst, a larger dread lay underneath. It propelled me in the direction I knew, deep down, I wanted to go. It was a simple question that you may find useful, too: what would happen if I didn't go for it?

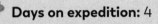

Days on expedition: 4

Location: heading upstream of the Essequibo River, south of Masakenari

Status: bricking it

I wish I could say I took to life in the jungle like a duck to water but, truthfully, it took me a little while to get used to it.

"Watch out for the bamboo…" Nereus Chekema warned as I picked up what I thought was dead wood for the fire. "It's like a bomb."

He said it just as I'd placed the sticks on the flames. Too late – the bamboo was alight. I beat a hasty retreat from the fire, bracing myself for an explosion. When I realized that a Hollywood-esque *boom* hadn't yet catapulted me from the camp, I tentatively turned around. My teammates hadn't moved from their positions around the fire and were looking amused. The burning bamboo suddenly sprang into action: a wheezing noise followed by a short, sharp "pop". It turned out it was more of a firecracker than a bomb.

I breathed a sigh of relief and tried to style out my overreaction by pretending I was on the way to get something from a bag next to my hammock. Judging by the laughing I heard as I rummaged around in one of my large dry bags, I'm not sure I pulled it off. On the plus side, I hadn't blown up myself – or my teammates – so I took that as a win. We'd survived, for now at least.

"You're such a klutz, Pip," shouted my friend Laura from around the campfire, teasingly.

"Well, you invited me along. I hold you entirely responsible," I shot back, smiling.

I'm pretty certain everybody has a friend that gets them into trouble. You know the sort: the person who convinces you that one last drink on an already boozy night is a good idea or that you're entirely capable of running a marathon in three weeks with zero training. I have a friend like this. Her name is Laura Bingham.

Laura doesn't do things by halves. It's fair to say she is one of the most driven people I've ever met. Over the years Laura has sailed across the Atlantic and cycled across South America, with no money, to raise funds and awareness for Operation South America, a children's charity in Paraguay. She's also got a sharp sense of humour and an uncanny ability to persuade people to do things – which is perhaps how we became friends. I found myself offering to help change her baby's dirty nappy at Campfire, an adventure festival we were both speaking at less than a year before.

In all honesty, I'd rather change a nappy than engage in small talk. I'm not very good at it and I'd rather know the content of your soul than bore you to death with chat about the weather. On this particular occasion I chose to get stuck into the contents of her son Ran's nappy. Laura's soul would have to wait. Getting to know each other over poo – particularly yellow poo, if I remember correctly – perhaps wasn't the most promising start to a friendship, but it created an immediate bond between us.

Two months later, I received a call from her just after lunch, while I was sitting at my desk at Red Bull, where I was working as their Adventure Editor. I didn't make a note of the conversation, so forgive the creative licence, but I am pretty sure it went something along the lines of:

Laura: "How do you feel about attempting a world-first expedition through the Guiana Shield – 'the greenhouse of the world' – and part of the larger Amazon biome? Paddling down the Essequibo, Guyana's largest river, through dense rainforest, from source to sea? Around three months? We will need to hike to the source, which is exceptionally mountainous and located in the Acarai Mountains, but we should be physically fit enough after the training. Oh, and it's a fairly quick turnaround – we're talking in eight months' time…"

Me: "Floating down a river, watching wildlife, with a piña colada in hand, no experience required? Yes, brilliant. Sign me up!"

I am not a natural office person. In fact, 20 minutes doesn't go by without me standing up, pacing the room or making at least one cup of tea. It's not that I'm avoiding work (well, not most of the time). Movement just helps my mind. Clearly, on the day Laura called, I had been sitting down for far too long and my brain had addled. However, our conversation made me realize that I was craving a new direction in life.

Set your compass in the rough direction you want to travel

It was only when I had put down the phone to Laura and called my partner Charlie that the reality of what I'd just agreed to began to sink in.

"You hate kayaking," Charlie reminded me when I started to explain the plan. "I remember you saying, when you tried it in New Zealand, that it was – and I quote – 'a rubbish sport, and I can't understand why anyone does it', and that your shoulders felt like they were on fire."

It was also around this time that words from my conversation with Laura, such as "caiman", "piranha", "machete", "waterfalls" and "jungle training", began to emerge through a post-lunch-induced brain fog.

"Who else is on board?" Charlie asked.

"Laura's best friend – Ness Knight. You know, the one I have a girl crush on, the woman who was the first female to swim the River Thames."

I'd never actually met Ness, but if she was anything like how she came across on social media, I knew I'd like her.

"So, in summary," Charlie clarified, "in eight months' time you're planning on kayaking a river through the rainforest with two women – one of whom you've only recently met and the other you don't know at all – for three months, and you don't currently know how to kayak, let alone take on white water. Good luck!"

Thankfully, Charlie – my partner of 12 years – is both used to, and supportive of, the adventures I get myself into. Together we cycled home from Asia, where we'd been living for five years, to London: a journey that took us 13 months and through 24 countries. I hadn't had much experience when we set off. I'd only ever really cycled around in a city, while I was at uni, so I was hardly a pro athlete. In fact, the whole journey nearly ended in disaster when, three weeks in, at the sight of our first small incline (I can barely call it a hill), I threw an absolute tantrum, flung my heavily loaded bike to the ground and declared that Charlie had picked the wrong woman. I wasn't capable of this and there was no way I was continuing either with the journey or the relationship. The reality of the situation was that I was embarrassed: I was unfit. I'd told my friends and family that I was going to "cycle halfway around the world" and, when push came to shove, my legs burned, my chest wheezed and my bloody inner critic set in.

Don't let your inner critic take over (it will try)

To his credit, Charlie handled my snot-filled meltdown brilliantly. After nearly three hours (yes, three!) of trying to calm me down on a Malaysian side road, he offered to take me to the nearest airport, although we had no option but to cycle there. He then said something to me that I've never forgotten and have repeated to myself on every subsequent journey: "Pip, these are not physical journeys; they are mental ones."

Something switched in me that day. I knew that if I could spend 8 hours a day at work, I could spend 8 hours a day on a bike. I realized that if I could quieten my inner critic that told me I was "too slow, too unfit, too fat, too much of this and not enough of that" then perhaps, just perhaps, I could do what I knew deep down I really wanted to. After 13 months, a few days before Christmas Day 2014, we cycled to Big Ben in London, where our family and friends were waiting with banners of congratulations. We'd done it. Through tears of joy, it dawned on me that we'd experienced a journey of over 10,000 miles that would stay with us forever; a journey that was possible because I'd pushed through my own fear and self-doubt.

Break your goal into smaller chunks and work on what you can control

I didn't overcome fear on that expedition; I just learned to live with it. I began to realize that whenever I made a decision that would alter the path I was travelling on – be this a massive expedition, or a change in a job, a relationship or a flat – uncomfortable feelings would always arise. You too may find that, at times of upheaval, fear will often pop up and announce that it has come to move in with you for a while. It's a blooming annoying housemate but, in a sense, it shows we're alive, and are fully functioning humans with the prerequisite insecurities that ultimately serve to keep us safe and out of trouble.

Even though fear had taken up residence in my brain since signing up to the kayak expedition, I focused on what I could control. I'm not a natural planner, but fear propelled me to take action. For an expedition of this magnitude, we needed to plan and prepare properly. In the build-up to the trip,

Laura had done the bulk of the heavy lifting when it came to organization.

First up, we needed permission for our journey. The headwaters of the Essequibo and the surrounding 625,000-hectare area of pristine forest are protected by the indigenous people of the community of Masakenari. We needed their authorization to enter for the expedition. Their village is the closest settlement to the river's source and it was the place where we were planning on starting our paddle. We connected over Facebook to Paul Chekema, the leader of the village (known as the Toshao) and used fixers on the ground in the capital Georgetown.

We also had the backing of the then First Lady of Guyana, Sandra Granger. She had heard about our trip and said it was a great thing for young women to see other women embarking on such "out-of-the-box" adventures. She even agreed to be a patron of our journey – and asked our fixers to pass on the message that we were to put every possible safety procedure in place, as the Essequibo was the country's biggest and mightiest river. As well as highlighting possibilities for women in adventure, both in Guyana and elsewhere, the joint expedition also offered opportunities to showcase, explore and document the incredible natural beauty of the nation and its rainforest. The country is one of South America's most heavily forested and has one of the world's most flourishing jungles. The Tourism Authority asked us to share with them, on our return, our thoughts and insights about what we witnessed on the journey.

Once we were granted the necessary permits from the village, as well as from the Ministry of Indigenous Peoples' Affairs and the Protected Areas Commission, we were left with the small matter of working out how to pay for the expedition. Like many large-scale projects, unless you're utterly minted, you need to find sponsorship. Given the remote nature and inaccessibility of the trip, Laura was looking to find around £30,000. This would be used to cover the cost of flights – both to and from Guyana, and internally – guiding fees, food en route and hotels in Georgetown, as well as any kit that we couldn't get sponsored. Often, getting these trips off the ground is as hard, if not harder, than the actual journey. Our success in this instance was down to Laura; she produced a stellar pitch document, outlining who we were, what we were doing and what companies could expect in return for their support (e.g. social media posts, their logos on our boats, and talks and blog posts that we'd produce for them when we returned).

Then there was the mind-boggling task of organizing logistics: arranging flights, internationally and locally, getting the right travel jabs, learning about navigation and remote, emergency medicine, preparing our kit, and figuring out how much food we'd need. There was also the small matter of actually getting fit enough to manage the journey. The list of things to do seemed endless. Laura farmed out a few tasks to Ness and me but, for the most part, she pulled the whole thing together. How she managed to do it while looking after a young baby is beyond me.

I realized how incredibly driven she could be when Ness and I went to stay with her around Christmastime to do some kayak and jungle training. Thankfully, Ness was just as I imagined her to be: ballsy, charming and up for a laugh. The expedition prep also meant I got to know Laura's husband, Ed Stafford, better. Ed was the first person to walk the length of the Amazon River. Following such an incredible feat, he made a TV career out of adventure and one journey took him to Guyana. Apparently, after this trip he told Laura that the rainforest there was like nothing he'd ever seen – "Disneyland for animals" was how she described it to me. His description of how remote the Essequibo was planted a seed in Laura's brain. The comment had clearly taken root, as the idea turned from concept to reality. Slowly, step after step, it morphed into our source-to-sea expedition.

Having settled into my room at their house in Leicestershire, I pottered down to the kitchen, where Ed was fixing us up a cup of coffee with a dollop of coconut cream.

"I'm on a keto diet," he said, "trying to get in shape for *First Man Out*." His new series involved pitting himself against other world survival experts in a race to get out of hostile environments. It was during his break from filming that we were attempting the expedition, so that he could look after Ran.

Given that Ed was both a world expert in jungle survival and Laura's husband, I asked him how the preparation had been going since we last spoke.

"I don't know. She won't let me look at it," he said, shrugging and handing me a surprisingly punchy coffee.

"Damn right," said Laura, coming through the kitchen door after having fed the chickens in the garden. Winston and Maggie, their two large, beautiful – but seriously slobbery – Newfoundland dogs, were in tow. "Although I have said he can help us with a jungle survival lesson." She added, "You get used to the dribble," as one of the dogs made its way straight to my groin. A massive drool patch now covered my crotch.

"Before we get cracking with the lesson, we've got you some presents," said Ed, as Laura disappeared off to get them. "You'll need them where you're going."

"Aw, mate, that's so kind of you guys," said Ness, when Laura returned and handed over two parcels. I reiterated the sentiment.

We opened a small box first: an electronic Casio watch from Laura.

"It's not sponsored or anything," she said. "They're not expensive but they're waterproof and the light function is super useful. I love mine and my bridesmaids even had to force me to take it off for my wedding."

Ed then handed us both a long, thin parcel. "Careful how you open it."

Ness and I slowly unwrapped a machete in a leather sheath.

"I picked these up in Brazil. I used the same for the Amazon. Hopefully, they won't let you down."

The gifts spoke to the very generous and thoughtful nature of the couple.

"Right, let's get cracking!" said Ed, once we'd thanked them again. We were going to disappear into the woods at the end of their garden to string up hammocks and tarps, learn how to find material to light a fire in the jungle, and practise using our new machetes.

"Not you, Winston," said Laura, shoving the dog back into the kitchen. "We'll be back soon."

That training day seemed like a world away, as I stood in the middle of the rainforest in Guyana, fiddling around in my hammock. It felt as if a million cicadas were buzzing and clicking around the canopy. I knew we had done all we could in the build-up to the trip. Our team had trained through the cold winter days. We asked for assistance from the outdoors community and received more than we ever could have anticipated, including fitness training, survival tips and help with analyzing topographical maps to gauge how big the rapids might be. But I'd still been nervous when getting on the flight to Guyana, as this was the most dangerous journey of our lives to date. Fear left me acting in peculiar ways.

Before we left, I was having nightmares and lashing out at the people I loved the most. I felt as if I had been put in a washing machine and churned around. Matters didn't improve when we visited the helicopter rescue team in Georgetown, who had agreed to ensure that a medical evacuation plane would be on standby during the expedition. As we were shown around the chopper they'd use in an emergency, we were told that rescue was entirely possible but there were a few issues. One: they didn't currently have a winch operator in the country. Two: they wouldn't fly at night. And three (the final nail in the coffin, so to speak): in order to land, they'd need either a sandbank or an area slightly larger than the chopper's rotor blades and tail. Given that we were heading to dense primary rainforest, the subtext was quite clear: get into trouble deep in the jungle and you're stuffed.

Thankfully, we weren't entirely on our own. After leaving Georgetown, we headed in a small chartered plane to the village of Masakenari, where we would meet our guides from the Waî Waî community, who would help us on our journey to the Acarai Mountains. This mountain range also serves as the modern border between southern Guyana and northern Brazil, and we were hoping to find the source of the river there. We expected the journey to the source to take a few weeks and then we would begin our paddle to the Atlantic Ocean. As the plane took off, I saw the ocean stretch before the capital city. Only around 800,000 people live in Guyana – a country of a similar size to Britain – and 90 per cent live along the northern coast we were flying over. The plane turned and headed to Guyana's interior.

I spent a good proportion of the three-hour plane ride watching the numerous waterways winding through the lush green terrain beneath us. To think we would spend months paddling back was mind-blowing. Looking down at the rivers beneath, I could understand why Guyana is an Amerindian word for "land of many waters". For better or for worse, in so many ways, water links us all.

Guyana is one of the greenest and most forested places on Earth and, although it is naturally resource-rich, it has historically been one of South America's poorest countries. It has had a turbulent history: it was colonized by the Dutch and later the British – in 1814 it became known as British Guiana – until independence was declared in 1966. Venezuela and Guyana are still locked in a long-standing border dispute over the territory to the west of the Essequibo, which makes up a large proportion of Guyana's current land mass. The impact of the centuries-old division of land by Spain, the Netherlands and the United Kingdom can still be felt today, as Venezuela refuses to acknowledge the border. Similarly, the diversity of Guyana's current population – indigenous Amerindian, African, Indian, Chinese, Portuguese and other Europeans – has its roots in colonial rule, the forcible moving of people across the globe for slavery and indenture, and a colonial plantation labour economy that helped fuel an empire.

I peered out the window, at the very waterways that gave life to the British Empire. Demerara sugar comes from the river of the same name. Rubber and gold, and other precious metals, flowed from Guyana's rivers into oceans and onto British shores. We had yet to realize it, but the twists and turns of our journey down the Essequibo River would reveal some uncomfortable truths about life past and present.

Now, fully immersed in the jungle, I stood by my hammock and looked up at my tarp. Small spiders seemed to be building a home for the night there, too. *At least my mosquito net should protect me*, I thought. After a few nights in the jungle, the journey had gone from being theoretical and conceptual to being very, very real. The fear was still there but I was getting more comfortable with it. I reminded myself that I just had to implement what I already knew and listen to what our Waî Waî guides were teaching us. We had brought with us a Garmin inReach Explorer for sending and receiving messages, as well as for navigation.

We also had a satellite phone for emergencies and a BGAN – a Broadband Global Area Network – a nifty device that provided broadband if there was enough clear sky for us to point it toward. We also had our mobiles and a generator to charge electronics. However, despite safety precautions, we knew there was little chance of rescue if something went wrong on this section of the journey, as it was so remote. We had to rely on each other.

I looked over my shoulder at the team gathered around the fire. Ness and Laura were chatting away to Cemci Suse, the oldest and most experienced member of the group. Next to him was his 16-year-old grandson, Nigel Issacs. It was his first time joining an expedition and you could tell he was excited. He'd made me chuckle earlier in the day; he shared that when the village was told of our expedition, he'd assumed we'd be men, so he was quite surprised to see three women step out of the plane.

I watched as a bright orange firefly flew past his face, perilously close to the fire and into tomorrow's potential breakfast: armadillo.

Brothers Jackson and Aaron Marawanaru were checking on how it was cooking. The armadillo had been shot with a bow and arrow earlier in the day and was now in halves, roasting. From where I was standing, I could see pools of blood and juices collecting in its cavities. Jackson had mentioned that armadillo usually takes a while to cook but should be ready by the morning. It was also, apparently, a highly unusual catch, as armadillos tend to clock up around 16 hours of sleep a day. This one had been spotted running out of its burrow and we were told that it had probably been under attack from a jaguar – a theory made even more likely when Cemci pointed out some fresh, distinctly cat-like paw prints on the sandy riverbank near where we'd set up our camp.

I rejoined the campfire in time to hear Nereus, the son of the village Toshao, deliver some advice in the eventuality we ever did encounter a jaguar.

"Don't run away or it will get you. Instead, take out your machete and get ready to fight," he cautioned. It's fair to say, as far as bedtime stories go, I wasn't sitting comfortably for this one. The thought of encountering a jaguar, or "tigers" as our guides referred to them, wasn't exactly filling me with joy. It's not quite as relaxing as counting sheep, that's for sure.

"Oh, and always take your machete with you if you go to defecate alone," he added.

"Are you ever scared of the jungle?" I asked him.

"No, the jungle is my home. I've been going into the forest on my own since I was 14 or 15," he said, staring at the stack of bamboo that I had mistaken for dead wood. Nereus gestured to it.

"When I was little, my grandfather burned bamboo and smeared the ash on my face. He told me that tigers can't get through bamboo, so it will protect me. He's passed away now, so unfortunately my younger brother didn't get the ceremony. My grandfather loved the jungle. He taught me a lot."

The embers dimmed to ash and the team slunk off to bed. The next few weeks, as we made our way to the source, were going to involve very hard, physical labour. Any sleep we could get was precious. In the brief period we'd been in the jungle, I had learned not to panic if I heard a low-pitched, other-worldly growl; it was likely just a howler monkey, not a sign of impending death and doom. That being said, I looked at the fire and pondered tales of jaguar. I wondered about retrieving the ash from the now exploded bamboo – I would happily receive all the protection I could get for this journey. As fate would have it, we were going to need it.

Patience

(noun): the capacity to accept or tolerate delay, problems or suffering, without becoming annoyed or anxious.

We let a flower blossom in its own time, yet we don't often seem to extend the same patience to ourselves. We feel so much pressure to achieve instantaneous results – be these mental, physical or material – and much of modern culture is geared toward quick fixes, fast delivery and overnight transformations.

In a world that encourages everything to be done as quickly as possible, I think there's much to be said for positioning yourself in the direction you want to go and then taking your foot off the gas (a little bit at least), allowing for setbacks and giving yourself permission to let things unfold in due course. Changing ingrained habits takes time and patience; you can't expect to be transformed immediately, so have a sense of humour about it. Reflection is a key part of the process, too. Take time to look back – in a week, a month or a year – as this will help you to appreciate the journey you've been on already. This is why at the end of each day in the jungle I'd ask my teammates for their highlights and thoughts. Taking that moment to pause, reflect and learn opened up so many conversations and informed many of the reflections in this book.

There's tremendous power in making small, daily changes to your habits. Over time, results will come. Don't be disheartened if the "New Year, New You" bollocks doesn't materialize in one month or even 12. We tend to overestimate how much we can achieve in a year but underestimate how much we can achieve in a decade. Results born from effort are worth the wait. Removing that time pressure from yourself to achieve everything right now might even allow you to enjoy the journey that little bit more.

Days on expedition: 14

Location: the Sipu River, a tributary of the Essequibo

Status: barred from entry

As far as Valentine's Days go, this was certainly one to remember. I've never been a fan of the occasion, since I find it somewhat hollow being guilt-tripped into buying overpriced set menus, flowers, chocolates or gifts in order to show your love. I will salute Ed, however, who managed to pull off a truly romantic gesture. Before we left the UK, he'd asked me to smuggle both a Valentine's Day card and a birthday card for Laura. After she'd disappeared into the jungle for a morning pee I rushed over to her hammock and popped the card in it. The look of surprise and happiness on her face when she returned was heart-warming. The gesture was about the most romantic thing that happened that day, unless your idea of romance is spending hours – sweaty, odorous and covered in insect bites – in a dugout canoe.

"This is not Valentine's Day! This is obstacle day," remarked Jackson when we hit yet another river block. A fallen tree, swollen with water, lay across our path. There is a distinct smell to wet, rotting wood and, let's just say, it's not a scent you'd use to get yourself in the mood for love.

We'd been travelling for two weeks and were making our way up the Sipu River, a tributary of the Essequibo and the waterway we were following to its source. The narrowing river, and the merging of water and trees – creating an increasingly dark green sky above us – had thrown up a fair few problems for the team. It felt like we were slowly being sucked into the rainforest.

We were travelling in two traditional dugout canoes, each made from large, hollowed-out tree trunks. Considering there were four of us in each canoe – plus a generator, all our food supplies, medical kit, a chainsaw, an axe, sat phones and general equipment for life in the jungle – they were surprisingly roomy. The craftsmanship was beautiful, although they did require a fair bit of maintenance; a few leaks were beginning to appear at the base, as evidenced by our wet shoes. I made a mental note to dry them out by the fire that evening.

Ness, Laura and I had brought out two pairs each: one lightweight that was suitable for paddling and the other a leather jungle boot designed for life under the canopy. Our guides had asked us to bring wellies out for them for the trip, which they now wore when they weren't using flip-flops. On the subject of jungle attire, Laura had made me laugh when she'd appeared a few days earlier wearing a long-sleeved floral top and Ed's oversized jungle trousers.

"I had so much to organize in the run-up to the trip, my outfit choices weren't top of the priority list," she said, as Ness and I ribbed her for wearing a shirt that screamed: "Eat me now, insects of the jungle!"

"Admittedly, it probably isn't the best pattern, but at least it keeps the sun off. I also brought a skirt to change into in the evenings," she added, smiling.

"You're joking, right?" said Ness.

"No, really, I have. It will keep me cool and it's good for aeration."

I had to hand it to Laura: it wasn't packing advice you'd find on any websites, but I'd come to learn she did things her own way. Most of the time this paid off although I was still unconvinced by the floral shirt...

Some very useful bits of kit were the outboard engines attached to the backs of the canoes, which we had hoped would take some of the strain out of our journey toward the source. We planned to use these engines to power upstream for as long as the fuel would last, and only switch to paddle power when the water became too shallow. At least, that was the plan. But given the size of the rotting tree currently in front of us, I began to wonder if we'd ever even make it *up*stream, let alone down.

"Obstacle number one hundred and one," said Laura, who had been keeping a log of everything blocking our path.

"Technically, it's one hundred," corrected Ness. "I don't think we can count that vine we just chopped down."

Navigating up the river had become a puzzle, an exercise in pitting tools against obstacles. Sometimes it would be the chainsaw. Others the machete. Sometimes the best thing was good old-fashioned body weight: jumping up and down on a log, in order to create enough depth for the heavy canoes to be pushed and hauled over the top. The worst instances by

Setbacks will always occur, so figure out how to overcome them

far were when there was just enough space to squeeze under a log. This involved us lying as flat as we could in the canoe and sliding underneath. Inevitably, we'd pick up a fair few unwanted stowaways in the process. It wasn't uncommon to find spiders as large as our hands in the boat. Not what you want to be eyeballing when lying flat on your back, under a log, in a wet dugout canoe.

"A chainsaw for this one," Jackson said, looking at the log. The requested tool was duly passed along the canoe. Jackson lowered himself into the now waist-high water and started it up. The engine roared to life, sawdust flying all over the place and the residue clinging to his face. Two cuts at different angles were made into the wood.

"These cuts help to stop the chainsaw jamming," Cemci explained.

This was stage one of clearing the obstacle. We waited while Jackson sliced away. The two dugouts were lined up next to each other and I found myself sat next to Nereus in the other boat. We began discussing the rivers of Guyana.

"Where the Essequibo split back there, if you take the other route you end up in Brazil. That's the way I go to see my aunt and uncle." As well as Guyana's Waî Waî community north of the Acarai Mountains, a larger number of Waî Waî people also live south of the mountains in Brazil. They remain connected to each other via historic family ties.

"Would you ever leave Masakenari?" I asked Nereus.

I got the impression it wasn't a straightforward question. He told me that his sister, Bernicia, lives in Georgetown and that there is little work in the village. He shared that he'd thought about moving elsewhere to set up a business – he'd even considered buying a dredger to mine, but he didn't think there would be much money in it. Seeing that Jackson had completed the cuts required for the first stage of "Operation Sink the Log", he then made his way along the canoe to the tree.

Stage two of clearing the obstacle involved body weight. As many people as was deemed safe climbed onto the log and started jumping up and down. As this was obstacle 100, we thought it was only right to commemorate the occasion, and "Eye of the Tiger" was belted out on the small portable speaker that Laura had brought with her. I watched as Ness and Laura jumped and squatted on the log in time to the beat. Finally, it sank into the river, although not fully. Thankfully, we had the precious centimetres needed for the canoes to pass – albeit with the help of shoves from those in the water and some bobsleigh-style push-starts from those of us who were still in the boat, as we passed over the top of the log. Ness and Laura, already wet and bobbing about in the river, proceeded to have a mini water fight.

Jackson climbed into the canoe and emptied his welly boot full of water back into the Essequibo.

"F-ing obstacles!" he said, cursing the log. "Although I thought that was serious fun," he added as he put his now damp welly back on. "I've never seen foreigners playing in the water. This is amazing for me."

It's remarkable how quickly people adjust to the circumstances they find themselves in. It had taken us just a few days to go from watching open-mouthed as Nereus stood at the end of the canoe's narrow tip, brandishing a chainsaw, to jumping in with our machetes and getting involved – albeit with some guidance, initially. Our life choices for the day now consisted of staying in the boat and taking on spiders and scorpions when going under logs or getting into the water and taking on caimans and piranhas.

Allow time to adjust to new habits and routines

"It's amazing to see you using the machete, but I think you need more practice," Jackson told me. "When we saw you cutting, we thought you might make a mistake. Your positioning needs work. I taught my son when he was six. He's now seven and he can chop wood," he shared proudly over a fish dinner that evening. Apparently, if cutting overhead, you should always do so in a forward motion, in case the blade drops and lands on you.

"I like how you can light a fire without help. I was watching you, thinking you were going to ask for help, but you didn't…" Jackson continued, clearly in a bid not to dampen our enthusiasm entirely. "And seeing Ness finally break a tree was my highlight today."

"Ha ha, yes, I must have tried cutting that tree about thirty times." Ness recounted her battle with the log to the rest of us.

"Jackson was chopping one side while I tackled the other and, after what seemed like ages, it *finally* gave."

Time and patience, I reminded myself. You'll get there in the end.

Are you as patient with yourself as you are with others?

It's fair to say I didn't have the most auspicious start to learning to kayak. I struggle with any task involving spatial awareness. I am also unbelievably clumsy. If you ever want a good laugh, watch me try to parallel park. Therefore, learning how to turn a kayak was somewhat more complicated than it really should have been. We began our training in October of 2017, six months before we were due to set off. Chris Murnin, of the Leicester Outdoor Pursuits Centre, took us through the basics of learning to kayak. Thankfully, the man has the patience of a saint, and he explained over and over again how to manoeuvre a boat and what an efficient paddle stroke looked like. Laura and Ness seemed to pick it up immediately, which didn't exactly stop me from feeling like the weakest link in the team. (At this point, I should also point out that Laura and Ness are both tall, beautiful specimens of humans, who wouldn't look out of place on a catwalk. I am 1.6 metres tall and like to eat cake.)

Once we'd nailed the basics, pro kayakers David Bain and his partner, Gabi Ridge, helped us to familiarize ourselves with white water on Wales's River Dee. We also enlisted in a white-water training course with the English Canoe Symposium. Let's just say I swam more than the others, but in doing so I learned some valuable lessons.

In many ways, training in the cold and rainy UK over the winter months was about as far away as you could get from paddling in the hot and humid jungle. However, it was where I stumbled across the mantra: "Focus on the rock if you want to hit the rock." It turns out that where your focus goes, so too does your boat.

Focus on the rock if you want to hit the rock

While getting to grips with the basics of white water, we were taken down a gentle route. We'd scouted it from the riverbank before running it. A rather large rock jutted out of the river, and fast-flowing water rushed either side of it. Essentially, all we had to do was pick a channel, either left or right, and avoid hitting the rock in the middle. Easy, right?

The problem was, as I got in my boat, I kept repeating to myself: "I must not hit the rock." Predictably, I found myself pressed up against it, with water pouring into my heavy boat that wasn't self-bailing. It was filling with water at such a rate that meant I could no longer flip it. I could feel the raw power of the river bearing down on me. To both my dismay and eventual relief, our instructor came to rescue me and talked me through how to deal with a capsize situation. To add insult to injury, I was soaked. I'd borrowed a male drysuit and realized I hadn't properly done it up in the crotch area (in my defence, I don't have a penis, so a penis flap – not the technical term – wasn't an obvious place to check). When I finally flopped back into my boat, I was cold, bedraggled and deflated.

"Yes, mate!" Ness exclaimed when I finally made it to where she and Laura were waiting downstream. "That was awesome."

I was somewhat bemused by the reaction.

"At least we know what to do if we do capsize," Laura clarified.

From that moment on, I knew that the team would hold together well in the jungle. I'd also learned that there was no use in comparing myself. It might take me longer to get there, but with time, effort, humour and teamwork, I'd arrive in the end: focus on your path, not the rock, and have patience.

Even if you mess up a few times along the way, you'll be a step closer to where you want to be.

Start small and build up   It was a lesson I would be able to put into practice when trying to learn a pastime that has never appealed: fishing. In normal life, if I was after a bit of peace and quiet, I'd prefer to just sit by a river rather than deal with all the faff and set-up of dangling a line in the water. But, in fairness, I understood the need to fish more now that our meals depended on it. We hadn't brought enough dehydrated food for every meal, since we knew we would catch fish and supplement that with rice or the traditional Amerindian staple, *farine* – a gravel-like flour made from a starchy root known as cassava. For dinner on Valentine's Day, the team were hoping to catch a particular type of fish known as the *aimara* or, more alarmingly, the wolf fish. It's how Ness, Laura and I were roped into an impromptu fishing lesson.

The *aimara* is a large, meaty freshwater fish found in many of South America's rivers. And when I say large, I mean *large*! They can grow to be around a metre long, have exceptionally sharp teeth and can top the scales at a whopping 40 kilograms. I decided not to overthink this, given that we were spending a lot more time getting in and out of the water.

I'd come across the fish a few years previously while filming *Transamazonica* with my friend Reza Pakravan – a documentary about the impacts of deforestation in Brazil and Peru. We'd learned that *aimara* are easily contaminated with the mercury used in gold mining, yet they remain a major food source for many who live along rivers. I recalled the heartbreaking tale of a young man who had told us how he'd lost his 24-year-old wife as a result of mercury poisoning.

Thankfully, that wasn't something we had to worry about – not yet at least; we were in pristine jungle, with no dredgers in sight. Finding an *aimara* would provide us with enough food for the evening.

In a change from the usual bait of rolled-up *farine*, Nereus had found an old wasp nest, which he dangled into the water. Small fish approached and were duly caught.

"We use the belly and the guts for bait. The *aimara* smell them," Nigel said, as he approached with the entrails of the smaller fish.

"My philosophy is the more fish there are out of the water, the less there are to bite me," Laura said.

Nereus twisted the entrails onto the fish hook, accidentally piercing his thumb as he did. No emotion showed on his face.

"Ow," I said, wincing. "You OK? Did that hurt?"

"Yes," he smiled. You'd have never known it.

"It's amazing how you can start off with something small and, using the right tactics, end up with bigger and bigger things," said Laura.

Bait in place, we waited. We spotted three capybaras, the largest rodent in the world, swimming in the distance. They looked like massive guinea pigs, with barrel-shaped bodies. Or, as Laura put it, little hippos. A speckled caiman was hiding a few metres away, in tree roots woven into the riverbank. Closely related to alligators, caimans are one of the planet's oldest species, believed to have evolved little over the last 200 million years. Depending on the species, they can range in size – the largest being the black caiman, which can often grow to around 5 metres. Thankfully, the one watching the proceedings was only a tiny wee thing, its orange eyes and snout inquisitively sticking out of the water.

While we waited for signs of movement on the fishing line, Cemci told us more about his community. The late 1940s and 50s had seen the arrival of American missionaries in the Essequibo area of Guyana. They'd established a permanent outpost on the banks of the river and called it Kanashen, which in Waî Waî means "God loves you here". Around the same time, many Waî Waî people from the Brazilian side of the Acarai Mountains moved to Guyana. Then, after the country declared independence in 1966, there was a period of political upheaval and Cemci shared that, in the 1970s, many Waî Waî people left for Brazil. Only five families remained in Guyana.

"Now the population is growing again. There have been six babies in the village so far this year," he said as he watched the little caiman disappear back under the water. "I heard some babies are due, too, so maybe there will be seven. There are between two hundred and fifty and three hundred people in the village, mainly Waî Waî, Wapishana or Macushi."

A pull on the line. A flurry of activity. A large fish was wrestled from the water and placed on a bed of prepared palm leaves. An *aimara* had been caught.

Nereus quickly cut a line from the jawbone along the belly and split it open. The teeth were fang-like and of varying sizes. With over 100 teeth, they have four times more than the average piranha. You could quite easily see how they'd take a chunk out of a leg. After removing the guts, Nereus took his knife up and around the gill to slice the meat, before removing the heart. It continued to beat in the palm of his hand. Ness and Laura examined it, and I was hit by a rush of emotion. Before this journey I'd never witnessed the killing of what I ate. *Should I eat the flesh if I wasn't OK with killing the source of it?* I wondered. A debate ensued and it was put to me that, in many ways, you are more respectful and mindful of what you're eating when you've taken part in the whole process. I understand this viewpoint and, to a large extent, I agree with it, but the incident made me think. I still eat meat but far, far less of it, and only if I feel my body craves it. I scooped up the gutted smaller fish, carefully trying to hold together the insides that hadn't been used as bait, and passed it to Nigel. Using the top of the machete's blade, he showed us how to scale it. Laura was already a dab hand at this, as she'd scaled and filleted a fair few fish in her journey across the Atlantic. All the pieces were then skewered and roasted on the fire.

Before dinner I took my wet jungle boots off and placed them on an upturned stick by the flames. I suspected they might end up smelling of roasting fish, but I hoped they'd at least dry out.

"Watch out for your boots, Pip," Jackson warned me, as he touched one. "They're very warm. A friend of mine once did the same thing, and they fell into the fire and burned."

I quickly retrieved them. It may have been Valentine's Day, but I didn't want to bring a new meaning to the phrase "too hot to handle". We needed boots where we were heading.

We bowed our heads in grace that evening, as we did for every meal, following the Waî Waî's Christian ritual. The tiny heart was etched in my mind.

"Today was so good," reflected Cemci. "There was no rain. The food we had was delicious. We are safe. Every day we've managed to get through the holes in the trees. Every day we move. The only thing that disappoints me is that those boys are sick."

It was more than disappointing. In an exceptionally worrying turn of events, that evening both Aaron and Nereus said they felt feverish, and were complaining of aches and pains, as well as being sensitive to light. Having witnessed Nereus place a fish hook through his thumb and not flinch, we knew it must be bad.

After digging out the extensive first aid kit we were carrying, Laura fished out rehydration salts, paracetamol and ibuprofen. We all desperately hoped it wasn't malaria. We decided the best course of action was to eat, sleep and reassess in the morning. If they weren't better, we would have to turn back. It was possible the expedition was about to end before it had even begun, but there was nothing else we could do; we just had to wait.

Appreciation

(noun): recognition and enjoyment of the good qualities of someone or something.

There is such overlooked power in focusing on the small things, in appreciating what we may have come to see as mundane. It's ironic that so many of us (myself included) feel the need to travel to experience the world, when there's so much beauty and awe to be found in our own backyard: the way weeds can weave themselves through pavement cracks or how art is etched on the underside of a leaf. I remember when one winter's night, under a full moon, I left a pint of water outside. By dawn, it had transformed; shards of ice cascaded and criss-crossed through the water like miniature suspended wands. Perhaps unremarkable, but exceptionally beautiful to me. It made me realize that, somewhere along the way, between a childhood spent digging for worms and an adulthood of paying off debt, we've lost some of the magic of life.

Exploration isn't just about travelling to far-flung corners of the world; it's about seeing the world with new eyes. Travel can give you amazing, memorable, once-in-a-lifetime experiences. However, by exploring in our daily lives – by finding and appreciating the beauty that's already there – the everyday can be transformed into an incredible adventure, too. Life layers dirt on everyone, and when it does, perhaps it's time we learn to dig for worms and try to conjure up that magic once again. Don't overlook the little things, the tiny moments that make up a day, a week, a month and, ultimately, a life. They usually turn out to be the big things, after all.

Days on expedition: 15

Location: Sipu River

Status: peeing down with rain

There's nothing like a bad night's sleep to make you appreciate a good one. This is especially so if you're sleeping in a hammock, in a downpour, in the middle of the rainforest. I say "downpour", but to get a more accurate idea of what this was like, imagine waking up at 3 a.m. to someone dumping a bucket of water over your only protection: a thin polyester tarp. (At this point you pray that when the manufacturers described the tarp as "waterproof", they really meant it.) Then picture yourself spinning around in the hammock, totally disorienting yourself in the pitch-black to the point that you no longer know where the zip to get out is. Add in so much water noise from the rain and the river that you can no longer tell which is which, or where your boat is. Finally, throw in a panic about flash floods and rising water levels, and the occasional unidentified growling noise, and you can understand why I didn't get much sleep on that particular evening.

Cemci clearly had the same worry about the rising river. I heard him get out of the hammock next to me and then saw a bobbing torch heading in the direction of what I assumed was the riverbank. Content that he'd returned and gone back to sleep, I tried to do the same. Something funky happens when you're awake in the middle of the night at the best of times. Worries that you'd brush off at 3 p.m. with a cup of tea and a Hobnob (or three), at 3 a.m. become almighty monsters that threaten to disembowel you. At home, my personal tried-and-tested, fail-safe technique for getting back to sleep is to keep my eyes open for as long as I can. Invariably, I find they begin to feel heavy and I doze off. Unfortunately, this didn't work in the jungle – my worried brain had other ideas. Any insomniacs out there who struggle with those intrusive 3 a.m. thoughts may be able to relate (on some level anyway) to the types of conversations I was having with myself:

"What's that noise?" said Scared Brain.

"I'm sure it's a twig," replied Rational Brain.

"Phew, you're right – it is a twig."

"Go to sleep. It's unlikely to be a jaguar, and even if it is a jaguar, it's probably more scared of you."

"I doubt that. What if I get eaten?" Scared Brain piped up again.

"Well, if you do get eaten by a jaguar, there's nothing you can do about it. Maybe it's just a monkey?" Rational Brain reasoned.

By this point, Scared Brain was on a roll.

"Are monkeys dangerous at night? What if the river rises some more? Argh! I left my hat by the river. What if it washes away? Perhaps I can wear a bandana on my head to stop my skin burning? But what about my nose? A hat is a key bit of kit! Maybe Charlie can bring me another one? What's that noise? If I shine my torch out of my hammock, will that scare off or attract a predator? Balls, where the hell is my torch? Why am I sleeping on it? How did it get from one end of the hammock to the other? Have I broken it? Could I use the broken remains as some form of weapon? If I did, would the batteries fall out? My body would decompose but batteries don't. I'd be dead and littering. Christ."

"GO TO SLEEP, WOMAN!" screamed now exasperated Rational Brain.

Thankfully, I did manage to nod off and woke to find that I hadn't been eaten by a jaguar – or a monkey. And I hadn't washed away. I also located my hat. The movement of the torch, however, remained a mystery.

No one had slept well, as it turned out. Laura had spent most of the night scratching bites. She pondered whether mosquitos were really fairies, stabbing us with their swords to get us to go away. The image of Tinkerbell donning fencing gear tickled me. I loved Laura's imagination. If she was right, those fairies were savage. They'd clearly dug their swords in, as she was covered in bites.

I shared with her the Dalai Lama's thoughts on his own run-ins with these flying swordsmen, one of my favourite quotes: "If you think you are too small to make a difference, try sleeping with a mosquito."

"I woke up so cold this morning," Nigel said, as we loaded the bags onto the canoe for the day's exertions.

"Yep, it was like someone turned on the A/C," Jackson replied, organizing the bags in the centre of our boat. "I got up first and went to look for firewood but it was all wet. I tried my best, but it's a rainforest – and it was raining."

Focus on what you have, not what you don't

Jackson had hit the nail on the head. It was a rainforest – so, of course, it was raining. Each night we would try to collect as much dead wood as we could for a fire and store it under the tarps to keep it dry. But, if things got wet, they got wet. We didn't have time to chop the soaked logs and salvage the hopefully drier core. There was little to be done other than to accept the situation and crack on. It reminded me of a piece of advice Ed gave us before we left. While walking the length of the Amazon River, he was infuriated by the attitude of his walking partner, Cho, when things didn't work out. Apparently, he would often say: "When there is, there is, and when there isn't, there isn't." Yet, Ed said that since the trip, it was a mantra he'd returned to again and again. I took it to mean: don't focus on the things you don't have; instead, appreciate the things you do.

The rain had eased for a while, and we counted that small blessing, but Jackson told us it wouldn't last.

"It's going to rain again soon," he said, looking at the river. "You can tell it is raining further upstream, because the fish are coming to the top of the water, swimming in a group. They're trying to find fruits and lay eggs."

Aaron and Nereus said they felt well enough and wanted to continue, despite not being entirely better – but, seeing them, you'd never have guessed that they were sick at all. They were both still attacking fallen trees with all the zeal of someone doing a HIIT class. We came up to one particularly difficult submerged log that we needed to chop. It was tricky partly because a large wasp nest was dangling from one of its higher branches. Aaron told me that they're known locally as *marabunta*.

I offered to take over but Nereus smiled. "I enjoy cutting wood. I like to clear the road."

From behind me in our boat, I could hear Jackson chuckling away. I was getting the distinct impression my assistance was not only not required but could potentially do more harm than good.

"When we are tired, we will rotate," Jackson assured me.

The tree dispatched, there was now space for one canoe at a time to squeeze through the gap that had been created. Nereus's boat had passed with ease and they disappeared around the river bend. It was our turn.

"Be careful: these *marabunta* can be your enemy. Jump in the water if we come under attack," Cemci warned, as we watched the large nest wobble precariously. We knew the stings of so many could cause anaphylactic shock. I made sure my shirt sleeves were rolled down, wrapped my bandana around my face and completed the protective look with my sunnies. Pretty much the only part of me showing was my unwashed, matted hair, sticking out the top of my ensemble.

"You look like some sort of strange pineapple," Laura commented, as we assumed the fetal position at the bottom of the boat.

Cemci started up the engine, slowly easing our way over the chopped log toward freedom... until we got stuck on some tree roots. We watched as the wasps slowly started to swarm out of the nest. Cemci tried the engine again. *Vroom*. Nothing. More and more wasps joined the swarm. *Vroooooom*. Still nothing.

Balls, I thought. *Is this the point we jump?*

VRRRRRRRROOOOOOOOOOMMMMM. We shot forward. Cemci had done it. We were free.

"They were a friend to us today, not an enemy. They didn't sting us," Cemci said, relieved.

As we rounded the corner, we saw Nereus diving into the water from the riverbank. We strained to see what was happening. The rest of his team in the boat were lined up on the shore, watching him. Had he been stung? Was he OK? Were there more wasps up ahead? He re-emerged, smiling.

Seeing my confusion, Cemci explained that apparently Nereus had just found a tree known to the Waî Waî as the "ants ants tree". The tree contains small ants with orange heads, known as "painkiller ants". Cemci told us that, formerly, people believed that if you had a fever, you should wet yourself with water, shake the ants over you and allow them to sting you. You take the pain for as long as you can bear and then jump into the water.

Nereus had climbed out of the river by the time our boat reached him. We pulled over for a quick rest and a chance to look at the ants ants tree.

Cemci suggested we experience the painkiller ants for ourselves. For some bizarre reason Ness, Laura and I agreed. I'd noticed Aaron hadn't given it a whirl. From the look on his face, he knew something we didn't. I felt my heartbeat begin to rise.

I held my arm out to the tree, and a few climbed on. Cemci squished some on the underside of my forearm and they bit me as he did. A scream may have escaped my lips, followed by a few choice words from Ness and Laura. I've got a pretty decent tolerance for pain but, wow, it was sore – a bit like being stung by a few angry bees. I flicked the ants off but two swollen white bite marks surrounded by a red ring remained. Pain-giving rather than painkiller ants. I wondered if the point was to distract from the other aches and pains you already had?

Don't overlook the small things in your life

Over the next few days the bites from the supposed painkiller ants would begin to get more and more swollen. It was then ironic that it wasn't the fear of a jaguar attack or a rising river that now kept me awake. It was the itch from tiny bites.

Ants are so numerous in the jungle. They inhabit pretty much everywhere you look. It was almost because of their frequency in our lives that I'd totally overlooked them. Perhaps you've seen stunning photos of the leafcutter ant hauling something so much larger than itself; or you might have heard of the sting of a bullet ant, which is so called because the pain is akin to getting shot. These creatures are small, but they have the capacity to completely shape their landscape. They're powerful alone and incredible en masse.

The fire ant is perhaps one of the best examples of this. To survive rising water levels, they link their bodies together to build a floating raft for the colony. Rudderless, and at the mercy of the current, when they find something dry, they swarm up it. Seeing as the average colony contains 100,000 to 500,000 ants, they were definitely something we were keen to avoid bumping into on the river. Thankfully, though South American in origin (and skilled enough to have found a way into the US, the Caribbean, Australia, New Zealand and several Asian countries), we didn't encounter any in Guyana. As awesome as their survival skills are, we didn't want them making a home out of our paddles.

The painkiller ants, however, had clearly had a good effect on Nereus. That afternoon, he demonstrated how to retrieve fruit from a tall turu palm.

The turu is like a smaller version of the açai berry. The circular fruits hang in ponytail-like clusters, and they have little black-purple nut-like seeds that dangle off numerous stems, like plump pearls dotted along a chain. But, unlike a pearl, they are tasty – and useful.

Nereus first hacked off vines at the base of the palm, so he could get a decent foothold. Then, machete in one hand, he propelled himself up the tree using what looked like "bush rope" – a vine we'd been using a lot in camp for tying together wooden structures. This time, it had been fashioned into foot straps. Once at the fruit, he hacked down a massive cluster and passed it to Aaron who was waiting below, who then threw it over his shoulder and carried it back to the boats. Later, the fruits would be boiled, mashed up, mixed with river water and turned into a jungle smoothie. It was a hefty haul, perhaps unsurprising, as the turu palm is one of the highest yielding palms in the Amazon. An average bunch weighs about 3–4 kilograms and contains around 2,500 small berries.

Having sourced the raw material for our very own energy drink, we took to the water again. Aaron passed me a berry to try, as he loaded the rest into the canoe. I was told to keep it in my cheek and that, after an hour or so, it would start to break down naturally. Mine came apart after 20 minutes and all I could taste was shell. Thankfully, the smoothie we made that evening was much nicer.

Just before we made camp that evening, we heard, and then saw, a commotion.

"Capuchin monkeys, and maybe a whole village of squirrel monkeys," Jackson said.

Find the remarkable in the everyday

A troop of about thirty monkeys, some with smaller ones on their backs, were leaping from tree to tree. Their massive jumps made them look almost like kamikaze frogs. Capuchin monkeys are super-cute, sporting a brown hat-like crown on the top of their heads. Portuguese explorers likened them to the monks in the Order of Friars Minor Capuchin, due to their brown robes with big hoods, and it's how their English name came about. (Turns out those monks have a lot to answer for; they were the muse behind the name cappuccino, too!)

Then, one of the monkeys must have landed on a dead branch, because we heard a crack. We watched as a group of them – and the branch – fell through the air. The monkeys made an unceremonious crash landing onto trees far below where they had expected to find themselves. Nereus, Ness and Jackson chuckled from the front of the canoe.

"That was amazing," said Jackson, as the monkeys regained their composure and went on their way. The scene was hilarious – the jungle equivalent of when you face-plant in the street and quickly stand up in the hope no one saw you. Despite the fact that your tights are now covered in dirt and holes, and blood is streaming from your knee, you saunter off like nothing has happened. But hey, you're still cool. Totally cool.

"It's the spider monkeys you need to watch out for," Cemci warned us. "They can be pretty naughty – they play around by pelting you with big branches."

I made a mental note to add "branch-throwing spider monkey" to our jungle risk assessment.

That night, Jackson lit the fire using something that looked like a small black and white rock. He held a match to it and then it suddenly caught light.

"A tree candle," he told us. The hard sap from this particular tree was used as a natural firelighter. Just like the sap from a pine tree, when lit, the resin was flammable.

We sat around the campfire, discussing our highlights. So much had happened that day, I commented, but Nereus just shrugged. "This is our culture," he said.

We continued to share tales of falling monkeys, storms in the night, stinging ants and near misses with wasps. I noticed my emotions in each moment had been heightened – with excitement, joy or fear. They'd been things that had happened to us and pulled our focus. To a large extent, they were things we had no control over. The events were remarkable and stuck with me in the way people tend to remember their first day at work, a wedding or that disastrous date.

Equally remarkable, however, were the things we deliberately chose to focus on. I noticed it was often the little, inconspicuous details that piqued our interest the most: the silhouette of an ant on the underside of a leaf, illuminated by the water's reflection dancing underneath. A dead beetle, whose shiny, mesmerizing body shimmered like a green oil slick, cradled by the water yet poised to sink. The way mushrooms jutted out of a dead tree like plates stacked haphazardly in a rack. Light ricocheting off a cobweb, moonlight entangled. Or, most intriguing of all, an abandoned wasp nest; it was crispy, dry and brown, yet when dipped in the river, silver rings emerged around the holes, shining as if diamonds were being offered up from below.

"Magical," said Ness, as we watched them appear. I was inclined to agree.

When we made an effort to appreciate what was around us, and specifically the small things, the world became more vibrant. Colours, textures, flavours, smells – all far richer. By cultivating my inner landscape, rather than relying on external cues alone to attract my focus, I found I was able to tune into more moments of joy. They didn't rely on something extraordinary happening. I wondered how much I'd missed in my everyday life, while sat on the Tube or whizzing through London's thronged streets at the top of a double-decker bus. The smells in the coffee shops. The sounds of the Underground. The sight of rowers gliding over the Thames in the early hours. The rustle in London's 8 million trees and the bustle of one of the most multicultural cities on Earth. Londoners are constantly reminded to: "Please mind the gap", yet had I even acknowledged there was one? I wasn't sure. Just as I hadn't noticed the ants in the jungle, I wondered what I'd failed to notice at home, as I scurried around, mindless busyness taking up bandwidth.

While we relived the events of the day, the fire burning well thanks to Jackson's tree candle, Cemci had been chopping up some heart of palm – a long, pale, smooth, crunchy strip cut from a palm tree – and Jackson lightly salted it. It tasted vaguely like artichoke. The macheted branch fanned out, white cuttings splayed on the floor. There was an artistic quality to it, almost like a clock face without the pressure of time. We were only disturbed by the whirring noise of the generator as it charged our camera equipment and whose noise cut through the calls from the jungle.

I shared with the group that one of my highlights had been watching the beautiful light that pierced the jungle at around 4 p.m. The falling rain blurred the dappled sunshine, giving the palm leaves a violent green hue. It was as if the beating of the rain heaved the landscape into life; every branch, every leaf, every droplet diving into the river – each dancing to their own flow. A soft glow seemed to shine from within the heart of the jungle.

"My highlight is a simple one," Cemci said, just as a glistening orange firefly darted over the fire. "I'm thinking about the journey all the time, where our landing is, how you girls are doing. I am really enjoying the trip with you all. The food was nice."

His comment made me smile. He was right; the food was nice. I inhaled the smell that arrived with nightfall. To me, it seemed musky, full of the dirt that the day had thrown up. I usually prefer the smell of mornings. The top notes of daybreak's perfume always smell fresher, cleaner; the dust seems to have settled overnight and your nostrils land on a blank canvas from which to start the day. The smell doesn't linger – it's a treat for early birds, and its fleeting nature is perhaps part of the appeal for me. Yet, on that particular evening, I breathed it all in: the base, woody, vegetative, soil-and-moisture-infused smell of a day in the jungle; life's simple pleasures were only a breath away.

Commitment

(noun): the state or quality of being dedicated to a cause, activity, etc.

"Happily ever after..." The ending that applies to no one. Ever. Although, I suppose, "And they all had interesting ups and downs ever after" doesn't have quite the same ring to it. Sticking to something is bloody tough, whether it's a relationship, a work project, looking after yourself or a lifestyle change that benefits the planet. Admittedly, it's much easier not to quit something when you're smack bang in the jungle, without any chance of rescue. The only way we could call time on the expedition was to keep paddling until we found a village with transport links once again. By which point we figured, if we were still alive, we may as well crack on. (Incidentally, for anyone trying to give up sugar, turns out it's a piece of cake. All you have to do is run out of supplies and isolate yourself from the rest of the world for a while.)

It was an interesting lesson for me – commitment is not a bed of roses, and complacency wasn't going to get us where we wanted to go. Unfortunately (or fortunately, depending on how you look at it), some changes that are needed in life are things you actively have to commit to. To show up even if you're uncomfortable. To question your goals and yourself. To accept that there will be days when you cock up or fall off the wagon. There will be times when you can't see the wood for the trees (quite literally, in the jungle). If it's something worth pursuing, you have to be able to recalibrate and actively make that commitment day after day. Just like a garden, our responsibilities – our mental and physical health, our relationships, our work, our planet – are things that require tending. And, although you still can't guarantee your "happily ever after" – the bugs and frost have a say in your garden, too – things will start to grow, and when your work pays off, you begin to appreciate that, however small the fruits of your labour may be, beautiful things can happen.

Days on expedition: 16

Location: Sipu River

Status: moving upriver. Slowly – very slowly

It turns out revenge isn't best served cold; it's best served barbecued. As we found our boat's path blocked by yet another log, I looked back to talk to Cemci about what kinds of wildlife call the river home. He pointed at his welly. I looked down to see that it contained bite marks. Apparently, an *aimara* we'd eaten for dinner had tried to take a chunk out of Cemci's calf a couple of days before, biting right through his rubber welly. No wonder Cemci said the food was so good – the fish, with a slight dusting of added salt, tasted of retribution.

"Did it hurt?" I asked, wincing at the thought of it.

Cemci looked at me steadily. "Yes," he said, a flicker of humour behind his eyes. "*Aimara* can take chunks out of your hands and feet. I told the boys to make sure they caught it." Luckily for Cemci, not so much for the fish, the team were incredibly skilled fishermen.

As we carried on discussing the power of a bite from a wolf fish, Laura, who had been waist-deep in water trying to chop through a log, suddenly flew into the canoe at speed. She'd just clocked one *aimara* next to the boat.

"It's amazing how much motivation you've got to move when you think you're about to be bitten," she said, hunting for the fishing gear as she did so. Having located the wire and fish hook, she began to dangle it over the side of the canoe.

Ness was less than amused. "Seriously, let me get out of the water before you start fishing for them," she said, as she hauled herself back into the boat.

Laura gave her a cheeky grin. "Sorry!"

I was staying firmly in the boat, since I had started my period the day before. After a day of getting in and out of the river, the thought had dawned on me that blood and piranha-infested waters probably weren't the best mix. I figured it might be worth checking what the Waî Waî women did when they were menstruating.

"They don't get in the water," said Cemci, deadly serious.

I was glad I'd let the team know I was on my period, as I was beginning to feel like a bit of a lemon, sitting in the boat while everyone else tried to cut through a log. Thankfully, Cemci was resting, too, so I had someone to talk to. I voiced that I was lucky the blood hadn't attracted anything sinister the previous day and he agreed. He told me that, in the past, the Waî Waî used to smear a red fruit on their forehead for protection against evil spirits.

"You'd put it on in any strange place," Cemci told me. "The men would put a straight line across the forehead and the women would put a cross."

I made a mental note to look out for that red fruit. I was also feeling slightly nervous at the prospect of emptying out my Mooncup in the jungle. Since we were on the topic of my uterus, Cemci then asked if I had any children.

"Not yet," I replied. "We'd like some, though."

"If your life is spared by the jungle," he said with a chuckle.

Enlist others to help you keep your commitment

Laura asked if there was a Waî Waî ceremony for boys to become men. Cemci shared that, once men learn to shoot, they can be with a woman – although very often their aim becomes squiffy as a result.

"When they start missing the target, they have to put ants and wasps on themselves. It numbs the nerves and it helps them shoot straighter," Cemci explained.

It appears that the jungle has its own ways to make sure you stay focused. From behind me, in a calm, low voice, Ness uttered the words: "Don't panic..." (Incidentally, if you don't want someone to panic, my advice would be to not say: "Don't panic.") It was quickly followed by: "But look behind you."

When I turned around, there was a spider with a huge brown body – far larger than a male hand – on the bag behind me. Feeling my eyes widen, I immediately stood up and grabbed my paddle. I figured it might offer some element of protection – or at least serve as a long-armed flicking device.

"Is that a friend or an enemy?" Laura asked, as the spider started to move.

"An enemy," Nigel said, "although it's never bitten me."

"Well, if you start missing your shots, we will put it on you and try," joked Laura. The spider had other ideas, however, and scuttled off the front of the boat and disappeared somewhere. It didn't look like it had gone in the water, so we spent the afternoon keeping a watchful eye out, in case it popped up again.

In fairness to Ness, being the bearer of panic-inducing information was a tough position to be in. Despite having been on the receiving end of such news, I was still unsure of the best way to deliver it. This was unfortunate, as it turned out that I was soon to be the person who had to deal with one of the most alarming moments of the trip so far.

After 20 minutes, just when I thought it was finally safe to fully relax my sphincter, Cemci made a bizarre guttural noise from the back of the canoe. It was sufficiently strange for me to turn around. Ness, who was sat behind me, did too. Without saying

Ask yourself if you're committed or complacent

a word, Cemci nudged his head, gesturing for us to look ahead, and I tried to find what he might be indicating. All I could see was Laura's floral shirt. Then, amid the swirling flowers, I saw why Cemci had sounded so alarmed. He gestured toward a small brown, almost translucent, scorpion that was working its way up Laura's arm and toward her neck. Worryingly, smaller scorpions often tend to be more venomous.

My initial reaction was one of horror as I realized that: a) I was the person closest to it, and so I had to deal with it; and b) the scorpion had its tail up and looked agitated. Adrenaline running, I grabbed my paddle (fast becoming an object of duel rather than travel) and gently told Laura to "hold still and relax". I calmly tried to wedge it between her ear and the scorpion, in the hope it might fancy a ride on a paddle rather than my friend's arteries. Thankfully, it walked onto the bright orange surface without fuss. Rather like a chef manoeuvring a pizza-oven shovel, I rotated my body slowly, so as not to unbalance the scorpion on my outstretched paddle. Once clear of Laura's body, rather unceremoniously and with haste, I chucked it into the river. Laura laughed somewhat manically and then went exceptionally quiet. It seemed both of us had retreated into our thoughts.

Half an hour passed before she spoke. When she finally did, her words were slow and deliberate. "I don't really know what to do with myself," she said. "I still feel like I don't want to move. I haven't wanted to touch anything since the incident. It was a real adrenaline shock. In the moment it's a bit like, 'Ha ha', but then the severity of it kicks in. I'm glad you didn't tell me what it was, initially. If you'd said there was a scorpion on my back, I would have panicked and it would probably have stung."

"I know what you mean," said Ness. "It's one thing seeing a scorpion on a log, but it's very different when it's on your friend's shoulder."

Laura winced slightly. I, too, felt a trickle of apprehension slip down my spine.

"It's easy to get complacent. Then, suddenly, you're like *wow*. This is jungle. This is the f-ing jungle. It's human to find this environment scary. To stay safe we've got to remain calm. We talk and laugh a lot, but we also need to *look*, talk and laugh a lot. Cemci spotted the scorpion from the back of the boat. It reminded me we've got to work as a team," Ness continued. Cemci nodded and Laura reiterated her thanks.

The scorpion served as a wake-up call for me. I'm one of those people that likes to live in my head. I'm an idea generator. A daydreamer. In many ways, sitting in the canoe for long stretches of time was the perfect opportunity to zone out and get lost in my thoughts. Yet, it was not the time or place for it. Our safety was on the line. If our team was going to make it out of the jungle in one piece, we all needed to show up for each other. Cemci's watchful eyes and Ness's words served as a real reminder that we should refocus on our shared goal – and, most importantly, the welfare of our group.

When you think you're never going to get there, reframe and refocus

Everyone was getting tired. Nereus, usually full of beans (even when sick), mentioned that he was looking forward to the trekking section for a change of scenery. Over the previous few days, the water had been getting shallower. The fact that we could stand in parts was testimony to how far we'd already come, albeit gradually. The sky had been grey and cloudy, as if time had been captured, cocooned and suspended in the canopy. Days were blurring. We hadn't, however, lost track of how many obstructions we'd cut through, as Laura was still keeping her "obstacle diary". She looked at her GPS.

"Pip, we've been on the water for two and a half hours. Guess for how many of those minutes we actually moved?"

Considering all the trees that had blocked our way, I optimistically estimated half an hour.

"It's twelve minutes."

"Well, we're twelve minutes further ahead than we were two and a half hours ago," I replied, trying to perk us all up. Maths has never been my strong suit so I didn't even try to estimate how much further upstream we had to go or how long it would take us.

For my part, this is how I was dealing with the slow pace. I tried not to think too far ahead and to take things day by day. Asking how long things would take seemed to produce different answers, so I settled with my own: "We'll get there when we get there. Each day we're moving that bit closer." I figured that putting a time on it would only lead to false expectations and disappointment. The reality was that we didn't know what obstacles lay ahead or how long they would take to overcome.

Take one action each day to move toward where you want to go

Taking one action each day is a technique I used at home, too, while figuring out how to go from my old job to doing more of the work that I found more fulfilling. I didn't want to just quit my reliable nine-to-five and find myself struggling to pay bills. Instead, the plan was to save some money for a buffer, while I got my writing, expeditions, social media and public speaking up and running. I then tried to do one thing every day to get me moving in the direction I wanted to go. It might have been sending an email, meeting someone for coffee, pitching an article or composing a social media post. Ultimately, those small steps paid off.

Before I sound all holier-than-thou, I should say that this approach took work. I am not naturally so chilled or patient, although I would like to be. In the jungle, I actively had to remind myself of my desired philosophy. Not least when Nereus announced that a log we had just come up against was going to take 5 hours to cut through – and that someone had just dropped the chainsaw's petrol cap in the water (a key bit of kit, as it turns out). A mad hunt ensued: Cemci put a weight on a fishing line to find the current and swam toward the river floor to see if he could locate it. Holding on to the line, Jackson dived down to follow it. The rest of our guides continued to chop the log with the machetes. After 10 minutes of Jackson and Cemci alternating between popping up for breath and scrabbling around looking for the missing item, Cemci re-emerged carrying something black. We all whooped, but the celebration was premature; we'd been cheering the retrieval of a small nut.

"Putting hands in holes, and in places you don't know, isn't fun," said Ness, as she and Laura hopped in the water, ducking down with outstretched hands and fiddling around to see if they could feel anything. Although my cramps were extremely painful, part of me was exceptionally glad to be on my period and sitting in the relative comfort of the boat. The other part of me felt that I should be helping the team, although I reasoned that drawing a school of piranha to help in the hunt for the cap might be more of a hindrance.

"Yep, this is the first lesson of jungle no-nos one-oh-one," said Laura, looking entirely uncomfortable in the water. "I've got a bit of a phobia of murky water – you never know what predator might be waiting for you in there," she added.

"Seriously?" I replied from the boat. "And you're leading an expedition down the Essequibo? You never fail to surprise me, Ms Bingham."

"I know, right? I'm trying not to think too much about it. I feel totally helpless at the moment, though," she said. "The cap is a little tiny thing in a huge area. The definition of a needle in a haystack."

She reached down into the water again, her hands empty when they reappeared. She shrugged, in the manner of a woman about to call it a day. "At least we're not at the start," she said, as she climbed back into the boat, a trail of water getting me wet as she threw her legs up and into the canoe. Cemci, Ness and Jackson called it quits, too.

"You are so helpful to us," Cemci said, trying to cheer everyone up. "Pulling the boat, going in the water – I like these sorts of people," he said as he retrieved his flip-flops, which were swimming around in a pool of water at the bottom of the canoe.

"I guess it's the nature of doing a lot of things in a day – things go wrong," Ness said, as she slumped onto one of the dry bags in the middle of the canoe and took a swig of water from her bottle. "The chainsaw is quite a necessary piece of kit. If we can't find the cap, we might have to trek to the source earlier than anticipated, as I'm not sure we can do a home-made job."

Cemci, however, had other ideas and had come up with a rather ingenious solution. Turns out we could do a home-made job. He had fashioned a cap by cutting a hole in his green flip-flop. The downside to this was that his shoe was now missing part of the sole.

"Don't worry," said Cemci, "we are nearly at the end of the Sipu River and it will soon be time to trek."

Commitment isn't always easy and it will be tested

Cemci's compliment about us being helpful was generous but not entirely accurate. As well as my boat-hauling skills being already out of action, my limited machete skills were about to be, too. Ness, who was trying to be helpful, had held a vine up so that those behind her in the canoe could pass. As she released the vine, it whipped me at speed and directly in the eye. The pain was penetrating.

After shutting my eye for a few minutes, I tried to open it. The little I could see was distorted and watery. It hurt to move, and every time I looked up, it felt like something was in it. Laura located some eyewash from the medical pack and I gave it a rinse. The team fashioned me an eyepatch using a wound covering plastered in medical tape. Let's just say that the incident wasn't ideal. It temporarily earned me the nickname "Pirate Pip".

I'm clumsy at the best of times, and working with one eye distorted my depth perception completely. Trying to balance along the log leading from the river to our camp that night was certainly interesting. Emotionally, it screwed me. That night in my hammock I sobbed, desperately worried that I'd done some damage to the optic nerve. My eye was so sore, I couldn't sleep. When horizontal, there was a searing pain behind my eyes, accompanied by the worst, sick-making headache I've ever had – sort of like a migraine, complete with runny nose and inflamed sinuses. Although there were many incredible things in the jungle, an optician wasn't one of them. Being so remote and isolated – part of the original appeal of the journey – suddenly wasn't a romantic notion; it was a terrifying one. The only people we could rely on for help were each other. All I could do was hope that the pain would go away. This "taking it day by day" bollocks was easier said than done. The next few days would give me an opportunity to put my money where my mouth was.

Belonging

(noun): acceptance as a natural member or part.

Whether it's at school, in the workplace, with your partner, friends or your family, there's something within most of us that makes us want to be unconditionally accepted. We crave that sense of fitting somewhere, just as we are. So often in life, I've tried to be a chameleon and adapt to situations in ways that I thought would make others accept me. The problem with this is that it's fake, and sooner or later the facade has to give. On expeditions, you're with each other 24/7 so, inevitably, people will see "the real you", with your strengths and your weaknesses. For people-pleasers this is terrifying but, ultimately, exceptionally liberating. This trip made me consider more deeply the importance of the communities we seek out or create, and what we can add to them. If you can find them – those places where you can truly be yourself, however bonkers you may be – then you're on to a winner.

In the aftermath of this expedition, I left my job and moved from London to East Wittering (a small beachside village in West Sussex), in search of a community rooted in nature. After such an intense experience in the jungle, returning to a big city felt too jarring. For all its buzz, excitement and freneticism, I found the impersonal, faceless Tube rides and the lack of human connection unsettling.

Admittedly, I was partly to blame; I could have made more effort to get to know my immediate neighbours and neighbourhood, and perhaps moving was a tad radical. However, after my smiles of acknowledgement got ignored one too many times, I found I was plugging myself in and tuning out the world, imitating those around me. It was all too easy to make no effort to talk to people. I'd convinced myself I was just one of millions, so what did those day-to-day interactions matter? Turns out they really do matter a great deal. At least to me. I only realized how much when I found a community that welcomed us. We are now surrounded by the most incredibly thoughtful neighbours. I always allow extra time when walking to the shops as, inevitably, we end up bumping into people and stopping for a chat. I love it.

When not taken to fanatical or harmful extremes, there is something wonderful about the groups we seek out or join: they offer a feeling of belonging, of safety. A notion of a common purpose. The sense that people have your back and you have theirs. This was something we experienced first-hand in the jungle. You're accepted not because you're the loudest, the wealthiest, the prettiest or the wittiest, but because you're part of something greater than yourself. You belong because you make up something so much more interesting – a community.

Days on expedition: 19

Location: Guyana's southern jungle

Status: hiking to the source

At 5.50 a.m. on a Sunday, Jackson started singing. I slowly opened both eyes and watched my mosquito net sway under the olive-green tarp. Thankfully, after a bit of rest, my eye under the patch felt much better. The morning coolness kissed my face, while the rest of my body was safely tucked up in my hammock. Most guidebooks tell you to take a lightweight sleeping bag to the jungle but, as someone who really feels the cold, I'd taken a four-seasons one which I opened up like a duvet, and I could kick on and off, as required. Although taking a sleeping bag suitable for winter might seem like a bizarre choice, I knew myself well and didn't regret it for a second.

Morning brought with it a sense of excitement for me. Once the water had become shallow enough for it to reach the top of our knees, we'd decided to switch our paddles for our walking boots. It was time to hike to the source. Over the course of a day and half, we'd set up a mini base camp; our canoes were hauled off the water and into the jungle, and wooden structures had been erected to keep any kit and dried food that wasn't vital for the hike under shelter. We anticipated it would take just under a week of travelling. Cemci had warned us that the maximum mileage per day was around ten kilometres, given we would have to chop our way through vines and foliage.

That pause in the trip felt like the calm before the storm. I had been looking forward to the hike but there'd also been a tinge of apprehension as I tied my machete sheath to my belt hook, hauled my large dry bag onto my back and set off behind the others into the jungle. Perhaps it was all that extra oxygen going to my brain from so many ancient trees – some with huge buttresses – but I felt exceptionally insignificant in the grand scheme of nature. There was a sense of magic to the jungle and every day felt like one worth getting up for, especially on mornings like this one.

I recognized the song that Jackson was singing, as I had first heard it during a Sunday service in Masakenari, before we embarked on our journey. The church had been next to our wooden guest house and, as Laura, Ness and I had finished packing and prepping for the expedition – pulling taut dry bags and double-checking kit – the singing had wrapped around us. Many voices had become one sound, joyous and uplifting. Jackson had tried to teach us some of the words on the river. It was a story about **Look out for your communities** Jesus, and the tune had now become a thread that connected our journey.

Masakenari is a remote village, and travel in the region is both expensive and sporadic. Lethem is the nearest large town where food and goods can be purchased, but it can take up to several weeks – using quad bikes – to make the journey through jungle trails and roughly paved roads. On average, there are around six flights a year to the village, with small propeller planes chartered by either government officials, anthropologists, tourists or scientists. Visitors therefore offer a valuable opportunity for the inhabitants of Masakenari to receive more resources from Georgetown. The Waî Waî had offered to guide us on our journey through the jungle and, in addition to payment, we were also asked to bring supplies for the community. Before we left the capital, we dashed around stores looking for the items that the Toshao had asked us for – rice, soap, footballs and volleyballs, as well as wellies for the team joining us. We'd already brought out with us extra hammocks, life vests, helmets and kayaking equipment from the UK for our new teammates.

When we arrived at Masakenari, our plane touched down on Gunns Strip, an earthen runway only accessible during fair weather. A few people greeted us when we got off the plane and loaded our bags onto the quad bikes that would take us the 3 kilometres to the village. It was a ten-minute ride to the plaza and en route we passed several wooden houses elevated a few metres off the ground, providing shaded space underneath for hammocks or storage. The roofs seemed to be made from either zinc or palm. As we approached the village centre, we passed a group of young men playing on a football pitch, the primary school and the guest house we would later be taken to.

In the heart of the village was a large, beautiful conical structure, known as the *umana*. It was made entirely from natural materials and the plaited palm leaves were the jewel in the crown of the massive thatched roof. It was relatively new; the community had moved there in 2000 after flooding forced them to relocate 6 kilometres from their previous location. The current village of Masakenari was previously the site of an old farm and its name means "mosquito hill" in Waî Waî.

It looked like the entire village had congregated in the communal, open hall to greet us. The Toshao asked us to make a speech for those who had gathered, explaining what we were doing and why we wanted their help. Although, in theory, our trip had been agreed to, the community would have to be consulted before it finally went ahead. We were asked to help out for a day in the local primary school, which we were more than happy to do. Then, having been formally introduced to the village, it was agreed that assistance would be given and that the expedition could go ahead, but only after the church service on Sunday.

With logistics organized and our guides introduced, the supplies we had brought were shared among the group. Villagers would come up to a long, central table and a scoop of rice shared into the containers they'd brought with them. An old man, wearing shorts and green socks pulled up to his knees, as well as a necklace made of safety pins, collected his portion and wandered out of the hall, only to be jovially beckoned back by the community – there was more rice to share. My dad was a Harrier pilot and so my sister Jo and I grew up on military bases where everyone tends to know everyone. When immersed in such a close community once again, I realized how much I missed this neighbourly spirit.

Afterward, we chatted to the old man and his wife with the help of the deputy Toshao. Unlike the majority of the villagers we met, they didn't speak English. They explained that they were part of the Waî Waî indigenous community, but had lived in Brazil and had travelled to Guyana with a Christian missionary. They told us they had no idea how old they were, as they couldn't read or write. However, the lady said she was old enough for her knees to hurt.

Now, at 5.50 a.m. and deep in the rainforest, that Sunday church service and the people of Masakenari felt like a world away. The further upstream we had gone, the more the jungle had encompassed us. I felt like I was becoming part of it, or it was becoming part of me. The canopy had been slowly closing in – our sky had become a network of greenery – and rain had been drenching the jungle for days. I'd read a *National Geographic* article explaining that, due to the thickness of the canopy, it could take around ten minutes for the raindrops to reach the jungle floor. I could quite believe it. Sunlight had been elusive – great news for our skin, but less so for staying dry! When light did break through, only narrow shards made it to the river, which was down to about ten metres wide. Following a few days of having been damp, our dry sleeping bags became a refuge – enveloping and warm, like a comforting hug of sorts.

Anyone who has camped might know what I mean when I describe that warm, happy, tranquil feeling that comes with waking up outside. That experience of discovering the freshness of a new day in its rawest form. I felt content as my hammock gently swayed from side to side, slowly waking to the morning's song. I found that Jackson's voice made a truly beautiful alarm clock. As a dim dawn broke through, you could almost pluck his notes from the leaves above. I recorded the song with the thought of using it as an alarm back home, so it could gently stir me from whatever sleep I had been in.

I sensed movement around me. From my hammock, I watched as my Waî Waî teammates assembled themselves near Jackson, who was sitting on a log.

Become part of something greater than yourself

When the singing stopped, Cemci began reading from a tiny, pocket-sized Bible that he had brought with him. He read in English and then explained further in Waî Waî. His head torch illuminated the words, as the others sat around on trees that had been fashioned into low benches.

I'm not religious but I do admire those with faith in something greater than themselves. I began to love the daily ritual of giving thanks before we ate. It was a chance to pause and reflect, to be grateful. I'd asked Jackson if he had always been religious and he told me he was born into Christianity. It was now very much part of the village and Waî Waî culture.

Although I don't believe in a god, I do find great comfort in nature, probably because we are all part of it in some shape or form.

Inspired by the daily saying of grace, one time I even attempted my own version of prayer – offering one up to the jungle as I bent my head to pass under a log. Unfortunately, I brought my head up prematurely and was blessed with an almighty wallop to my skull. My personal hunt for prayer went on.

"Whether you're religious or not, that singing was really beautiful. It gave me goosebumps," Ness commented, as she sipped a black coffee over breakfast.

Beautiful as it was, however, Laura wished the singing could have waited a few more minutes. Our usual wake-up time for the group was 6 a.m. and on that particular day she'd woken up groggy, missing those precious 10 minutes of sleep.

"At least you got to lie in your hammock and not do things for ten minutes," Ness teased her.

Laura nodded and rolled her eyes, a small smile trying not to show on her lips. Jackson chuckled, before tucking into his breakfast of *farine* and a piece of a large bird called a powis. In appearance, this bird is roughly the same size and shape as a turkey, but far better looking, sporting a crest of black feathers and a bright yellow bill. Apparently, their flight feathers can also be used for stabilizing an arrow. Unfortunately for this bird, it had been on the receiving end of one, as Nigel had hit it the day before.

"It was a lucky day," he told me. "I had a really good shot. It was far away on a high tree and I shot it. I called myself Robin Hood."

Jackson handed me a bit to try. It was better than I had anticipated but I passed on the offer of more, and tucked into my oats and cinnamon instead.

"What do you pray for, Jackson?" I asked, as we chomped our way through breakfast.

He wiggled his bare toes. "For the journey. To make sure the things I can't see, in and out of the water, don't bite me."

"Sounds sensible to me," I replied.

Since setting out together, a routine had settled into the camp, from prayers before eating to recounting our highlights each day. We'd started to work as a seamless unit. When we set up camp, the area would be cleared for our hammocks. Dead wood for the fire would be found. Fish would be caught and prepared, and water boiled, before we tended to our individual needs and wants. If it had been a particularly wet day, clothes would be placed on sticks and vines by the fire to dry, before being checked, beaten and put on the next morning. We seemed to have found our own little rhythm.

There was something incredibly comforting about habit. Tasks were done, and no one shirked from or avoided responsibility – everyone mucked in. Laura remarked on it as we made the fire one day.

"I love doing this, getting involved and having a part to play," she said. "It makes me really happy."

Given that I am a believer in equality, I felt surprised that I was more drawn to chores such as cooking, washing up or making the fire, rather than the manual tasks of moving large logs and setting up for camp. At home, the washing-up is something I like to avoid like the plague – partly because I don't enjoy it and partly out of a reaction against traditional gender roles. Thankfully, Charlie is great at it! However, for the first time I was in an environment where I felt like physicality and strength really did make a difference. When I set off on the journey, I was keen to prove that I could be as capable as everyone else to take on all tasks. However, the reality was that, in the division of labour, I probably was best placed to do the less manual jobs. Unless we had years to wait for my skills and strength to improve – which we didn't.

What are your strengths? What can you offer those around you?

I voiced the concern to Ness that, in gravitating to stereotypical gender roles based on assigned sex, I might be a rubbish feminist. But Ness, one of the strongest people I know regardless of gender, pointed out that she enjoyed the physicality of so-called "masculine pursuits", so it really came down to what we're drawn to as individuals.

I realized that, like everything in life, it was about playing to our own strengths. My takeaway? Just do you – however you choose to define yourself and your strengths.

I'd noticed, too, that, on a basic, human level, I felt so much more protected – and more fulfilled – in the group than alone, and I was reluctant to stray far from it, which surprised me, given how comfortable with being alone I usually felt at home. I wondered if this was one of the ills of the urbanized world; on a very intrinsic level we feel safer, more included, more protected in groups, yet increasingly we are building fortresses to lock ourselves away from one another. My time with the team forced me to be more social than I'd otherwise be and I began to realize that, when I returned home, I wanted to seek out, or create, more of a community. The feeling of being part of a team made me feel like I had more of a purpose.

I received so much from being part of a team, so I also wanted to give back. However, I was acutely aware that teams are only as strong as their weakest link. I've found that being physically the weakest one in the group – as has often been the case for me – is both a blessing and a curse. A blessing because, if I'm in a good team, it means I won't be left behind. However, when you are the one that's struggling, it's also easy to feel like a complete drain, a failure, the one bringing others down. If you

You always have something to add – even if you think you don't

75

let that thought develop, it's easy to spiral into a place of low self-confidence.

I've personally found that in such a situation it is useful to have a sense of humour about it, and I try to focus on the contributions I am able to make. For example, "doing a Pip" became shorthand for anything clumsy that happened on the trip. I would regularly, and accidentally, kick sand or mud into someone's food as I got up to move around camp. There were several times when I ended up extinguishing the fire by pouring water all over it. On one memorable occasion, I clattered down the riverbank after having somehow managed to trap one of my bootlaces on the other shoe. In many ways it is a wonder that I am still alive.

However, my blundering inelegance gave the team something to laugh about. When I thought hard enough about it, I realized there was genuinely lots I did add, if I chose to focus on my positive contributions. I may not be the fastest or the fittest on any trip, but I am gritty and will keep pushing on. I might career down a riverbank but I will stand up, hold my hands aloft, and finish with a smile and a bow. I think about and document what I see. I like to do things for others, to listen, to make people smile, to be there for them when they need a chat. In a funny way, my slowness enables others to feel stronger; it lifts them. I'd hazard a guess and say there's lots you add, too, even if it doesn't always feel that way. Perhaps your perceived failures aren't actually failures at all?

With the Sunday service and breakfast over, it was time to start moving and continue on our hike to the source. Our guides had adapted our dry bags to make them even bigger, by weaving palm leaves up the back and giving them a sort of crown effect. Extra pots and water containers were then strapped on. As Nigel went to hitch his exceptionally heavy-looking pack onto his shoulders, he spotted a discarded tortoise shell on the jungle floor. He reached down and picked up a thin branch, which he then speared into the ground, before placing the shell on top. It looked like a signpost of sorts, marking out our camp for the return journey. I pointed at it.

"It's like me – a tortoise," I smiled. "Slow and steady, but I'll get there in the end. I know you've told me several times, but what's its name in Waî Waî again?"

"Try to remember," Nigel said.

"*Wagnoo*?!" I offered up to an unamused face.

"Try again."

Eventually, after many attempts, it was decided that I wasn't going to get it and Nigel typed *wayamoo* into my phone.

"I think that's how we spell it in Waî Waî," he said. "My mum is great at spelling, so we will have to double-check with her."

With that, Nigel hauled the bag onto his back; I followed suit and we began our movement into the jungle. Tropical rainforest blocked our view but I knew that very soon we would be beginning our ascent into the Acarai Mountains. The low-lying range forms part of the border with Brazil and is the northern watershed of the Amazon basin, running 130 kilometres from east to west. They're not beastly high peaks, as they rise only to around 600 metres from sea level – around half the height of Ben Nevis, give or take 100 metres. However, throw in hot, humid jungle conditions, torrential downpours, steep slopes and little chance of rescue if something goes wrong, and it's definitely a challenging climb. Unlike some mountains, you're also unlikely to be rewarded with a view, owing to the constant canopy cover.

It definitely took a while to get into the routine of walking through the forest. For a start, "walking" was probably the wrong term. We had to cut a path through the jungle with our machetes, so it was a slow, steady, uphill slog. Cutting was difficult and back-breaking work, so we agreed to take it in turns, walking single file in order not to disturb the wildlife around us.

I realized we also had to lift our feet up much more than it felt natural to do, lest a rogue vine whipped them out from under us. After a while, thoughts of spiders, snakes or scorpions hiding in the rotten wood began to dissipate and I really started to enjoy being on foot, despite the heavy packs. Given how much it had rained during the hike, it was often hard to tell if it was sweat or the downpour that had soaked us through.

"It feels amazing to have more of an understanding about what Ed went through when he walked the length of the Amazon," Laura remarked, as she sliced through a vine, a mixture of rainwater and sweat dribbling down her face. "Now I am like, *wow*, you really are hardcore."

"Yep," I replied. "I can't believe he did this day in, day out for two and a half years." Thinking about what Ed had done was incredible and I could see that it gave Laura motivation, as we got used to hiking through the jungle. Ness had brought Ed's book out with her and would often read it aloud to Laura as a sort of bedtime story. As we moved through the terrain, it was bizarre to think back to our jungle survival lessons in their garden.

It has to be said, I wasn't moving as fast as everyone else. Cemci, Laura and I were bringing up the rear. The others were moving at such a clip, they were nowhere to be seen between the thick trunks.

Lift others if you can

"I read somewhere that wolves often put the slowest at the front, as most predators attack from the back. Apparently, it gives the slowest a fighting chance to get away," Laura shared with us as we trundled along.

"I didn't know that," I replied. "I'd be alright in a wolf pack then."

Cemci added that when working with tourists, you had to look after the weakest and make sure you went at their pace.

The benefit of walking with Cemci was that he was trying to teach us how to read the environment and how to figure out where our teammates had gone. To start with, when I looked around the rainforest, all I could see was a mass of trees, leaves and bushes.

"It feels like we're looking for a grass path on a lawn," Laura quipped, as Cemci asked us to tell him which way we thought everyone had gone. Slowly, though, Laura and I began to get the hang of it.

First, we'd scan the ground, looking for signs of trampled ferns or small shrubs (and to check that we weren't putting our feet on anything vaguely dangerous). Then, we'd scan at eye level, checking any vines or slender trees for the telltale sign that they had been cut by a machete. We were looking for slight, angled, pointed slices taken out of the vegetation. The hacked remains could often be blooming painful! The sharpened spike of a cut vine had already speared my trouser leg pocket – making a clean hole right through it. I'd shown Jackson at the time and he shared a cautionary tale. His friend had sliced through a bamboo stalk, whose pointy end ended up spearing one of his balls. Apparently, it was excruciating.

During the early days of the expedition, those of us new to life in the jungle had taken to asking if certain creatures were a "friend or enemy". Cemci had replied that everything was a friend unless you disturbed it. Now we were deeper into the rainforest, I asked if there was anything particular we should be watching out for.

"Snakes in the trees are usually less dangerous than ones that curl up on the ground," he said, gesturing to the forest floor.

Among others, one of the floor-dwelling snakes we particularly had to look out for was a pit viper known as the lancehead. This species is responsible for the majority of attacks on humans, as they tend to lie in wait for prey, out on jungle trails. Unfortunately, they are hard to spot, as their colouring is beautifully camouflaged to the jungle floor. I didn't fancy coming across one of these.

A few days previously I had, however, identified an iconic snake correctly: the anaconda. In a particularly macabre turn of events, we found it trying to strangle the most powerful and biggest raptor in the jungle – the harpy eagle. It is a bewitchingly beautiful bird, with the largest talons of any eagle, and is usually at the top of the food chain, feasting on monkeys, sloths, macaws and snakes. Just not when we saw it.

Don't underestimate the fight in an underdog

From our position in the canoes, we watched as a symbolic battle played out in front of us – the anaconda that the eagle had gone for was fighting back, and the two were locked in a battle for survival, wrestling on a log on the river. The anaconda was wrapped around the eagle's neck, its tongue tasting the air. In many ways we were lucky to spot the bird, because deforestation is bringing the ecosystem and the spectacular creatures within it to near breaking point. In Central America the harpy eagle is almost extinct. The anaconda clearly didn't have any sympathy for its plight.

"I've never seen anything like it," said Jackson, as we watched the hunted become the hunter, life draining out of the eagle's blinking eyes, "The eagle should eat the snake, not the snake the eagle."

The flapping of wings decreased, as the vigorous fight slowed to a weakened wave; there was a letting go, a surrender to death.

The eagle's body finally relaxed, life squeezed from it, head fallen, almost a warning: one false move can be your downfall. Things can turn quickly in the jungle. Never underestimate the underdog.

Back on our jungle trail, I was snapped out of my thoughts of snakes as we heard Aaron and Nereus talking up ahead. The team were gathered around a surprisingly clean brown patch, free of leaves, on the forest floor.

"A hog has been here," said Aaron.

I have to say, I was mildly alarmed at the finding because, of all the things I least wanted to meet in the jungle, the piglike animal known as the peccary came pretty high up on the list (especially the white-lipped peccary, as they tend to stick together in packs of between 40 and 200 and apparently, en masse, they are extremely aggressive). Ed had warned us before we set off that if we saw any, we were to climb a tree.

"Let's crack on," suggested Laura. For once, I was entirely willing to sacrifice a rest stop. About half an hour later we did stumble across a hog, albeit a dead one. Apparently, Aaron had shot two of the animals the day before when he'd gone hunting with Nereus and Nigel. One had been brought back to the camp and, although the other had been wounded, it had managed to get away. We now found it lying dead on its side, at the mercy of the jungle floor. It had a swollen stomach, and was already covered with flies and yellow globules of tiny maggots – almost like a dusting of fish eggs – on its snout and bum. After having examined it, Jackson declared that the boys loved to eat the liver and that the hog would still be OK to take with us.

Taking his machete, he sliced it open slowly and delicately, as if scoring leather, trying not to pop the stomach sack with the built-up gasses inside. Jackson warned us to move further away from the carcass – good job, too, as he accidentally nicked the stomach and the air became saturated with the smell of decomposing hog. It was the sort of stench that sticks and threatens to cling to you for a lifetime. It was utterly rancid. It was all we could do not to retch.

He then reached into the carcass, and started pulling out the innards and laying them across a large fern leaf that the Waî

Your contribution in life doesn't have to be conventional

Waî tend to use for everything, from prepping and covering food to putting under hammocks to prevent creepy-crawlies working their way into their bags. A handy jungle carpet, chopping board and food protector, all in one. Jackson checked the liver – and after all that, it was no good. It had developed black spots, a sign it was already too far decomposed to eat. While Jackson chose the cuts that were edible – the more muscular meat, the legs and the ribs – Cemci had found some palm leaves and was weaving a full-on backpack for them.

Ness offered to carry the hog until we camped. I tried to keep ahead of her on the hike, as the carcass absolutely stank. Escaping juices had leaked down her back and all over her bottom. It's fair to say she literally stank like a pig.

After setting up camp by a small stream only inches deep, I found Ness sitting in the water, looking utterly miserable, wearing just her bikini top and pants full of holes. Her arms were wrapped around her legs, and she was sitting on her blue trekking shirt. Even this seemed to be trying to escape the stench, bobbing to the surface of the water in what seemed like a bid to break free. Her big blue eyes stared up at me, mimicking a puppy dog. She was a sorry sight.

"Ness, what's wrong?" I asked.

"I stink of hog and I can't get the smell out of my clothes or myself," she said, looking utterly dejected. "I also touched a gland and this yellow liquid let out a smell like a skunk.

Apparently, it's what conditions fleas and other critters to stay away."

I couldn't really sugar-coat things. "Yep, you're right, Ness, you do stink. In fact, you, my dear, are possibly the most odorous human I have ever had the displeasure of encountering," I replied, sensing that humour might be the best way to deal with my pongy friend. Even being close to her was making me want to gag a bit.

"At least I didn't get any ticks on the way here," she consoled herself, her mood becoming marginally lighter. "And Cemci was gentlemanly enough to find me some jungle soap, which is a bark that lathers up," she added, holding it aloft, the beginnings of a smile starting to spread across her face.

I offered to help her scrub and essentially ended up squatting to her arse height, lathering up her bum with soap suds and scrubbing her pants.

"Pip, this might sound a bit weird, but can you do me a favour?" She then proceeded to ask me a question I never thought I'd hear: "Can you sniff my pants to see if I still smell of hog?"

It went from bizarre to ridiculous, as Ness's beautifully soapy bum was suddenly in my face and I sniffed around her hole-laden pants, searching for any residual pig smell. We looked up and noticed that a crowd had developed on the riverbank.

"It's not what it looks like," I shouted up to them all who, by this point, were doubled over in laughter.

With Ness as clean as she was ever going to get, we decided to join the others. The smell lingered but at least it was becoming more tolerable – or perhaps I'd gone nose blind. While I'd been scrubbing Ness, Laura had been scrubbing, too: helping to prepare the hog for the fire by scraping off the fur with her machete. A few bits of wiry hog hair clung to her trousers. She wiped sweat off her brow.

"I much prefer preparing meat in the kitchen, but I think I did OK for my first hog," she said, looking pretty proud of her effort. I looked at the carcass that was going to sustain us for the next few days and considered that the hog had been a life and was now a meal, touched and made possible by many hands.

Laura handed the meat to Aaron to put on the fire and she caught a whiff of Ness as she did. "You smell marginally better," she said, before adding, "which is a relief for the rest of us."

"I will never make the same mistake again," Ness sighed, now resigned to her perfume for the evening.

Jackson clearly found this hilarious, as he made a point of seeking me out that evening to tell me that I needed to write down his very specific highlight: Ness offering to carry the hog. With the exception of Ness, I think it's safe to say the rest of us were all in agreement on this. If I ever need cheering up, the image of Ness in her smelly, holey pants is a memory I still go back to. It works every time. A true team player, Ness certainly had our backs that day. However, in the most unexpected way, it turned out I also had hers...

Problems

(plural noun): a matter or situation regarded as unwelcome or harmful and needing to be dealt with and overcome.

In the same way your to-do list never seems complete, problems will always exist. Like the jungle, life is not something you can be in total control of – whether you're dealing with a constant barrage of snakes, spiders and scorpions, ever-looming work deadlines, or worries about health, money, family or friends. Rather than try to wish your problems away, ignore them or bury them so far down that they'll pop up in therapy years later, perhaps it's best to try to acknowledge them, share them and, if possible, reframe them. If you can't change your problem, can you change your thinking?

Sometimes opening up and admitting you're struggling – in whatever form this may take – seems like an impossible task. What if I'm judged? What if I'm burdening others? What if people laugh at me? Extreme situations can bring about extreme reactions, and so often on my adventures I am forced into admitting I need help. I've come to realize that there is no shame in this. In fact, it is wonderfully freeing to be vulnerable enough to ask for support. There's also the added benefit of building even stronger bonds with those you open up to. The friends, and the teams, that have seen me at my most vulnerable and to whom I've shown all sides of myself are the ones I feel most connected to. If there's something you're struggling with in life, whether personally or professionally, open up to someone, seek the help you need. It's the bravest thing you can do.

Days on expedition: 20

Location: Guyana's southern jungle

Status: about to sit on death

In many ways it's probably a good thing that life-changing days start out like any other. If we knew what was coming for us, chances are we'd refuse to leave the confines of whatever cosy cocoon we'd found ourselves sleeping in, stick two fingers up to the world and proclaim: "Not today, thank you. I'm going back to bed." Unfortunately, life doesn't operate like that. The jungle certainly doesn't.

For starters, you can forget waking up slowly. None of that hitting the snooze button, groggily wandering to the kitchen bleary-eyed, tripping over the cat or the kids and making yourself a coffee malarkey. No, the jungle rouses you into the day with an almighty challenge: are you ready to survive? The morning roars of the prehistoric-sounding howler monkeys are a reminder that you are merely a guest in this environment. That you should be alert and respect the place you are travelling through. A weird dichotomy exists in the jungle: life and death sit side by side. Nowhere on Earth have I been so consistently on edge. The place exploded with life, yet on a daily basis we saw things that had the potential to end it. On that particular day it turned out it would be luck, not awareness, that kept me alive.

Admittedly, the day started out better than the previous one. For starters, I didn't find a spider as I tentatively removed and inspected my upturned shoes off the long stick I'd placed next to my hammock. The day before there had been a small black one lurking in there. As I was trying to smoke it out over the fire, half-wondering what the hell you'd do if a hot and bothered spider came screeching out onto your hand, I asked Jackson about the best way to remove it. It transpires that smoking them out is exactly what you do. As for the protocol for an angry, steaming spider, I guessed the only thing to do was to apologize profusely for waking it up in such an aggressive manner, pray it didn't bite and try not to drop your only jungle boot on the fire. To double-check the spider had left, Jackson then bashed my shoe against a tree and, with unbelievable nonchalance, fiddled around the inners of my smelly boot with his hand. He couldn't find anything and so concluded it had gone. I still took a sharp inhalation of breath as I lowered my foot into the shoe…

Unfortunately, over breakfast, Jackson diagnosed me with "mosquito worms" in my hands and shoulders. He had noticed me scratching a cluster of small, red-and-white bites that I had thought were harmless. However, left unchecked, these seemingly innocuous bites could hatch into maggots. Apparently, the sneaky botfly will immobilize a mosquito, deposit some of its eggs on its victim's legs and then bugger off, waiting for said mosquito to find a nice, juicy host and implant their offspring. Both lazy and undiscerning parenting on the part of the botfly, if you ask me. Also, bloody inconvenient for the said host, as I really didn't fancy squeezing maggots out over my porridge. Extra cinnamon? Hell, yes. Raisins? Load me up. A plump, juicy maggot? No, thank you. Not even if it was dressed up as a wellness trend. You don't mess with breakfast.

Thankfully, there is a simple jungle hack for dealing with uninvited guests – duct tape. The idea is that you suffocate the larvae over a few days and then try to rip them out with the tape. Given how nonchalant Jackson seemed about maggots potentially hatching out of my body, I, too, was remarkably unfazed. The discovery also meant I became part of the duct-tape crew. Ness and Laura had a line of tape covering similar bites on their bums. In fact, on this particular morning, Ness remarked that she may also have one patch on her coccyx and "wouldn't mind someone checking it out". She was quickly outdone by Laura, however, who claimed: "Mine's in my bum crack." Joyous. Amazing how quickly you bond on an expedition...

Taped up, we were all ready to go at 7.40 a.m. I always find it amusing when people give exact timings, as I'm sure it's of no consequence to you to know precisely at what time we set off. However, on this occasion, I feel it is important to stress that before most people have even fully opened their eyes, or made it into work, by 8.20 a.m. we had trekked over three hills in dense, humid, suffocatingly hot jungle, were absolutely knackered and felt ready to go back to bed. That I was unwittingly dragging various bits of jungle foliage around with me probably didn't help matters.

"Mate, I swear you're like walking Velcro. You seem to pick up most of the forest and don't even realize it," Ness exclaimed, as I tentatively fished a rather sticky vine off the back of my trousers.

Sensing we were flagging a bit, Jackson reassured us that the açai juice we had for breakfast would be helping us.

"Makes you sweat – but will give you a lot of power, a lot of energy."

Ness snorted. "Does it? I'm still trying to find it."

"It will come this afternoon," Jackson replied with confidence – or perhaps it was hope.

If you can't change your situation, change your attitude

Later that day I realized how poignant his comment was. Our energy levels and our afternoons were far from guaranteed.

You can strive for goals over years – decades even – every day inching closer to what you think you want. Yet in mere seconds, life can have you by the scruff of the neck. Everything can change in a moment. *You* can change in a moment.

Hiking through thick jungle is not for the faint-hearted. Unstable ground, no discernable paths, the place teeming with life – some of which is deadly. Jackson's promised "power and energy" of the açai had failed to kick in for me that afternoon, and I found my movements cumbersome and slow. This is probably how I managed to get my foot wedged between a gnarled, rotting tree trunk and a twisted vine. I must have spent a minute or so struggling, shaking and tugging to free my limb. As I did so, it crossed my mind that I had become amazingly comfortable with the environment, clambering over fallen trees that, just weeks ago, I'd have been scared to put my hand on. I even briefly considered having a sit-down, given that I was stuck anyway, but I thought better of it. Finally, my foot came loose and I cleared the trunk – sweaty, victorious, elated. If only for a moment. Just as I moved my leg, Laura cried out: "Oh my god, there's a snake."

Mere inches away from where my bum and leg had been flailing around seconds earlier was a mottled black, white and grey snake. I'd clearly disturbed its peace, as its diamond-shaped head now reared up and its tongue was out. It wasn't just any snake, either. It was highly venomous – one of the specimens you pray won't bite you in the jungle. Least of all when you are several days' hike from medical help. It was a lancehead.

Also known as the labaria or fer-de-lance, the lancehead is responsible for more human deaths than any other snake in the Americas. Turns out that an irritable disposition and fast-acting, powerful venom is a potentially lethal combination for anyone who happens to stumble across one. As the *Guyana Chronicle* put it, "Once they feel threatened, they would bite you fast, fast, fast; before you even realize it, they could bite you five times already. They are very hot-tempered and most people that get bitten get bitten by that same snake-type."

However, when you're in its vicinity (or indeed waggling your bum over one), I can confirm that you don't need the *Guyana Chronicle* to alert you to the dangers. Let me assure you that your survival instinct kicks in well enough to tell you to get as far away as you can, as quickly as you can. We'd discussed with Dave (a medic who had run us through basic emergency medicine and was on hand to help remotely if we needed), about taking antivenom with us, but there was little point. There are several different types of serums and most needed to be refrigerated. To be blunt, we knew that if something happened to us on the hike to the source of the river, we were stuffed. To be bitten by a common lancehead so far from help would be fatal. As soon as I'd heard the word "snake" uttered in my direction, I'd bolted as far from the log as I could. From what I felt was a safe enough distance, I looked back to Jackson, Laura, Ness and Aaron, who were stuck behind the log.

"That's definitely an enemy," said Jackson, who at this point had drawn his machete and was holding it at arm's length from the snake. "An oval head on a snake is OK, but not a diamond. If it gets your veins, it will kill you. If it gets your muscle, you will be very sick. It's very tiny but very poisonous."

His elaboration was unnecessary, as I was already keeping as much distance between myself and the snake as possible.

"Pain, pain, pain," said Cemci, standing next to me, shaking his head. "This is one of the bad snakes of the jungle."

We watched as Jackson covered the hole it had been hiding in with the machete, so the others could climb over the log unharmed. I couldn't bring myself to watch, still trembling with a mixture of terror and adrenalin. Slowly, and to my great relief, the others joined us. Before Jackson crossed the log himself, all I heard was the dull thud of the machete on wood. The sound

Be honest with yourself. When you say, "I'm OK," are you really?

was deliberate, purposeful, and a sense of finality rung through the trees: an unexpected death knell. The snake was dead.

"I thought it was dead, initially," said Laura, as we all regrouped. "I saw the snake's skin but thought it was discarded. Then I saw it move, looking around, and its tongue was flickering. Its senses seemed to be heightened."

"Yes, it was getting ready to attack," Jackson clarified.

We didn't hang around at the scene for long and continued our trudge down the mountain. I tried to focus on just putting one foot in front of the other, but my mind was whirring, struggling to process what had just happened. My eyes darted all around me, suddenly unsure of the ground in front. I think I was in a state of shock. To think that I'd been hovering just inches from something that could have easily killed me was terrifying. I was also exceptionally thankful to it for not attacking. I tried to act like everything was fine, to brush it off and tape over my emotions, just as I did with the botfly eggs. Yet, inside, I was the one suffocating. There are so many moments in life when we try to put on a brave face while, underneath, we are a mess. This behaviour is often likened to that of a duck – serene on the outside, flapping around under the surface. I felt like a duck on speed – a mechanized, wind-up bird that couldn't control what the hell was going on underneath. It was only when we came to rest at the bottom of the slope that I fell apart and broke down in tears.

I had been mere centimetres over the snake. Had it struck, the fer de lance could have killed me. But it didn't and, to this day, I'm thankful. I was ALIVE. I was, unbelievably, ALIVE! I was also exceptionally sad that, though it had spared me, we hadn't returned the favour. It had done me no harm and

I felt uncomfortable that it had been killed because it had had a chance encounter with a human on a hike. I asked Jackson why he'd had to kill it.

"I killed it because it's poisonous," he said. "I was bitten by one once. I didn't feel sick immediately. After fifteen minutes I tried to open my eyes and they were swollen already. I ended up in hospital. I was there for a long time."

This was the first time of many on the trip when I would be confronted with my own ego. Had I not been there, the snake would have still been alive. I clearly saw how our life choices have an impact far beyond what we can imagine, both positively and negatively. That day, my own insecurities and the desire to prove something to myself and perhaps to those around me – that I was "tough", that I was "capable", that I could take part in something far more extreme than I ever thought possible – had led to the death of a snake that could have attacked, but didn't. If anything, I came to realize that I was the "enemy" in the jungle – a sobering truth and one I am still wrestling with. Should I have even been there in the first place? When does the desire to explore and learn about the world go from being helpful to harmful? Can you attach morality to travel and, if so, how do you stay on the right side of the line? The fer-de-lance had slithered its way into my psyche and refused to leave. I knew that the snake – and those questions – would stay with me forever.

"Pip, don't think too much about snakes," said Cemci, as he watched me zone out during our rest. To help me, the team then proceeded to tell me all about their own snake encounters. I can only imagine this was an attempt at reverse psychology.

"I am scared of snakes," said Nigel, "they're dangerous."

Apparently, one woman had been bitten by a bushmaster close to the Waî Waî village. In my dazed state, I did not manage to grasp what had happened to her. I am not entirely sure it was a happy ending…

Jackson's story at least lightened the mood. On his way to answering the call of nature, he had spotted a snake and jumped a mile. His learning from the experience? Always clear the jungle floor with your machete and check around first.

Jackson also informed us that if you dream of needles, you'll see a snake. Quite bizarrely, Laura said she'd had a dream about mending a shirt the night before. At least she didn't dream about a vagina. Apparently, it's a sure sign you're about to make a big mistake, according to Jackson.

There is great power in being vulnerable

"What does it mean if you dream of things that don't exist?" Laura asked.

"No one has ever asked me that," he said.

Our rest stop over, it was time to get moving again. Panicked, shaken and full of self-doubt, I knew I couldn't change my situation – I could only change my response to it. The only way out of the jungle was to keep moving. I literally didn't have any other choice, much as I wanted to run home and quit at that moment. The only thing I could control, or try to at least, was how I processed that event.

For weeks afterward, though, it seemed that my spirit wouldn't settle. I would wake up after the most visceral night terrors – dreams of being attacked by a jaguar or capsizing. So situational, so painfully real. On one occasion I woke the entire camp up with a scream. But, rather than complain, someone would always hop out of bed, offer a hug and check I was OK. Previously, my hammock might have hung on the edge of the group, closest to the jungle. Now, however, the team made sure that my hammock would be placed nearer the centre of the camp, so that I would have people sleeping around me. An extra few logs would be added to the fire before bed to keep it burning longer into the night. Every act was a great kindness that didn't go unnoticed. It was the team that got me through the aftermath of the snake incident – their humour and their thoughtfulness. I've always found being an agony aunt a fairly natural role, and one I enjoy, but ironically I've always struggled when it comes to talking about my own problems. I think one of the bravest things I did in the jungle was admit when I needed help and allow myself to be open to receiving it. As a result, the jungle slowly became that little bit less terrifying and transformed into a place I relished sleeping in, a place I loved and was ultimately sad to leave.

Contrary to Cemci's advice at the time, I did think about the snake that day, and have done most days subsequently. If I'm honest, a shiver still goes up my spine every time I think about it. But I'm grateful to it. The snake has now come to represent the fragility of life and the twists of fate on which it hangs. The river shaped me, the journey humbled me and the team caught me, but it was the snake that made me feel most alive. In that moment, it was all I could ask for.

Growth

(noun): the process of developing physically, mentally or spiritually.

Everyone and everything can teach you something if you're open to listening. Listening allows you to hear the nuances of life. We are all products of the environment we were born into; there is no perfect way to be or think, so taking other people's thoughts and opinions into consideration is helpful in many ways. This is especially true when they conflict with your own ideas. Really listening involves humility: the ability to accept that we may need to re-examine some of our own views and actions, and not force our preconceived ideas on others. Rather than getting stuck in our ways as we age, perhaps we should think about refining our ways. Great growth can come from approaching life with an open heart and mind.

I've found I'm most self-critical when I think of myself as a static entity: someone who should be perfect, or continually acting, thinking or being a certain way. This rigidity is not helpful; we are evolving beings. We track children's milestones – their first steps and first words are all celebrated. However, as adults we perhaps don't tend to appreciate our own breakthroughs, developments and learning as much as we should. Adopting healthier habits, understanding and moving on from failures, acknowledging why you behave in a particular way in a relationship or why certain things trigger you are all things to salute. You're growing and evolving. So give yourself a break. If you're learning, you're growing; you're not perfect and you shouldn't have to be, either.

Days on expedition: 22

Location: heading up the Acarai Mountains

Status: taking it in turns to cut
a trail through the jungle

Laura raised a bow in front of her and pulled the arrow toward her chin. Nigel and I watched and laughed as it fell off the string and landed between her feet.

"You've told me everything except how to actually do it," Laura quipped, as she whacked her hand with the string of the bow for the umpteenth time. She had yet to fire a single arrow and her arm was now beginning to turn the colour of a raspberry.

I wasn't faring much better. My wrist, too, had developed a rash, threatening a bruise, and there were cuts across my index finger. Nigel chuckled as he resumed his coaching, watching our failed attempts and offering up guidance.

For the last few days we'd been slogging away at the painfully slow pace of 4 kilometres an hour. Our slower-than-anticipated pace meant that we were also running low on food. Breakfast had been half the porridge we'd usually have. After a few nights of just eating rice, the now few-days-old hog was starting to seem more appealing. Watching Laura eat a piece for breakfast, I experienced my body sending a clear message, and what I can only describe as a deep, primal urge rose within me. "Can I have some?" I found myself unexpectedly asking, before ripping meat off the bone with such intensity it shocked me.

"Whoa, for someone who said they didn't want any hog you're making fine work of it," she commented, as I devoured what was left of it.

We were about to embark on another day and, given the physical exertion required, we'd decided to take turns to cut the trail up into the Acarai Mountains. The hope was that while one half of the team forged the way, the rest could relax and restore their energy. Thankfully, it was my turn to rest, which explained why I was also not fully dressed yet. I'd intended to lounge in the hammock for most of the morning and was still wearing my pyjama bottoms when I decided to join Nigel's impromptu archery lesson.

Laura's archery skills were not destined to improve that day, as her lesson was cut short. She didn't seem overly disappointed as she handed Nigel back his bow and swapped it for her machete. Together with Jackson and Cemci, she went off to cut a path through the jungle. The rest of us would move to join them in a few hours. Ness, Nereus and Aaron decided to chill in their hammocks, whereas I reconvened my lesson with Nigel and resumed aim.

"The crowd booed as Pip took a shot," Nigel teased, as the arrow fell through the bow and landed at my feet.

Serves me right for laughing at Laura, I thought.

"When I was six, I learned to shoot by firing at a target and competing with my friend. Why don't we try that?" Nigel suggested, picking up a large leaf and skewering it through a small branch.

Be open to trying new things – and realize they may take a while to master

So that's what we did, me with my right hand and Nigel with his left. I secured the end of the arrow to the bowstring, put one finger above and two below, and pulled it back. I looked down the arrow shaft, squinted as I tried to visualize the tip piercing the leaf and released. Bollocks.

"You only have three chances. Concentrate next time," Nigel goaded, as his arrow whistled straight through the centre of the leaf.

Finally, after an hour of trying, *ping*. My arrow hit the mark I was aiming at. I was ecstatic. There may have been a somewhat exaggerated victory celebration, complete with singing and the sort of dance moves familiar to every drunk person on a Friday night. I heard Ness chuckle from her hammock.

"Well done," Nigel said as he handed me a fallen branch. "Your trophy."

Needless to say, I didn't win the competition and decided to call it a day with the archery. I made the error of showing Nigel, the joker, my archery wound. Instead of sympathy, he took one look at my cut finger and promptly walloped it. He let out a cackle that would be fitting of a Bond villain.

My poor aim meant that I'd shot several arrows way past the target and so we ventured deeper into the jungle to find them. Locating them among the forest floor was surprisingly difficult but luckily we spotted them, including one caught in a tangle of vines and another in a pile of crunchy dead leaves. As we headed back to camp, Nigel remarked that the forest's aroma was different.

If you don't understand something fully, ask someone who does

"Fruits," he said, turning his head to try to establish the source of the fragrance. "Can you smell them?"

For the first time, I could; my senses were clearly improving. We decided to follow our noses, and we trudged over fallen branches and dead logs to find some yellow plums on the floor. Nigel picked some up but, as he did so, maggots and worms slithered out.

"Best not to eat these ones," he told me. However, poking around further, we discovered a few fresh-looking ones that didn't appear to have been munched.

Nigel ripped a palm leaf from a nearby plant and took it over to one of the fallen logs. He grabbed one of his flip-flops, placed it on the tree and plonked himself down on top of it. I watched as he started to tightly weave the shiny, thick but flexible fronds into a basket. He began by crossing the two parts at the apex of the leaf. Then, methodically, Nigel took one strand from the right side and passed it over and under the frond on the left, pulling it tight as he did. He repeated the process on the other side, bright green woven into bright green. It was hypnotic to watch.

"I'll show you how to do this when I've finished," he said.

My trance-like state was short-lived, as I soon realized I was sitting directly on a log in just my pyjama bottoms. I was beginning to get fidgety and keen to get moving. I calmed myself by thinking about a stat that Laura had given me that morning: 90 per cent of scorpion bites happen on the hand, so presumably my bum was safe.

I asked Nigel if we should be worried about a jaguar sneaking up on us, given we were away from the group.

"There are birds that warn you. You just have to listen out for them," he replied.

I was about to suggest that we abandon the basket, and just wrap the plums in my bandana and take them back that way, but caught myself. Phrases like "just a sec" or "in a minute" had no relevance in the jungle. Things were done when they were done. Food took time. Water had to be boiled. Fires had to be tended to. Days slowed and elongated to a blur. Perhaps 10 minutes weaving a proper basket was time well spent. At the very least, it meant I wouldn't be getting plum juices and maggots seeping into my bandana. I remarked that Nigel was a very patient man and a good teacher. He asked me to explain what "patient" meant. *It's something I hope to get better at,* I thought as I did so.

The palm was remarkably resilient, and I watched him gently pull and tie off the ends to secure the shape of the basket. Nigel had finished, and it was a work of art. We then filled it with the plums. I say *we*; I added five, after first poking them (and then the ground around them) numerous times with the tip of the arrow, in case of scorpions. Of the five I did contribute, Nigel questioned why I had picked some that were mouldy.

Everyone in the camp was asleep when we returned. I picked up the empty bucket we had been using to make açaí juice and sat on it. It was black and white, and, in another life, it had been a farmer's motor oil bucket. As the fire crackled, Nigel boiled up the plums and unceremoniously flung the beautifully crafted basket back into the jungle. I thought about retrieving it but figured it would just be another thing to carry. We fished the plums out of the water and allowed them to cool in our Tupperware. Once the fruits were lukewarm, Nigel offered me one. They were delicious. Turns out it wasn't the yellow flesh but the skin that was the tasty bit: once cooked, it peeled off easily and was beautifully sweet.

Be willing to listen to new ideas and ways of doing things

"I watch you sometimes, looking around as you type on your phone, master of the writing. I admire your skill," Nigel shared, as we nibbled the plum skins.

I told him that, of all the skills to have, writing was unlikely to save me in the jungle. Although, in some ways, words had become part of my own survival toolkit.

"You teach me," he said, giving me an element of hope that I was adding something to the team. "I like listening to you speak, to the words you use."

Nigel asked what the biggest words I knew were. In return for genuinely useful survival skills, I offered up "discombobulated" and "iconoclastic" – perhaps a fair indication of my time in the jungle so far.

Nigel went quiet for a while. I would say it was a comfortable silence, but the squawks and chirps of our jungle surroundings meant it was anything but noiseless. I found the atmosphere incredibly restful and felt no urge to speak.

"Do you cry a lot?" Nigel asked, when he did talk again.

"Yes, if I feel like I need to," I replied. "It helps me to process things and wash them away."

"I feel something inside but I don't like to cry," he shared. "When you climb up the mountains, you must only look up. Take a deep breath and don't look back. If you do, then you will cry." He paused. "I miss my mum. She really looks after us well, as a mum, you know?"

Understanding that you always have more to learn helps you to grow

I did know. We were all missing something.

"I feel like you're a good friend," he said, warming my heart. "I've enjoyed every moment playing with you and teaching you archery. I teach you something, you teach me something – I love that."

I smiled. "Me too, Nigel."

The rest of the camp had now begun to stir and Ness came to sit with us.

"Have we received a message on the Garmin for us to leave camp yet?" she asked. The plan had been for the cutting team to send a message once they'd made decent headway. Worryingly, hours had passed and we'd heard nothing.

"We should try to find them," Aaron said as he began to pack up his hammock and get ready to hit the trail once again. The rest of us followed suit.

As we scanned the foliage for signs that it had been trampled by the others, I considered how much better my bushcraft skills were becoming. Over breakfast, Cemci had talked about the benefit of sharing knowledge between cultures. He explained how the Waî Waî had helped a German team film a documentary about the source of the Essequibo a few years previously. Cemci said he had hoped that more people would come to the area off the back of it, but they hadn't.

"The white man has skill in technology but cannot move. The Amerindian can move but we need skill in technology," he said.

Cemci was definitely a gadget man. Over the last few weeks, he'd wanted to get to grips with the GPS we'd brought out with us and was eager to explore the features that differed from his. He'd also been keen to discuss the latest iPhone and the cost of phone contracts back in the UK.

"We need more technology," he continued. "I'd like to learn more about it; see the different models of GPS."

In my case at least, Cemci was right about not being able to move. Moving felt like a struggle. I had to fight every urge my body had to stop, just to keep going. I occupied my mind by trying to familiarize myself more with the flora and fauna. Along the journey, Cemci and Jackson had pointed things out to test our knowledge and so that they could tell us more. So many trees, flowers, berries and animals had their own unique story or use.

"I'll pass on all my knowledge to you," Jackson had said. "If I know it, I'll tell you."

I tried to keep my eyes peeled for a thick, twisted vine that he'd chopped up the day before. Jackson had told us to hold it aloft and let the cool liquid drip into our mouths. A deliciously sweet, clear liquid briefly flowed from it – a potentially life-saving source of water if we ever ran out. However, there were also vines that, when cut, yielded a stickier, milky sap – a good sign that it would be poisonous. I just needed to remember which was which and what they looked like…

"I love going out into the wilderness and learning like this…" Ness said, briefly pausing to feel a tree with a particularly gnarled bark. "You know, by touching, tasting, smelling. I find it's the best way to learn. I wish we did more of this back home." I knew exactly what she meant but, unfortunately, we didn't have time to linger, as we were keen to locate the cutting team.

After 2.5 hours we finally caught up with them. Turns out they were absolutely fine and had made great headway. They'd sent a message a few hours into their cutting but, probably given the thickness of the canopy, it hadn't been received. Although it was important to take potentially life-saving technology on the expedition, the slow delivery of the message served as a reminder that we also needed to be able to look after ourselves if something went wrong. We needed to have our wits about us. I was pooped from the hike – and I hadn't even been cutting a path through the jungle. I was full of admiration for the work that the team had done. I told Cemci I thought he was unbelievably strong and fit.

If someone is prepared to teach you something, receive their wisdom gratefully

"It's not strength," he replied, without a hint of arrogance. "It's just a skill."

As we had a brief pause to catch our breath, Jackson sliced a diagonal cut into the bark of a tall mottled white-and-grey tree we were standing next to. Red, sticky sap flowed from the incision and Jackson rubbed it into the small cuts on his hands. Apparently, it had medicinal properties and, once dried, it acted as a sort of second skin.

Cemci then pointed out a thick vine near where we'd stopped. According to the tales of our teammates, the vine could make you feel a bit giddy. The people of Masakenari made it a rule in the village not to drink alcohol but it sounded like the sensation was similar to getting drunk.

"You're lucky to see this," Cemci said. "It's hard to find this vine, even for us. I've heard from some miners that in Brazil they're trying to collect it, as it's said to help cure HIV. It can also be used to poison fish."

Cemci told us he'd heard that it was first discovered after two men who had HIV came to the jungle to kill themselves but, after drinking from the vine and surviving, went home and tested negative.

While I can't confirm the accuracy of the story, I can believe the sentiment. It's estimated that about 25 per cent of all the drugs used today are derived from the 80,000 plant species that call the Amazon biome home, as well as 70 per cent of plants with anticancer properties. I thought back to a conversation that I'd had with Cemci's wife, Deli, back in the village. It was about the jungle being "nature's supermarket" – turns out it's the world's medicine cabinet, too, and so much is still to be discovered.

Over the centuries, fungi from temperate climates have been used to create antibiotics and statins, so the medical possibilities from specimens found in the Amazon are exciting. The venom of Amazonian scorpions is also now being researched to gain insights into pain relief, as well as its ability to kill parasites, viruses, fungi and bacteria. With less than 5 per cent of the properties of plant species in the Amazon having been researched, and considering the numerous poisonous animals and fungi that call the jungle home, it not only operates as the lungs of our planet but it may help us all to live longer on it, too. That is, if we don't destroy it first.

"I've never tried alcohol," Cemci said, as we looked at the thick vine, "but when you drink this, it feels like when you take malaria tablets: your eyes turn a bit."

It was an interesting comparison, especially when you consider that one of the first antimalarial drugs came from the jungle. Quinine is made from the bitter bark of the cinchona tree; it has been utilized for centuries, after its beneficial uses were discovered in Peru in the seventeenth century. When mixed with sweetened water, it became known as tonic. British colonialists later added gin to it. Thus, the rainforest spawned not only a life-saving drug, but also gin and tonic.

"Want to try?" Nereus asked, an amused expression on his face.

"Sure, but maybe after the walk, so that I can go in a vaguely straight line," I replied.

Everyone giggled, but I didn't intend it to be funny; I was deadly serious. It was now my turn to cut a trail and I didn't feel that a perception-altering vine would aid my machete skills. Not least because I was knackered from the morning's hike, which had seemed to involve climbing and descending slopes that appeared around 45°. I was also hungry, bordering on hangry, but it was agreed that Jackson and I would go ahead and start cutting a path for use the following day, while the rest of the team set up camp.

"I feel like I'm about to do an exam," I moaned as I set off.

"You came for it," Nigel pointed out, as he waved us off jollily.

I'd like to say I looked badass, chopping my way through the jungle, but in reality I looked like a right wally. Since I had lost weight, my trousers were now far too big, bunched around my waist and held in place with a belt. Whenever we were going downhill, I'd hold my arm outstretched, worried I might drop the machete and then land on it. Combining a clumsy disposition and sharp blades wasn't exactly ideal. I remembered Ed's sage

Listen to Mother Nature's lessons, too

words before we left: most accidents in the jungle are self-inflicted. He also mentioned that we should keep our knives sharpened. Doing this means you need to put less force behind them when you chop, which helps to reduce the chance of a messy mishap.

"You're only as sharp as your machete," he'd said, as he taught us how to sharpen the blades with a metal mill file. That constant improvement of our tools was an action we had to perform most days in the jungle; the shaving off of the old, dull, blunt edge to produce something sharper, and more effective. As our little team of two chopped our way up and down mountainous ridges, I did give myself a pat on the back about how far I'd come since that training with Ed. I was by no means the sharpest machete in the group, but I wasn't quite as blunt as I used to be. Little by little, my skill set was growing.

Just as I engaged in a spot of self-congratulation, my phone buzzed in my pocket. It was a period tracker app, alerting me to the fact that I was at my most fertile time of the month. Apparently, "my flowers were blooming". I literally jumped a mile.

"You're frightened of a porcupine," Jackson teased, seeing my body involuntarily jerk as my phone went off. *Aren't porcupines covered in sharp quills?* my brain responded. I kept the thought to myself.

As tired as I was, it turned out to be an exhausting but magical afternoon. We'd hiked over three hilly ridges, cutting a trail for everyone to use the following day. The light was incredible, and a welcoming and rich warmth penetrated the canopy. Beams radiated around us, surging through the gaps in the trees, and the forest took on a mystical hue. The two of us stopped and looked up at the canopy that was now such an intense green, illuminated by the sun's slow descent.

"You are the first foreigner to step foot in this primary rainforest. We took the German team another way," Jackson said, as we marvelled at the astonishing surroundings we found ourselves in. It was perfect. If only for a moment. Above our heads, we heard a noise, almost like a dog's bark. Jackson imitated the call and slowly the sound grew in volume.

"Spider monkeys," he said, as the creatures began to gather overhead. "They come slowly, slowly. I think there's about six up there now," Jackson estimated.

The spider monkeys are often called ecosystem engineers, due to their important role in the rainforest. This is down to their bowel movements. Creatures of habit, they tend to go to the loo morning and evening, depositing the seeds from the fruit they eat in the same predictable place. Admittedly, a jungle latrine is not everyone's first choice of venue for breakfast or dinner, but their loo does attract an array of insects and other animals that consume, and then spread, the seeds even further around the forest. Sharing is caring and all that.

There's a slight problem with this system, however: humans. Cattle ranching, mining, logging, crop plantations and road building have all caused the deforestation of their environment, and the species is now under threat. In many ways we were lucky to see them.

The spellbinding magic of their appearance was soon broken by a piercing yell.

"Move!" Jackson commanded, as large branches started to fall around us. We were literally under attack. The monkeys in the canopy above were marking their territory, using their disproportionately long limbs to rattle the trees above and pelt us with branches. A large piece of wood whistled past my ear, missing me by millimetres. A not-so-subtle lesson from above: respect our home. I could quite understand why they wanted us to leave. We didn't hang around and instead beat a hasty retreat back to the others.

"Phew, that was a lucky escape," I voiced when it felt safe enough to do so, sweat streaming down my face. I thought back to when Laura asked me to join the expedition. Naively, I thought I'd be sitting in a kayak for most of the day. Running through hilly jungle while under attack wasn't quite the same thing...

As the adrenalin subsided, we began to walk at a slower pace back to camp – far easier now that we had a trail to follow. Occasionally, we'd widen the parts that needed it. I reflected that I had learned more about the world around me in a day than I had for years. Being in an environment where the advice you're being given can potentially make the difference between life and death definitely forces you to pay attention. Approaching the world with a willingness to learn and grow was unbelievably rewarding. Genuinely listening to the environment and the conversations around me helped to give me a fresh perspective on life. It also made me realize that we shouldn't be so hard on ourselves. There is always something we don't know. There is always someone more skilled or more knowledgeable. If we constantly strive for perfection, comparing ourselves to other people, we are likely to always be disappointed. However, we could compare ourselves to our past selves – that's where we could learn and develop. I raised my machete and sliced clean through a vine in front of me. Slowly but surely, I was getting better. I was growing.

Storytelling

(noun): the activity of telling or writing stories.

Have you ever spoken unkindly to yourself? Not put yourself forward for something because you didn't feel good enough for it? Or not tried to make a change because you felt like your contribution wouldn't make a difference? If you can answer "yes" to any of these, I'd hazard a guess that you've been writing a self-limiting narrative. Once again, I found nature provided some answers about how to change this.

Before this trip I hadn't realized that rainforests have many layers. There's the dark forest floor, home of the decomposers. Just above there's the understorey layer, which lies beneath the canopy – as it's humid and has little light, plants that make their home there have large leaves to catch what sun they can. Then there's the sunnier canopy, the home to most of the animals of the rainforest. And, finally, there's the overstorey, the place where giant trees look down on the rest of the forest. If you take a vertical section of jungle, you could write several different stories about what it's like, depending on which layer you're looking at. The same is true for us; there are many possible ways to interpret ourselves and the events of our lives, depending on the narrative we choose.

Stories have tremendous power to shape how we think about things. We can tell ourselves that we're useless, unlovable or unlucky and, because we're looking for proof of it, we can even find the evidence to back up these claims. It's the emotional equivalent of spending too long staring at the forest floor, allowing those darker narratives the time to crawl into the mind. If these negative stories are the ones we're constantly feeding ourselves, the chances are we're not giving ourselves the sunlight we need to grow. Next time you beat yourself up, it's worth examining why. Where has this thought come from? Does it serve you? Is it limiting you? Is it worth looking at yourself and what you're capable of from a different perspective? I'd wager if you asked a friend whether you were really as useless as you thought, they'd tell you you're actually pretty darned awesome. We can't change the past, but we can try to shift the meaning it holds for us going forward. A life is made of highs and lows, and events that we can't control, but we do get to choose how we define what they mean to us. We get to write the story.

Days on expedition: 23

Location: Guyana's Acarai Mountains

Status: nearly at the source

The good news was that we were nearly at the source. The bad news was that, because hiking was taking far longer than we'd anticipated, food supplies were running dangerously low. Alarmingly for someone like me who adores breakfast, we had entirely run out of oats and cinnamon, and rice and *farine* staples were being rationed.

"I've got an idea," said Cemci, as he left camp and wandered into the jungle's interior. A few minutes later he returned, holding two shoots covered in thorns and a large, round, hard shell, not dissimilar to a coconut. He held out one of the shoots to me.

"A backscratcher," he said.

After examining it, I proceeded to whack my back with the spiny root. It was surprisingly good for relieving the itch of mosquito bites.

I clocked Nereus looking at me with a small smirk on his face and guessed that those shoots weren't intended be to used for scratching backs. Although, having tried it, I can definitely recommend it! What started as a joke actually became a pretty useful bit of kit for me.

Cemci then cracked open the shell with his machete, revealing a cluster of Brazil nuts inside.

"Yum, I love Brazil nuts," I said, as he offered me some.

"Guyana nuts, not Brazil nuts," Jackson joked.

Cemci held up the root to show me and then rubbed the nuts against the thorns, until they turned into a crumbly pulp.

It quickly became clear that the root was used as a natural grater. I followed suit and started rubbing the nuts against the spikes, the residue falling over a palm leaf. Cemci scooped up my pile and popped it in a pot of water over the fire. He then added some *farine* and, within 15 minutes, it had turned into a deliciously thick soup. When we least expected it, breakfast turned out to be surprisingly tasty, thanks to the jungle kitchen and its utensils.

As we ate, I studied the thorny root and considered its fascinating backstory. It came from the "walking palm", a tree with 1- or 2-metre stilt-like roots that make the base of it look like a man-made woodland den where children play. Scientists have debated (and generally rejected) the claim, but legend has it that, when the canopy becomes too crowded or the soil inhospitable, the 20-metre-high tree will amble around the forest looking for a new place to put down roots. The old roots that no longer serve the tree supposedly die off. In many ways, the walking palm set the tone of the day. Every situation can be told in a multitude of ways, depending on where you choose to stand. If your current position doesn't serve you – or those around you – perhaps it's best to find more nourishing places to root yourself.

Brazil nuts grated, backs scratched and breakfast over, it was time to get moving.

Question your own narratives – they're not always right

"What will you all do when you see the source?" Nigel asked, as we trudged uphill again.

"Turn around," I replied, somewhat flippantly, as I readjusted my tight bag straps.

It was an illuminating question. In the grand scheme of life, establishing where something like a river comes from, or how and why it starts, perhaps matters less than the fact that it exists.

However, for me, finding and documenting the source was like understanding the beginning of a story. It helps to explain the river's own journey, and illustrates the interconnected nature of wilderness and humanity.

"I guess, for me, the source represents not only an adventure but the start of something," I shared as we walked. "How something so small and easily overlooked can grow to become so vital, so mighty, so necessary to so many people; the power of little things."

A brilliant electric-blue poison dart frog hopped across our path, causing us to pause momentarily to admire it. As we watched the creature hop away, I considered Nigel's question some more. I thought about my teammates and what they'd told me about their motivations.

For Laura, this had been a trip she'd poured her heart and soul into, planned for months and said goodbye to her baby for; reaching the source was the start of her dream. For our guides, it was paid work and an opportunity to further explore their protected area.

"I'll be interested to see how you all react," Nigel concluded.

Honestly, so was I. I found it fascinating that, within our small team, we had so many different narratives and backstories about the expedition. Analyzing these differing perspectives made me question my own. If I was honest, I'd neglected to say that ego, and the desire to prove I was capable of something so extreme, also played a part in me wanting to get to the source. When I dug into it, and if I was really frank with myself, at times I was operating from a place of low self-confidence.

On the face of it, perhaps this seems counter-intuitive. I'm privileged in so many ways. I've got wonderful family and friends, and, outwardly at least, it would seem I have nothing to worry about. I moved around a lot as a kid, and I remember how scary the prospect of making new friends was. Like so many of us, I'd always try to be a more outgoing, fun version of myself. It worked, and in several ways it was a massively positive experience, which now helps me to adjust to unfamiliar environments, learn how to meet new

Focus on the best version of you

people and push through situations that feel uncomfortable. However, I realized over the years that, by doing this, my ego had written a more counterproductive narrative – that perhaps my shy, awkward and introspective side was less valuable, less liked, and that if I showed it, I wouldn't be accepted in the same way.

I'm guessing your head might produce unhealthy stories, too, at times. We all have these different facets of ourselves, and maybe accepting and embracing them all is key to showing up authentically. I've come to understand that, whether they're accurate or not, the pessimistic stories my brain sometimes cooks up don't serve me. So, instead of focusing on these, I find it more useful to gravitate toward helpful and nourishing ones.

Although rare, I reckon everyone has had at least one moment in life that felt like it was taken from a scene in a film. My freeze-frame happened a few days previously, when we crossed a steep riverbank, via a narrow fallen log. The jungle equivalent of a tightrope. Only, in my case, I was also fully laden, and dangling from my teeth was a leg of hog bound in palm for ease of carrying.

We'd been following a path through the jungle that Cemci and Jackson had cut earlier that morning, and we found ourselves back at the river. Although the water was shallow, the banks were incredibly steep. It would have taken ages to cross if it wasn't for a thin, but solid, 10-metre-long tree that lay across the water, spanning bank to bank. Using large pieces of bamboo cut and rammed into the riverbed at strategic points, Cemci and

Jackson had managed to fashion an incredible bridge of sorts. The only problem was that we could seriously hurt ourselves if we slipped and fell. I watched as my teammates crossed. I saw them swing the bamboo to those behind them to help stabilize their crossing. There were a few moments of jeopardy, when the odd wobble threatened to send them plunging into the riverbed 3 metres below, and there was exhilaration when they made it to the other side.

Then it was my turn. I was the last to cross. I looked down. The log could comfortably fit one shoe but two together was pushing it. *One foot in front of the other*, I thought. *Focus on the log, not the fall. You can do this.* I felt remarkably calm and courageous, and made it across without so much as a wobble. Indiana Jones, eat your heart out. I like to think it's the most badass I've ever looked.

I've tried to store this particular image away for the days when I feel overwhelmed. When those negative thoughts wheedle and wrap themselves around my brain. When I feel so scared of judgment that I want to hide myself, like a hedgehog curling into a ball. If I had lingered too long with these corrosive stories, this book would not have been written. Thoughts of everyone who reads it giving it a terrible review almost stopped the flow of words, a dam of my own making. Yet, as I stared at a blank page, I realized

Examine the language you use about yourself – especially if it's self-limiting

that another story was possible, just like when I balanced on that log, teeth clamped on a piece of hog, feeling far braver than usual. A "what if": what if I did get the words down? What if they resonated with someone? What if they inspired just one person? What if that one person started to believe in being capable of more than they thought? I still picture that version of me, every now and again – me at my most ballsy. It is the story of myself I try to focus on.

As the expedition went on, I enjoyed observing the stories my teammates were writing for themselves, too, especially when in uncomfortable situations. The stories we embrace have amazing power over how we feel about ourselves. I was fascinated by the way Ness dealt with feeling ill. A few days previously, when Cemci and Laura were cutting the trail, they had found two large eggs and carefully spent hours carrying them back to the rest of the team. Unfortunately, small as the portion was, the egg clearly didn't agree with Ness.

"I was feeling fantastic until just after the egg," she told me as we ate breakfast the next morning. "But I think it's on the mend. I had hot and cold sweats, but I will be alright. I just couldn't focus and it made me a bit woozy, but I think it's going out the system."

I found her choice of language, the words she chose to write her story, fascinating. "*It's* on the mend", "*It's* going out *the* system" – Ness hadn't internalized the fact she was feeling sick. It wasn't defining her. When she did refer to herself, it was positive and forward-looking. "I *had* hot and cold sweats" and "I *will* be alright". Maybe it's a subtle distinction but I think it's an important one. The entire team was low on energy but were using narratives about themselves to help put one foot in front of the other.

At another point on the hike, I'd noticed that Nigel was using a similar technique. I'd clocked that he was carrying two massive bags. I'd tried to lift his pack the day before and it was unbelievably heavy. Carrying two was impressive in itself, let alone up mountainous slopes. I offered to take one off him, or at least to share the load.

Nigel explained that the new pack was his granddad's. I held out my hand to take it but he pushed it back toward my body.

"I am strong. You be you," he said.

Nigel was strong. He was also telling himself that he was, choosing how he constructed his identity. Similarly, above my desk at home I have the words: "I am a writer." Psychologically, this helps me more than saying: "I write." Partly because there are days when the words fail to come – when they've buggered off on holiday and forgotten to leave a note. If I say, "I write," I can also say that sometimes there are days when I don't write. Saying I *am* a writer talks to something deeper. There's less of a get-out clause. It forms part of my core beliefs about myself, the identity construction that's put out into the world. If we define ourselves, choose how we write our own story, it keeps us moving in the direction of who we want to become.

"You'd make a good Toshao," I told Nigel, as we continued trudging up the mountain.

"I don't want to be a Toshao. I want freedom," he replied. "Anyway, right now, I'm thinking about mountains."

I was trying to think about anything other than mountains, as my legs were screaming at me. I was grateful

The stories we tell ourselves can impact society – so let's write more positive ones

when Cemci pulled some of the Brazil nuts from breakfast out of his pocket and offered us one.

"They're a good source of oil," Cemci said, chomping away. "The uncontacted are very strong. They live on these and starch."

A combination of living off-grid for a few weeks and Cemci's mention of indigenous peoples in isolation reminded me of the benefit of questioning not just our individual narratives but also, more broadly, our society's. As communities, our collective beliefs help to shape what matters in life and what we should value. Just as we can write ourselves stories that don't serve us, we can also write or perpetuate narratives that don't help the societies and world we live in.

I looked at the Brazil nut that Cemci had offered me and considered that over 100 indigenous communities in isolation are estimated to exist around the world, half of whom live in the Amazon rainforest. Many of these people disappeared into the jungle interior after the Amazon rubber boom of 1879–1912. There is little wonder why. In the middle of the nineteenth century, the desire for rubber grew after the American Charles Goodyear discovered that latex cooked from rubber trees had numerous uses. The invention of tyres by the Scotsman John Dunlop in 1888, and mass production of the motor car by Henry Ford, further increased demand. On the face of it, the narrative was that the discovery was great for business and development.

The account we hear less of in Europe was how the rubber boom fuelled crimes against humanity. European rubber traders not only exposed remote indigenous communities to illness, but also enslaved, tortured and murdered them. One of the most brutal cases involved the Peruvian Amazon Rubber Company, which was run by the Peruvian Arana brothers but had a British board of directors and was funded by the London Stock Exchange.

Atrocities committed against indigenous men, women and children were reported to have taken place. Evidence suggests that people were flogged, left to die, shot for amusement, dashed against trees and burned alive. Nearly 30,000 indigenous people were killed. It is a terrible and shameful period of history. The journalist W. E. Hardenburg wrote a book in 1912, *The Putumayo: The Devil's Paradise*, documenting the abuses of the rubber boom along the Putumayo River, one of the Amazon's tributaries that forms part of Colombia's border with Ecuador and Peru. As the book's editor put it in the preface, the atrocities were "perhaps the most terrible page in the whole history of commercialism". The Prime Minister at the time of the book's publication, Herbert Asquith, even set up a committee to look into the widespread human rights abuses. The conclusion? Those in the UK who attended board meetings and signed cheques funding proceedings also had to be held collectively and morally responsible. The case highlighted how interconnected humanity is. It is also why the collective stories we write, and what we choose to value and focus on, matter. Centuries on from the rubber boom, indigenous communities and their homes are still under threat from deforestation – another story that needs to be told and shared more to help make positive change.

Be comforted by the fact that you can shape your future narratives, if not your past

Thankfully, the Brazil nut that Cemci gave me sustained me for a few more hours of hiking. It was a welcome relief, though, to finally remove the weight from our shoulders and plonk our bags down for a breather. I rubbed my neck and back, feeling the indentation of the straps on my skin. Above us was what Cemci ominously dubbed "the evil tree". It was a large, chunky tree with peeling brown bark. According to Cemci, the indigenous people of Suriname will often pin a picture of those who have wronged them against this large tree and shoot an arrow at them. The person in the picture will then drop dead. Not wanting to experience the tree's temperament first-hand, we didn't hang around for too long. Unfortunately, the direction we were headed wasn't much more enticing.

"It's the stuff of nightmares," said Ness, as we came to a temporary halt in front of a fallen tree.

On one side was a huge spider's web – actually, lair would be a better description – strung across a large bush. It must have been about three metres wide and one metre deep. It was thick and foreboding, and looked almost like someone had thrown a bed sheet over the foliage. Given the size of the web, I wondered if it belonged to the largest spider in the world: the Goliath birdeater. This tarantula has legs that are nearly 31 centimetres long and fangs large enough to break human skin – and it calls the rainforest of Guyana home. The only consolation of coming face to face with something out of a Harry Potter book would have been that at least it's not deadly to humans. I needn't have worried, however, as apparently the tarantula inhabits burrows abandoned by rodents; a relief in one respect, although it left the maker of the largest web I have ever seen a mystery. Unfortunately, while focusing on the spider's web, I'd totally failed to look on the other side of the log, which turned out to be home to a nest of angry – and now disturbed – wasps.

"Run," came the alarming command from the front of the group.

At this point I managed to summon up more energy than I had had all day, as we hurtled back the way we had come. Frustratingly, we had decided that the safest course of action was to double back on ourselves and take a different route.

That's the thing with stories – you never really know how things are going to turn out. Who knows if the plot twists are good or bad? So often, it's the stumble that precedes the triumph – the classic hero's journey. At the time, our setbacks in life can seem like the end of the world, but perhaps it's just that we have yet to see how they can be the making of us. On this occasion, our long detour paid off.

We felt our campsite for the evening before we saw it. The air relaxed its stifling heat; a coolness breathed life back into us. We hoped this would be our last camp before the final push to the source. A creek was up ahead. A babbling, fast-flowing stream glistened in the afternoon light. Beautiful rock pools almost took on the green hue of the trees swaying in the wind around them. Pristine and untouched, it was one of the most beautiful places I have ever seen.

It's amazing how a good wash can remove the stresses and dirt of the day – both literally and metaphorically. The water was clear enough to feel safe in and us ladies floated, watching the trees wave above us and feeling the chill rush over our naked bodies. It was glorious. When we returned to camp, the men went to wash, and Ness, Laura and I had a good chuckle listening to them messing around in the rock pool. There was lots of giggling as we heard someone counting Nigel doing push-ups. When he got to around twenty, the counting started again at one.

Clean, having sourced some fish for dinner and with a sleep ahead of us, our spirits were restored. The following day we were to begin our expedition in earnest: we were going to make it to the source. However, like most of the best stories in life, it didn't go quite as expected...

Mystery

*(noun): anything that is kept secret,
or remains unexplained or unknown.*

In the age of Google, of instant access to information, of satellites beaming images from across the solar system, there is something humbling about a bit of mystery. In many ways, technology gives us a sense that we are in control of something beyond ourselves. Arguably, mastery of your decisions and of yourself is beneficial, but trying to control everything – your environment, those around you or what people think of you – is bloody tiring. Nature, once again, provides a solution: embrace the mystery in life. We are yet to know the exact hue of tonight's sunset, what shape the illuminated clouds will take as light scatters across the sky. There's a joy to that, a sense of excitement, something to look forward to.

MYSTERY

There is so much we have yet to learn as a species. If nature were a date, I'd hazard a guess she'd be a hell of an interesting one. Intriguing, beguiling and, at times, immensely frustrating. She'd be bewitching but vaguely dangerous, with a sting in her tail; a woman with secrets you'd never unlock. A reminder that however much we think we are in control of the planet, we're not. It's exciting. Mystery holds our attention – where water flows from and to; the berry that may or may not be edible; the fire that flickers between destructive and enabling. A bit of mystery has helped humanity grow and, equally, reminds us we still have far to go.

Days on expedition: 24

Location: Guyana's Acarai Mountains

Status: reaching the source

It felt like a very momentous day when we woke up, similar to being a kid and jumping out of bed on Christmas Day. I bounded out of the hammock. Jackson had even shaved for the occasion. Given we were so close to the source, we left the bags in camp. It was amazing what a difference it made to our speed and spirits. It was so refreshing to be travelling light. We'd estimated that, as the crow flies, it was nearly 16 kilometres from base camp to where we thought the source was. If we were right, there were only around 5 kilometres left.

At this point I will hold my hand up and say I was the least useful member of the team when it came to navigating. I can read a map (as long as I've oriented it first) but it isn't my strong suit. As someone who struggles with spatial awareness, I genuinely see the blue dot on my phone as a personal nemesis, shifting and moving all over the shop, as I try to turn my device to read the map around the streets of London. I have been told (on several occasions) that this is not how you use GPS on a phone. Call me old-fashioned, but I do love looking for street names on a map and taking note of where I am, rather than holding my phone and waiting for the annoying blue circle to pull me forward, as if it were a dowsing rod looking for water. In this instance, however, we were looking for water.

Mystery forces us to ask questions; curiosity can help us grow

It hadn't been easy to figure where our expedition would start in earnest, as rivers can have many sources. Where the Amazon

River starts, for example, has been a subject that academics have debated for centuries. It's now considered that there are potentially three main headstream areas rather than one specific source. Likewise, the Nile, the Yangtze and even the Thames have all had their sources debated. How quickly the river flows, the altitude, how far it drains and the distance the tributary is from the river's end are all factors that are considered when establishing a source.

The location of the Essequibo's source wasn't entirely clear, either. A British expedition in 1969 known as "Operation El Dorado" took geologists Dr Jevan P. Berrangé and Dr Richard L. Johnson to Guyana to produce the first topographical maps with the help of aerial photography. They took outboard canoes up the major eastward tributaries – the Kuyuwini, Kassikaityu, Kamoa, Sipu and Chodikar River – to check their observations of the physical features and geology of the area. The Chodikar has the largest water flow and was considered to be the source of the Essequibo.

Then, in 2013, the Waî Waî, including Jackson and Nereus, had led a Guyanese-German expedition to find the source. This team, using research aided by satellite photography and drones, believed that it was on the Sipu River. Since Ness, Laura and I aren't geologists, topographers or cartographers, we took a slightly different approach and asked the Waî Waî where they believed the source

Find romance in the mystery

of the river they called home was. This is how we also found ourselves on the Sipu River – albeit following a different route to a higher altitude than the previous team.

In some ways, not having a definite answer to: "Where *exactly* is the source?" was immensely frustrating, given the slog, effort and emotional energy we'd put into the expedition. But in other ways, I liked the romance, the mystery of the river. Seasons change, water ebbs and flows, and rivers can take a different course. In a world where we have so much at our fingertips, nature still keeps us guessing. The Essequibo made us work before she revealed herself. Despite carrying no weight during the hike, it took us 4 hours to move those 5 kilometres. As we ascended toward where we thought the source was, we started scrambling, literally squeezing through trunks, clinging on to vines, and shimmying under and over rocks, trees and all manner of foliage. I'm pretty sure whatever beasties the jungle had in it ended up in our hair. We were up close and personal in a way we never envisioned we would be. I made a mental note to get myself checked out by the walk-in clinic at London's Hospital for Tropical Diseases when I got home.

As the last to arrive, I found the rest of the team up ahead, gathered together, heads bowed. Orange leaves peppered the floor. Cemci and Jackson sat on rocks, the former holding the map casually slung across his lap. I followed their gaze to a tiny trickle of water running out from near the base of a large slab of rock. High in the Acarai Mountains, on the Brazilian border, a headwater of the mighty Essequibo River.

Wanting to double-check that there wasn't any water higher up, Laura scouted a few metres further up the mountain and concluded that even though she had initially been doubtful that this was the source, she was now elated. She and Ness logged the coordinates.

N1°24'52.43
W59°16'51.07

Months of hard work, of pulling together a team, and of organizing the logistics, training and sponsors were finally starting to pay off for our expedition leader.

Everyone was buzzing. We had achieved what we set out to do. Over 500 people have been in space. We wondered how many had stood in this spot over the course of human history.

"It was virgin forest we have come through; no one has ever been there. Nobody has come here," Jackson said. "From the mountaintop, it looks like a basin below."

We gathered together, and shot a group picture in various states of seriousness and silliness, before following the water down the gully. We stopped for lunch in a beautiful spot. It felt momentous, magical even. Up until this point, the source we were looking for had been a mystery to us. We'd been unable to google what it looked like or from where it emanated. We hadn't known what the cooling chill of the water would feel like on our fingers. We just knew it was a life source.

There is no greater surprise than nature

Cemci was thrilled. "This is the first time the Waî Waî have led a trek to the source. If any foreigners have come before, they've told us what coordinates to use. This is the first time we've used our own coordinates. I feel so glad to get to here," he said, brandishing his GPS device and map. "It wasn't as high as I thought, either – pretty flat, really," he added.

"You call that flat?" I exclaimed. "That was blooming hilly!" He chuckled.

"On the map the source looked like it was going into a palm swamp," Jackson said. "When I saw it wasn't like that, I felt good. We'd been chosen by the village to do this journey because of our skills. I've cut trails to Suriname and Brazil before. Now, when I go back to the Waî Waî, I will explain what the source looked like and show them the location on the map." He paused. "One thing, though, you guys didn't put up a little flag. I thought you'd do that."

We paused and took a bite of our rather uninspiring lunch of plain rice. We watched the tiny trickle of water running near our feet, occasionally letting it flow into our water bottles as we held them to the ground. I considered Jackson's comment about flag planting. I'm glad we didn't.

From the beginning of the fifteenth century until the eighteenth century, seafaring European nations (primarily Portugal and Spain, and later the Netherlands, Britain and France) were engaged in a race to claim and colonize land previously unknown to them. Flags would be planted, staking claim to territories for the kings and queens of the countries funding those expeditions. This period of history is sometimes referred to as the Age of Exploration or Age of Discovery. It explains why Spanish is the predominant language in much of South and Central America. Christopher Columbus unexpectedly landed in the region when trying to seek out a western ocean route to Asia. As the popular rhyme goes: "In 1492, Columbus sailed the ocean blue."

It is telling that the explorers and soldiers who partook in these expeditions were known as "conquistadors" in the Spanish and Portuguese empires – a term derived from the word "conquistar", Spanish for "to conquer". The language often used around exploration fascinates me, as so often it's a language of arrogance. In the same way people and nations have been controlled and invaded, mountains, rivers and oceans are often talked about as having been battled, conquered or tamed. Yet, little is spoken of how nature will reclaim the flag long after people have departed. If it is a battle, she will win every time. Flag planting has a long historical tie with exploring but it's one practice best left in the past. Admittedly, there was one thing I wanted to conquer that day – lunch, even if it was boring.

As we shoveled down rice with a side of rice, Jackson continued, "I shaved off my beard today because it is important for me to have a photo with you. I'm very happy that you ladies, not a male, reached the source. You never see ladies going like this. You are all very, very strong – stronger than me. The German team didn't cut a line, but you guys follow us and cut..." He turned his smile toward me. "Or just bat."

Jackson's words were generous in many respects. There was no way we were stronger than him, but we appreciated the sentiment.

"The girls want to try men's work," Cemci added. "You can be proud of yourselves. You've got better. Better than others. Slowly but surely."

"I am still in shock that we finally made it here," Ness said. "It's been a mega part of our expedition; the heart and soul of it; the richness of the community, the wildlife, the people – everything has been out of this world. We've given blood, sweat and tears to get to the source and we find it's a tiny, tranquil trickle. To think it's going to turn into a monster at the bottom. To see how much life it gives. It's pretty amazing. I really enjoyed taking that team photo together; you've worked your bollocks off, more than we have."

"If you came alone, do you think you could make it?" Jackson asked.

"Not a chance," Laura, Ness and I responded.

"How will people feel about it? Who will know about the source?" Jackson asked.

"Soon it will be everyone," Ness replied. "That information will be online because of us. I like the fact that we will give information to the world about where the source is. That's satisfying. That's what exploration is."

We now just had the small matter of hiking back through dense, mountainous jungle and then kayaking down the 1,014 kilometres of the Essequibo River, complete with its rapids and waterfalls. Our journey to the source may have been over, but the expedition was just beginning.

"It's comical that this is the start of the expedition after nearly a month of being in the jungle," Laura said, as we retraced our steps and started our descent back to camp.

"I think we will have good dreams tonight," Cemci replied.

What we didn't realize at the time was that Mother Nature had a few more secrets up her sleeve. Returning home in one piece, or even to camp that night, was far from guaranteed.

Map of the Essequibo's Tributaries

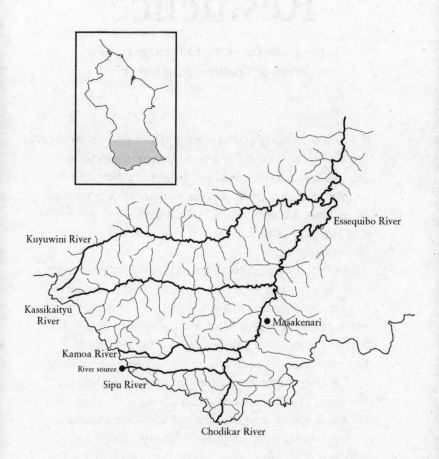

Kuyuwini River

Essequibo River

Kassikaityu River

Masakenari

Kamoa River

River source

Sipu River

Chodikar River

Resilience

(noun): the capacity to recover quickly from difficulties; toughness.

If you're old enough to be reading this book, chances are life has thrown a fair few unpleasant things your way. As a result, I'd guess you're already way grittier than you might think. Unless seriously lucky, most of us have to endure experiences we'd rather not, and learning how to cope when things are tough is resilience in action.

I like to think trees can teach us a fair amount about weathering storms, as they are battered by all sorts of bad weather. Some, like the oak, are stoic, strong, and just grin and bear what Mother Nature throws at them. Others, like the palm, flex and bend in the wind. Occasionally, the pressure might become too much and a tree might be forced to grow in a different direction. Worst case, a few branches might snap off. However, given time, the tree almost always begins to see new shoots of growth. In life, bad weather and setbacks will always occur, but we must try to find ways to adapt and remain rooted when they do. Just as different trees take different approaches, the tools we use to get us through tricky times will differ, depending on the individual. Humour, stoicism and reframing are some of my go-tos.

One of my favourite compliments in life is: "You're gritty." I'm drawn to gritty people. When life knocks them down, they are the ones who get up again and again. They are the survivors and the thrivers. More often than not, they can laugh at, and be kind to, themselves. I think, with practice, we can all become that little bit grittier. It helps if we accept that the most interesting journeys through life often involve a few unexpected twists and turns; no one lives a perfect life, even if it appears that way. Rubbish things will happen. Cock-ups will be made. You will fail at a fair few things. So when you fall – and you will – when you're flat on your face in the mud, look up. Channel the resilience of trees and remember that, even if you can't see it yet, sunlight still exists.

Days on expedition: 24

Location: Guyana's Acarai Mountains

Status: lost in the jungle

It was official: we were lost, deep in the Acarai Mountains, with the majority of our kit at camp. What was meant to be a short trip to the source and back was becoming more serious by the minute, as exhaustion and nightfall were setting in.

"I know we passed the trail, but I don't know where," Cemci said.

We all looked around – there were vines and massive trees, but none of the small, telltale machete cuts that indicated we'd been in the forest. The team were remarkably relaxed, considering. As Ness put it, Cemci and Jackson had been doing this for donkey's years.

Control what you can and accept what you can't

"We have a compass and a GPS," said Jackson, clearly trying to give us hope that we weren't about to be lost to the jungle forever.

"Even if we didn't," added Cemci, "we would just have to sleep somewhere and then cut a new line."

Spending the night without a hammock, mosquito net, warm clothes or food wasn't my ideal wild night out, it has to be said. However, a more pressing problem confronted us: exhaustion.

Nigel asked if I was alright at one point, as I kept swaying. I was so tired I fell over twice. Aside from refilling our bottles at the source, water had been hard to come by as soon as we deviated from it. I'd also been sweating so much that I hadn't peed for the entire day.

From behind me, Jackson tried to gee me along by making up some songs. He's got a lovely singing voice and his choice of lyrics did help to put more of a spring in my step. I tried to maintain a straight line by focusing on following Aaron's footsteps, as he walked in front of me. Jackson's words carried us along. Lyrics included: "Check your boots" (as my shoelace came undone), "Keep straight on your path; I'm always behind you" (as my walking became more metronomic), "Where else can you find a nice jungle? In Guyana, in Guyana" (as we descended down what Jackson described as an "f-ing 45° slope") and "Watch your step, baby" (as I got my legs tangled in a vine for what was the umpteenth time that day).

"I swear the jungle is trying to keep me here," I sighed.

Most of the day I'd had a stick in one hand and my bandana wrapped around the other for the occasions when I would inevitably lean too long on the rotten logs we had to clamber over. Many a time I lost my foot in one and prayed it would come out in one piece. I wasn't the only one in a bad way, though; everyone was shattered.

If things are becoming too much, stop, rest and reassess

At one point, Laura said she felt super dizzy and that her vision was black-and-white. Her eyes were wide and wired; she looked drained. She described the feeling as similar to being drunk. We stopped for a breather, and gave her the Brazil nuts and the remains of the water.

"I'm not worried that we are lost but my blood sugar is low and my depth of field is a bit off. The vision thing is scaring me a bit," she said.

It really hit home then how much we needed to get back to camp, in case something was more seriously wrong. Bizarrely, seeing Laura in such a bad way snapped me out of my lethargy.

It was as if my body was suddenly in survival mode. Given that I hadn't peed, drunk or eaten a great deal, I suppose it was. Ness walked ahead of her and I followed behind, making sure she got down the steep, slippery slope OK.

At the end of the slope was a small stream. It could be described as stagnant were it not for a tiny flow running through the shallow, predominantly murky water. I filled up my water bottle. As we didn't know how long it would be until we reached camp, I figured that it was better to have some water, albeit potentially dodgy, than none at all.

Thankfully, I didn't need to put my theory to the test as, within the hour, we'd found our camp. Never have I been so grateful to see a hammock in my life. Unfortunately, some of our tarps had been ripped to bits and spider-monkey poo was splattered around the shredded remains, but our relief was so great that even this blow couldn't dampen our spirits too much.

To celebrate reaching the source, and given we were now only a couple of days' walk back to base camp, we cracked open two of our emergency freeze-dried Firepot meals – each intended for a person – and shared them between the nine of us. Dinner time had become so one-dimensional it was doing my head in, both through boredom and lack of nutritional value. Having something other than rice, *farine* and fish was beyond amazing. "Snacks" (if you can call them that) had become unsoaked soya chunks sprinkled with either garlic powder or mixed herbs. Our jungle equivalent of popcorn.

"I wish they made chocolate flavour," Ness had said a few days previously, as she placed an exceptionally dry piece in her mouth. I double-checked the ingredients on the back: "Defatted soy flour and caramel colour."

"Sod it, it works for me," Laura replied, tossing her head back. In an exaggerated motion she threw the soya chunks into the air, leaned backward and tried to catch them in her mouth.

As she did so, our eyes fell on a stick, sharpened into the shape of a fork, that had been left on a dry bag behind her and was pointing directly at her skull. We'd been using it to prod the fire, but it now looked like it might end up skewering an open-mouthed Laura. Let's face it, it wouldn't be the best epitaph: "She loved MSG-laden soya so much she impaled herself." Thankfully, she missed being the latest addition to our nightly BBQ by mere millimetres.

You are capable of more than you think

Like many things in life, just when you think you can't take any more, you're handed something else to deal with. Turns out that our rehydrated chilli "we've reached the source" con carne and rice celebratory meal was premature. The following few days were to be physically the toughest (and sweatiest) of my life.

I'd had an absolutely shocking night's sleep. Scrambling and squeezing my way through the jungle to reach the source had left me feeling unbelievably itchy. My torso and the back of my legs felt like they were on fire with tiny red dots that were covering my body. I'd spent most of the night scratching – both consciously and unconsciously.

Nereus, meanwhile, was dispatching a large, 8-centimetre-long black scorpion that had made a home on the blue T-shirt hanging over his hammock.

"It's the biggest we've seen," said Laura as we watched it land in the fire.

The mood in the camp was definitely lower than usual and I noticed many of us, despite knowing we needed to eat, were finding it hard to get down our breakfast of *farine* and Brazil nuts. The environment slowly seemed to be getting to us all.

In many ways, retracing our steps and knowing what we had ahead of us was far harder to deal with mentally. Walking through our old camps was eerie. They felt like ghost towns. The jungle almost seemed to be clawing back any evidence that we'd been there at all. A reminder that we were simply guests and our presence was temporary. We passed what the guys had nicknamed "hog hill" and all that remained of the sliced-up hog was the skull. In nearly a week the forest had reclaimed what it had spawned.

One day, after a few hours of traipsing up and down, hillside after hillside, we stopped for a rest. I asked Ness and Laura how many slopes we'd hiked over. We reckoned we'd covered around eight hills: five of them exceptionally steep and three at more of an incline. We double-checked with Jackson – a futile exercise. "I'm just passing without checking," came the response.

It felt like we were in a sauna. Sweat cascaded from every angle. At one point I thought, *I never want to do a physical journey ever again.* My legs burned. Every step was a mental battle. Keeping myself upright was becoming a problem.

Humour is powerful when things get tough

I asked how everyone was feeling. The question was unnecessary: we all looked broken. Sweat streamed down our bodies, and our clothes were sodden; faces full of desperation and exhaustion looked back at me. Aaron stared deep into his water bottle. Jackson and Cemci lifted a fist in the air. What was meant to be a sign of strength looked more like a weary protest.

Ness called bullshit. "I'm at the point where I'm unable and unwilling to even speak. Running on fumes. Buggered. Empty right now. Can you teleport me?" she said.

"The speed that I'm walking is all the speed that I've got," Cemci capitulated.

"Well, I feel like I could get on a rodeo bull," Laura said.

Taking one look at her, you could tell that most certainly wasn't the case. Sweat seeped through her floral shirt, turning it quite translucent in parts. However, her gag raised a smile from us all. Humour had been a powerful force in helping the team put one step in front of the other. Be it Jackson's songs, Laura's quips or the general banter, it all helped us to keep moving. As a team we tried to focus on the small wins. In my case, it was the tiny bright-yellow pee I'd done a few hours earlier – an improvement on no pee the day before.

Ness massively got the giggles at one point, as I'd somehow managed to attach myself to the Amazonian equivalent of a spiky gorse bush. I was too tired to care and decided to drag it with me. I'd hoped it would fall off by itself. It didn't.

"Oh, Pip, I do enjoy walking behind you," Ness wheezed. "We're on our last legs, going down a steep slope and you've got a branch attached to what looks like your crotch. It's making a hell of a racket, tripping you up and every step you take it's just shuddering down the mountain with you. It's ridiculous."

She was laughing so hard I got the giggles, too, lost my balance further and – remarkably, given the circumstances – nearly peed myself. I informed Ness of this brilliant proof of my hydration, which finished her off entirely.

"I needed that," she said, as the hysterics came to an end. "I was so exhausted I just lost the plot. That brought light to my day just when I needed it."

"You need to do more Kegels, Pip," Laura laughed. "You haven't even had a baby."

It was those moments of light relief, those metaphorical glimpses of sunlight, that we'd been chasing. They invigorated us mentally, helped us to push on. At times things had felt so bleak it was hard to find anything positive or smile-inducing about a situation.

Sunlight always exists somewhere

Yet, it just took one of us to find something and everyone felt emotionally lifted. Like any challenge, sometimes approaching it with a sense of humour (however dark) can help things to feel less daunting.

Walking back to base camp seemed to go on forever. We went through all sorts of terrain: swamps – where if you stood in the wrong place, your foot, calf or knee would sink into the mud – steep slopes and rather pleasant meanders through the forest. At one point we walked through a break in the canopy and a tiny patch of sun welcomed us. Actual warming sunlight. It was such a shock I initially felt like a vampire, trying to hide.

"I'd almost forgotten the sun existed," Laura remarked, as she extended her arms and felt its rays caress them.

In the midst of our personal struggles, at times we'd all forgotten that the sun existed. However, deep down, we knew it had to be there somewhere. Words had become my sunlight. In the toughest moments I would often turn to my favourite poems, to passages that particularly resonated. As I trudged up and down hillsides, I was accompanied by poets past and present. Philip Larkin's ideas about beginning "afresh" in his poem "Trees" and the words of Lang Leav – "She will not only climb mountains – she will move them too" – were particularly helpful on the steep climbs. Using words, humour or conversations, the team had found distractions to keep pushing each other through the pain.

Then, after nine days of walking, there it was: base camp.

"It feels like coming home," said Laura. "No more walking tomorrow. This is it. We are going paddling..."

We all dived, fully clothed, into the water, although not before I'd had the chance to trip over my feet once again. The jungle had pushed me to the edges of myself. I felt like I'd experienced every human emotion. I was knackered.

Nigel, too, was pensive. He had been in a very weird, quiet mood for the last few days. As we waited for the water to boil for dinner, Ness and Laura suggested I go and talk to him.

"If anyone can get it out of him, you can," they said.

He was carving another cross-like symbol into some wood as I sat with him. I noticed he now had two on the bracelet he'd made out of hammock string. I shared that I was tired – a shell of a woman. He said he was tired, too.

"Are you looking forward to going home?" I asked.

"Sort of," he replied.

In a funny way, the knowledge that we were going to leave base camp was tinged with sadness. As Laura had remarked, it had begun to feel a bit like home. To lift the mood and to mark the occasion, I gave Nigel my phone, so he could choose some music. He loves music, devouring anything with a strong beat, which was lucky because my playlists mainly consisted of dance music. I promised to write down the list of songs and artists for him. The team all bopped about, torches attached to our heads on flashing mode. We must have looked ridiculous: matted hair, dirty, smelly clothes, covered in bites, limbs flailing, seemingly not a care in the world. It was good for the soul – and the appetite.

A supportive network can help you endure more than you think

Excitingly, dinner that evening was a celebratory freeze-dried "extra-large serving" of orzo pasta bolognese. We really pushed the boat out – one portion each this time – at 940 calories a pop. It barely scratched the surface of our hunger, so we made up more. We'd estimated we'd burned nearly 6,000 calories that day.

As we washed our Tupperware in the river, my thoughts turned to the next few days. Now that we'd located the source, the paddling part of the expedition would begin in earnest. First, we would take the dugout canoes back to Masakenari. It would be the last time we'd paddle as a team, before Ness, Laura and I would be in sole control of our boats. From there, the river would be wide enough that our inflatable kayaks wouldn't be punctured by submerged obstacles. Reaching Masakenari also meant saying goodbye to the team that had accompanied us in the jungle. Our river guides, Ant and Romel, would be taking their place. I asked Jackson if he'd enjoyed the expedition.

"Yes, you are phenomenal ladies," he added kindly. "This is my second expedition and, on the first, the team didn't integrate as much as we did."

We massively appreciated the Waî Waî sharing knowledge with us. From what Jackson was saying, it seemed that he had also appreciated our willingness to learn. I told him I'd miss him a lot.

"I think one of the greatest things has been our journey together, the friendships that have blossomed, reaching the source together. It's one of those milestones where you kind of take stock. We will have an incredible bond for life now," Ness said.

Later that evening, Nigel carved into the makeshift table that our guides had made from logs: "Maybe you will walk away."

"Forever in the jungle of my mind," I scratched back.

He smiled. Ness cried and gave him a big hug.

Nigel handed back my phone. "I've loved every minute," he said.

With the music off and the team getting ready for bed (a late night for us at 9 p.m., rather than our usual 7.30 p.m.), we heard a terrifying, nasal grunt close to us.

"It sounds beast-like," Laura exclaimed, her eyes wide.

A clattering sound of something lurching through the jungle was getting nearer. I froze, panicked. Had we made it this far to be charged by a peccary? Christ, which tree would we climb, if so? I looked to Jackson for help. He simply shook his head.

"The hoatzin," he told us, "the national bird of Guyana. We don't kill it."

Like me, it's a clumsy, smelly bird, known for its inelegant way of clambering through the foliage, hopping from branch to branch, aiming in the right direction and hoping for the best. The hoatzin is harmless and pheasant-like, with a featherless blue face, red eyes and a ruffled crest. It also has two stomachs, like a cow. When full, they have a rubbery callus on their breastbone, which handily serves as a sort of tripod. They rarely fly and, when they do, they're not the most beautiful to watch, due to their large wings, dumpy bodies, long necks and small heads. Yet, despite everything, they get to where they need to go, and they've become an icon for a nation. Similarly, our journey to the source had been a bit of a bumpy ride. Things hadn't gone entirely to plan. However, despite setbacks – and much like the hoatzin – we'd ultimately persevered and got there in the end.

As I lay in bed that evening, I looked at the trees surrounding our campsite. It was bonkers to think that the region was around 1.7 billion years old. I wondered how many thousands of years the ginormous trees I was looking at had been holding firm. We just had to hope that, over the coming months on the river, we could, too. One thing was certain: the jungle certainly wasn't finished with us yet.

PART TWO

LIFE ON THE RIVER

Kindness

*(noun): the quality of being friendly,
generous and considerate*

Watching the news, you'd be forgiven for thinking the world is in a shocking state. In many ways it is. But what conventional media misses is the kindness we're all capable of. The stories of generosity. The inherent goodness that exists within humanity.

Many moons ago I worked in Hong Kong as a news reporter. I loved the cut and thrust, the excitement of never knowing what story may appear in the day. Yet something was missing for me: the positive stories. Indeed, things only make the news because they are out of the ordinary in some way, so kindness never usually gets top billing over disaster and hardship. But so many stories of generosity exist buried within us all. I'd hazard a guess that, if I really pushed you, you could name someone within the last week who has been generous to you in some way. Perhaps it was an obvious act of hospitality or thoughtfulness, but it might have been something subtler that needed closer inspection.

You might have heard of the concept of a "love language" – the idea that people express and receive love differently. For some, this is done by performing acts of service: making sure that the house is tidy and well kept, chores are done, and breakfast brought to you in bed. For others, the huggers and the kissers of the world, it might be physical touch. You might identify instead with the gift givers or those who appreciate words of affirmation – the people most likely to leave notes scattered around or send you texts. Or perhaps, for you, love is about feeling listened to, knowing that someone is spending quality time on you and you for them. Everyone has a different combination and those around you aren't necessarily going to speak the same love language. Look again at the events happening around you. Analyze them with new eyes. If kindness is love in action, have you missed an expression of it along the way?

During our journey down the Essequibo, we witnessed and received so many obvious acts of kindness, of generosity: meals being shared, help offered and homes thrown open. However, the subtler acts were those that fascinated me. The daily interactions where each of us had the chance to be kind if we chose to be. How we expressed it was different for us all. Yet, when I looked for these expressions of kindness, of love, they were always there, even in the strangest of circumstances. So, if you despair at the state of the world, remember the times when people have been good to you. Pay it forward and remind those of us who have forgotten that there is still so much to smile about. Not all is wrong with the world. Kindness still exists.

Days on expedition: 31

Location: the Essequibo River, south of Masakenari

Status: returning to Masakenari

As I was winding down for sleep, the last thing I expected to see was Jackson, wearing only pants and welly boots, whizzing past me while clutching an axe. Since returning to base camp from the Acarai Mountains, we'd been paddling on the river for three days without a hitch. Yet, just as I slipped on my pyjama bottoms and hopped in my hammock, a commotion had broken out in the jungle. Instructions in Waî Waî were being shouted back at volume to camp. Picked out by my head torch, I watched as Jackson disappeared into the night, muttering something rude about obstacles.

With the exception of Cemci and Jackson, the rest of our Waî Waî guides were out on the water, hunting caimans. We were getting close to the Waî Waî village of Masakenari, and the plan was for Nereus, Aaron and Nigel to paddle and hunt for food for the villagers during the moonlit night. They'd then set up camp for us further downstream and we'd join them there the following day. However, from the sounds of it, they hadn't got very far at all. The dugout canoe had already found its path blocked by a fallen log that needed cutting. At least it explained why a half-clad Jackson was disappearing off to meet them with an axe, despite being midway through getting ready for bed.

I can't say I was overly enthusiastic about the coming days. Because the hiking section had lasted nearly double the time we'd initially anticipated, we were now at risk of falling behind schedule. Consequently, we'd committed to two pretty chunky days of paddling to get back to Masakenari. The news that we might have to chop our way through more obstacles the following morning wasn't *Kindness* exactly welcomed by Ness, either, who *comes* seemed to be aching all over. Her symptoms – *in many* headache, fever, aches – bore a remarkable *forms* resemblance to dengue fever. We hoped it was just exhaustion and that a good night's sleep would sort her out.

Unfortunately, the next morning Ness was no better. Those of us left at camp had taken our places in the dugout and were paddling hard to catch the others up. Ness, too, was clearly trying to pull her weight but, in spite of her best efforts, her paddle barely moved through the water. Slumped across dry bags in the middle of the boat, she was a shell of her usual Rambo self. Laura was insistent: Ness needed to stop.

"Getting Ness to stop working is a bit like getting a nun to have sex," she observed. She wasn't wrong. Unless it was absolutely necessary to remove weight from the boat, we banned Ness from getting out to push the canoe over the obstacles. We emphasized that this was a team expedition and, as such, she had to let us look after her. If that meant she could nap and recuperate while the rest of us paddled, so be it. Thankfully, Ness relented.

At my position at the back of the canoe I began to zone out. I stared at the water for a brief while and Jackson caught me looking.

"Don't worry," he said, "you'll see Charlie soon."

He was intuitive and his words kind; my thoughts had drifted to how much I was missing Charlie.

"You'll get to see your wife soon, too. It's been a few weeks – that's a long time," I replied.

"I'm looking forward to seeing her but weeks on expedition is nothing. When I've gone away before it's usually been three to six months – that's a long time."

That put things into perspective for me. His words were comforting. It wouldn't be too long before I saw Charlie again, as the plan was for him, Ed and baby Ran to join us in a couple of weeks. At that point, we would also be joined by Jon, a cameraman, who would capture the second half of our journey. They were all going to fly to Apoteri and then charter a boat upstream to meet us on the river – we just had to be there in time to meet them.

Jackson's eyes shifted to the riverbank. Then, like lightning, he picked up a long piece of bamboo we'd been using to help manoeuvre the canoe off obstacles whenever we became stuck. He raised it over his head and, with almighty force, thwacked it into the water.

Smash.

When the water calmed, we saw a caiman. Dead. Killed with one blow to the skull. Jackson pulled the bloodied reptile into the boat. Taking his machete straight to it, he severed the spine between its head, back and tail. The speed of the kill was insane. It was also the kindest way he could have done it.

After a while, pools of red appeared in the water on one side of the boat. It happened every couple of metres. I couldn't figure out what it was until I clocked Laura diligently bailing out a mixture of river water and blood that was swirling around at the bottom of the dugout.

The sight of blood churned my stomach. My breakfast of rice, salt and seasoning suddenly wasn't sitting so well. It didn't help that, when I looked down to my own feet, I noticed that the light-soled shoes I wore to paddle were soaking up the thick red soup of the caiman's remains. Let's just say it wasn't ideal. Not least because my feet were also suffering from the beginnings of trench foot.

Trench foot got its name because it was a common condition for the soldiers engaged in trench warfare during World War One. The constantly damp state of their feet would cause skin and tissue breakdown. It could lead to amputation and, in the worst cases, if the gangrene wasn't caught in time, it would result in death from sepsis. It's why Ed, during our jungle training, had been so insistent on us using talcum powder on our feet each night to dry them out. Unfortunately, during the hike, the constant walking in wet socks and jungle boots meant that my feet had slowly become increasingly prune-like and blotchy, and they were now permanently itchy. Despite trying to dry them out in the hammock each evening, they still felt as if lice had infiltrated my skin and were throwing an energetic dance party. I hoped the blood in which my feet were now bathing wouldn't make them any worse. I lifted my graze and asked Jackson if he had found his first kill difficult.

"I don't know what I killed first. I have killed many things," he replied. "The Waî Waî made a rule in 2006: don't shoot what you don't eat. People were just wasting before."

I tried to make conversation as the morning went on, but the constant paddling meant both my mind and body were beginning to flag. I needed to eat something. I could feel the telltale pangs of hanger creep up on me. My limbs were moving my paddle but didn't feel entirely connected. Ness was still in a shocking state and had spent the day lying down. We clearly all needed a rest and a sleep. Even the caiman seemed diminished. One of the most notorious predators in the Amazon basin now resembled more of a cuddly-toy imitation, after any signs it had once been alive had slowly drained away. Its head lolled to one side and its small claws seem to have wrapped around its body. I felt so sad every time I looked at it.

Unfortunately, by the time it came to lunch we still hadn't found the others, so we decided to press on. Usually, we'd stop, have a decent meal and continue refreshed but, given that we didn't know how far Nereus, Aaron and Nigel had paddled, we didn't have the luxury of stopping. I've never been a fan of eating on the move, as I love the ceremony of sitting down together, but on this occasion our meal of *farine*, soya and *aimara* would have to be on the hoof. I found not knowing how far or how long we would have to paddle psychologically tough. We couldn't ring ahead and see how far we had to go. We also knew that when we arrived, the day's physicality would continue; we couldn't just slump on a sofa and turn on the telly. Hammocks would have to be put up, dead wood for the fire found, and food caught and prepped. None of us were overjoyed by the prospect and we were beginning to give up hope that we'd even find the others before nightfall.

Even the smallest gestures can have a big impact

Then, at 5.30 p.m., just as we were considering whether the safest thing to do would be to set up camp and try to catch them up in the morning, we saw a flame in the distance. A fire was lit and friendly faces were waving from the riverbank. Aaron, Nigel and Nereus ran to greet us, pulled in our canoe and helped us unload the bags They'd set everything up. Our last camp together felt like a welcome home.

Laura remarked how lovely it was to see them. The welcome spoke of that innate human need to be cared for and to care for others. I thought of Charlie, and how nice it is when either of us comes home to the other, cuddles waiting, dinner on the go.

Apparently, the team had arrived there at 8 a.m. and had spent the day fishing. On the fire – which was more like a home-made grill with slats of logs fashioned across it – was a veritable feast of caiman and fish. It looked like some sort of all-you-can-eat.

I knew that this wasn't all for us. Food was being prepared for the village, which we would reach the next evening. What I hadn't expected to see, however, were the eight live caimans next to the fire. Their feet and snouts were bound with vine.

Our caiman was added to the fire, centre stage. Its large, dead eyes looked directly at us, its claws dangled nonchalantly and its teeth stuck out from its snout.

"Small caimans are better to eat," Jackson advised, pointing to the various cuts of caiman meat that had already been cooked on the home-made BBQ. "With the exception of the intestines, we eat everything; from head to tail, from source to sea…" he quipped.

Jackson picked a piece and tore me a bit to try. I tentatively put it in my mouth. It was a chewy white meat with no distinct taste. Looking at the array of food grilling before me, I opted to take a small bit of fish for dinner instead and made up some rehydrated spinach daal that Laura and I shared. I should probably have had a bit more, given how little we'd eaten that day, but it was hard to have much of an appetite in the heat. I felt more dehydrated than hungry.

"Stop giving me evils," Laura said to the live caimans grumpily shuffling about next to us as we ate. I clearly looked a bit uncomfortable, too.

"What are you concerned about, Pip?" Cemci said, watching me eye them up.

I asked why all the caimans hadn't been killed immediately and was told that keeping them alive preserves the meat. Given that one caiman can feed around 25 people, taking them back to the village would provide nearly enough food for everyone.

"This is a protected area and the farming is done in a very sustainable way," Cemci elaborated, explaining that, in 2017, Kanashen Amerindian Protected Area became Guyana's largest and first indigenous-owned protected area.

I knew he was right. Research has shown that when indigenous communities manage and own the rights to their land, habitats are more likely to thrive and deforestation is greatly reduced. It's why formalizing the land rights of indigenous peoples is seen as one of the most important ways of preserving the environment. It didn't stop the caimans eyeballing us.

Conversation then turned to the next step of our journey. Following our return to Masakenari, the next settlement we would encounter along the Essequibo would be the village of Apoteri. Interestingly, the village is very much tied to Britain's colonial past. Bookers – of the grocery and "Booker" prize fame – was one of the world's largest multinationals and dominated 75 per cent of Guyana's sugar trade. The company also traded in rubber, and Apoteri became a base for operations in the 1970s. The growth in the demand for rubber brought with it workers from around the region looking for employment. A new, nationally recognized airstrip was built and infrastructure, such as hospitals, housing compounds and water supply pontoons, arrived. In 1998, however, the rubber industry relocated and the population of the village decreased. Fishing, hunting and farming became the main means of income for those that remained.

"When you reach Apoteri, be careful you don't sleep so close to the river," Cemci warned. "A friend of ours slept on a rock there. The next thing he knew the caiman had whipped his hammock into the water."

Your actions can change someone's day

Lots to look forward to, then, I thought…

With the exception of the captive caimans, it was a stunning evening. The canoes were lit up in the moonlight, and the warm, flickering glow from the campfire caused shadows to dance and twirl on our faces.

Then the singing started. Melodic, uplifting hymns sung in Waî Waî became the audio accompaniment to the pirouetting flames. The final song was beautiful. "Goodbye brothers and sisters, until we see you in heaven" was how Jackson translated it. Although I didn't understand the words, we all clapped in time to the rhythm and the shuffling caimans added their own distinct riff.

The following morning, Nereus woke us all up at 5.19 a.m., singing as loudly as his lungs would allow. His voice warbled with a sense of excitement and finality. Our guides had helped us to the source safely, caught food for the village and now it was time for them to return triumphant. Our last day would be the longest one on the river in our whole expedition. We estimated that, paddling at our usual speed, it would take at least a couple of days to reach Masakenari, which would mean we risked falling behind schedule. Instead, we agreed to keep paddling until we reached the village. We would watch as dawn turned into dusk and then as dusk surrendered itself to the night. Moonlight would be our guide as darkness came. Feeling more comfortable in the environment, and with faith in the team and our skill set, the idea of paddling through the jungle at night thrilled me. Like Nereus, I was excited by what lay ahead.

Camp packed down, canoes loaded, we climbed into the dugouts for the last time. It was both an ending and a beginning. The next time Ness, Laura and I would put our paddles in the Essequibo it would be from our individual inflatable kayaks.

The caimans, still bound, seemed to be resigned to their fate. They were now lying still in the bottom of the canoe, four in each boat. I hoped their placidity would last the trip, as I didn't fancy capsizing, least of all at night. Our training on the River Dee didn't include what to do when live animals are in your craft. I looked to Jackson for advice on how best to arrange myself around them.

"Either put your feet on the wooden seat above them or place them on their back," said Jackson as I climbed into the dugout. "Just avoid the tail, as it will lash you very, very badly."

I opted to disturb them as little as possible and gingerly put my feet on the seat. Doing so made my core a little less stable for paddling but at least I wasn't at risk of being trashed by their incredibly powerful tails.

Thankfully, the day went without a hitch. Canoes stayed upright, Ness started to feel better, and the team felt united by memories, laughter and a common purpose. We'd been away for weeks but it felt like we had known each other far longer. As the heat of the day surrendered to evening's spreading coolness, our paddling had almost a ceremonial feel to it. Even though we'd been going for 12 hours straight, each stroke was almost an acknowledgement of all that had gone before and all that was yet to come. Even if just for one night, our hammocks would be exchanged for a bed in the Waî Waî's small wooden guest house. Our nightly fire would become a stove. The wooden walls of a dug-out loo a place to pause without the need to look around for predators.

Despite having paddled all day, there was an energy to our strokes. We were getting closer, mere kilometres away, and the twists and turns of the river were increasingly familiar to our guides. It wouldn't be long before we turned into the wide bend that signalled Masakenari. Our paddles worked in unison: catch, power, release. Catch, power, release. We glided across the surface of the river, picking up speed, its gentle breeze caressing our hair, like flags in the wind. We were but a moment in time, but what a moment it was.

The idyllic scene was somewhat ruined by the music that was playing to motivate us. From Laura's small portable speaker came Scooter's "The Logical Song". It's high-energy, happy hardcore music, more in keeping with a wild rave than the wild jungle. Yet the lyrics about life being magical seemed appropriate. I still smile when I think of Nereus sitting at the front of one of the boats, so animated, bopping away with his paddle, his grin the widest I'd seen it.

As we flew over the moonlit water, speeding toward the village, the sky brilliantly lit, it hit me that, in this freeze-frame of my life, everything (with the exception of the caimans between my legs) was perfect. Although we'd been paddling for literally the entire day, this was living; this was what it meant to be truly alive. The jungle was beginning to make a woman out of me.

We arrived shortly after midnight, sneaking through the village so as not to disturb those sleeping. Our guides crept back to their families, and Ness, Laura and I returned to our rooms in the guest house, where the rest of our kit was waiting for us and the next stage of the journey. We'd made good progress that evening so we would have some time in the village to regroup.

We went to the village office the following morning to connect to the internet and I spent an hour talking to Charlie. It was lovely to have a proper catch-up, and it warmed the soul to speak to him. However, in some ways, I was so reluctant to connect to Wi-Fi. The jungle had been both an escape and an awakening. The technological world is so rushed and so instant; it had felt so nice – weirdly normal and so human – not to be logging into emails, social media, admin. The internet enables me to do what I love, but my time in the jungle made me realize that I need to be in control of it, not the other way around.

Later that day, Cemci's wife, Deli, and her daughter-in-law popped over with some bananas for us. As we sat around talking, Laura showed us a very sweet video she'd just been sent of Ran trying to say "Mama". Seeing it, Deli suggested we should give up on the idea of paddling. She said a flight would be arriving in a few days and ventured that perhaps Laura should get on that. I don't think she was joking.

It was certainly tempting to stay longer than we'd planned. My feet were in a sorry state, flakey and full of red sores: the trench foot was getting worse. Walking around the village was agony – and exceptionally slow. It felt like I was walking on needles. As we went to wash at the creek, I was literally hobbling, and Ness and Laura joked that I looked like an old lady.

"You look like you need a Zimmer frame. I've never seen anything like it," said Ness.

"I have seen something like it before," Laura responded, "but she was eighty-nine and about to die."

Nereus came to join us for dinner. He gifted us a massive bag of mangoes: the ones in the village had been green when we set off for the trek, but had now turned into glorious golden globes. Given that we also hadn't had much fruit or veg for weeks, they were the best mangoes I've ever tasted.

Small acts of kindness don't go unnoticed

The rest of the team were eating at home, so it was strange not to be surrounded by them or listening to the daily saying of grace. Nereus sat next to me on one of the wooden benches that adorned either side of the table. The electricity was off but there was a beautiful red glow from Ness's torchlight, which gave the timber guest-house kitchen warmth.

"I'll pray every night for you to be safe. I hope I will see you again, or in heaven," Nereus said. Then, for the first time he proclaimed: "I'll miss you guys."

Nereus had been the strong, silent type on our journey. To hear his words, so genuine and heartfelt, was incredibly touching. We gave him a huge hug, and then Ness and I started crying. Nereus followed suit. Sometimes it is not what people say but their very presence that makes an impact. Nereus was the embodiment of this – a wonderfully kind man.

"I wasn't expecting him to cry," said Ness after Nereus left. "We didn't talk too much but he was always watching, always perceptive."

Laura nodded in agreement. I was somewhat lost for words; the encounter had been so moving.

The last few days, I'd been randomly bursting into tears – the smallest kindness, smile or gesture was enough to set me off. Ness was the same. Laura seemed more stoic – partly, I think, because her mind was with Ran and concentrating on getting to see him soon. For her, her baby was a large part of her motivation to get back on the water.

I didn't sleep immediately that night. I sat on the stairs to the guest house, looking at the moon, pregnant and round, the village lit with its light. The jungle played its tune, as stars glistened overhead. I pondered Nereus's heartfelt words, the kindness we'd received on this journey. The evening chill peppered my skin with goosebumps, yet I was filled with such warmth. Words, the best way I have of expressing love and myself, finally came to me as I sat there. I began to write…

> It was under a full moon
> that she said goodbye.
> "I will pray for you," he said,
> "every night."
> And as the tears flowed,
> and the clouds parted,
> under those faraway stars,
> that majestic ball of hope,
> she wondered if perhaps,
> just perhaps,
> there was something
> worth praying to.

Slowness

(noun): the quality of moving or operating at a low speed.

Slowness is underrated. A leisurely, relaxed journey is my favourite way to travel. In fairness, this is partly because, unless it is over the course of a 100-metre race, my body doesn't seem to travel fast. Rather than fight against it, I've come to accept this and have found great joy in slowness. Long walks allow for immersion in a landscape – a chance to envelop yourself in it, rather than just speed through. Or jaunts on a river where hours can be whiled away staring at the changing movements of the water. The best bike rides are ones that are punctuated by numerous pit stops, taking in a view as your cup of tea cools next to you. I am fully signed up to "Team Slow". You may well be in the team, too, or know someone who is. You can identify a member by their relaxed stroll around an airport – those smug types who have arrived with time to spare. Usually sipping a coffee, seemingly without a care in the world. Looking over the rim of their cup and taking a bite of their pastry, while watching those rushing to check in. Given half the chance I, too, like to be among the leisurely croissant eaters of the world.

However, Charlie was the total opposite, firmly in "Team Fast", when I first met him. A good day for him would be one in which he squeezed in meeting after meeting, careering around London, with minutes to spare between appointments. Inevitably, if we travelled somewhere, he'd want to arrive at the eleventh hour to feel as though he had maximized his time. Whenever I went along with this plan (relationships are about compromise, after all), we would be running to our plane seats pumped full of adrenaline. Victorious but also wired.

I reckon Charlie could have cycled back from Malaysia in half the time it took us (13 months), yet, physically, there is no way I could have done this. However, as he himself acknowledges, by slowing down he saw so much more. Rather than passing up conversations, we embraced them. We took up generous offers of hospitality and friendship. We were pulled off our bikes, sweating and muddy, and invited to dance in a wedding in Uzbekistan. We rode a cable car up a mountain with a young family in Kazakhstan and ended up in a joyous snowball fight, followed by lunch together. In Germany, a wonderful couple offered us a room for the night, and in the morning we found our shoes full of chocolate – we had been visited by St Nicholas. Arguably, by slowing down and taking the time to bond with people, everyone's experience and interactions were enhanced.

I'm pleased to say that, off the back of the bike journey, Charlie has converted to Team Slow. However, even though I fully subscribe to the benefits of slowing down, it is still something I have to remind myself of and work for. Over the years, my commitment to slowness has ebbed and flowed, but I always feel better when operating at a more relaxed pace. There are still the occasional days where Charlie and I cut things fine but for the most part we take things slower, especially the most important meal of the day – breakfast. Rather than wolfing our food down, we use it as a chance to connect, chat and contemplate the world over at least two hot drinks. We find it's worth getting up a bit earlier just to do this. If you're someone who loves to travel through life at speed, go for it – but I challenge you to take an hour to see what happens if you just stop and stay still. Breathe. Look about. Stare at the wall. See what comes up. In some ways, the kayak journey took this one step further, because fewer encounters with people – and 1,014 kilometres of river to paddle – meant much time sat with our thoughts.

This brings me to a warning: slowing down is not always comfortable, or at least it hasn't always been in my case. Just like standing still when you get off a teacup ride in a fairground, when you slow down, sometimes you're left feeling a bit weird for a while. The blur of life that was distracting you from yourself is suddenly removed. It might reveal things you haven't fully dealt with. If so, this could be the opportunity to do so. Yet, despite this, I find that stillness brings with it an element of clarity, creativity and awareness. Perhaps slowing down and doing less ultimately means you do more, better.

Days on expedition: 36

Location: the Essequibo River, between Masakenari and Apoteri

Status: getting to know our new teammates

"There." Romel motioned to the tree above with his paddle.

"I still can't see it," I replied.

For the last 5 minutes Romel had been patiently trying to point out a beautiful green iguana to me. As hard as I was trying, desperately scanning every tree, the canopy above had contorted my vision into a viridescent blur. All I could see were blooming green leaves. Romel had even stood in his kayak, waving a bright orange paddle in its direction, but still I couldn't see it. It was immensely frustrating, not least when you consider that the average green iguana grows to be around 2 metres. Romel, however, seemed totally unfazed by my inability to spot something entirely obvious to him. I thanked him for trying but gave up – clearly some things weren't meant to be.

In some ways, being back on the water was a strange adjustment compared to our time deep in the jungle. On the hike to the source, we were almost forced to engage with the landscape, it was so omnipresent. There was an urgency to being under the canopy, too – a need for alertness. Now, in contrast, somehow the sun on the open river had seduced us with its rays. We felt wrapped in its warmth, and it gave us a distorted sense of security. The river also had an openness to it. It felt freer in some ways, flanked by rainforest that stretched out across the horizon.

We had also exchanged the traditional and more social dugout canoes for individual inflatable kayaks. They were to become familiar territory – a place to zone out in on the flat sections, to get lost in the strokes of the paddles and to daydream. If we wanted to engage with others, or with the wildlife of the canopy, we had to choose to paddle closer to our teammates or the riverbank. It gave us a false sense of control; the ability to engage or disengage as we chose. The question was, when we did choose to talk, were we engaging with others or disengaging from ourselves? It was something we were going to have time to ponder…

Watch what comes up when you slow down

Nereus, as well as a fair number of villagers, had turned up at the river to wave us off. We'd brought out inflatable kayaks for our newest team members, our river guides Ant Shushu and Romel Shoni. Ness, Laura and I loaded our dry bags onto our kayaks, and secured them with a strap and a stainless-steel buckle. We watched from the riverbank as Ant and Romel practised manoeuvring the bright blue boats up and down the Essequibo. They made light work of it. We were in safe hands.

We then clambered into our own brightly coloured kayaks. Several people were filming the scene on their phones.

During the hike I'd asked Nigel if he could come up with a fitting name for my boat.

"So, what's her name?" I asked as I leaned forward in the kayak, double-checking I'd secured my dry bags properly.

Nigel flashed me a cheeky grin. "The sloth."

"And mine?" Laura yelled.

"*Wayamoo* – the turtle."

Brilliant. *This bodes well*, I thought. Nigel's confidence in our kayaking abilities clearly shone through. It did make us laugh, though.

Cemci, Nigel and Jackson joined us in one of the dugout canoes for a few kilometres. Jackson's young son, about three years old, had come too and was sucking on a blue lollipop, which he'd briefly stopped licking from time to time to flash us a distinctly discoloured smile. Then, up ahead, we heard a small rapid. I watched as the team secured the dugout canoe to some rocks and climbed out. Ant and Romel remained in their kayaks, clearly keeping their distance so we could say goodbye. Jackson waded into the water to see them. According to Ness, he was giving them instructions about making sure they looked out for us. I was the last to paddle in and Nigel helped me to pull my kayak up on the rocks. Having spoken to Ant and Romel, Jackson slowly made his way back through the water to join our friends who had lined up to say farewell.

Seeing Jackson, one of the strongest members of our team, waist-deep in water, with his usually twinkling eyes full of sadness, was horrible. He looked like a bedraggled puppy. I peeked at Ness and knew that she, too, was about to break and already tearful. There wasn't a single dry eye on the river that day; even Laura had cracked. With a final round of hugs, Jackson reminded us to carry on some of the traditions from our trip – including giving thanks before we ate. We promised that we would.

The guys stayed on the rock for a while, waving. We paddled off until all we could see in the distance was one of our bright orange kayak paddles swinging in the air. That particular one had been used to try to push our canoe off from a fallen tree. Let's just say it snapped after an unfortunate run-in with a combination of body weight, bad choice of angle and pressure. As we disappeared around the river bend, we ushered in a new chapter, one in which our minds were to be tested as much as our bodies.

"In the jungle there was so much going on: maps, people singing, stuff to do," Ness said as we left the old team. "On the outside, paddling seems really serene and beautiful, with the calm and glassy water. But on the inside there's the emotion of leaving good friends and getting your head around that. You've got a lot of time to think on the water. How do you make such good friends and then see them once or twice in your life at best? Honestly, I am still on a bit of a roller coaster."

Ness was right: there was going to be a lot of time to think. It's human nature to look outward to avoid looking inward, but with 8 hours of kayaking a day ahead for the foreseeable future, we were all going to get quite familiar with the notion of sitting with ourselves. Our days were to consist of getting up at 6 a.m., or earlier, and paddling until just before the sunset to give us time to set up camp. There would be moments on white water, or traversing waterfalls, when we could leave the roller coaster of our minds for a more tangible ride. However, for the most part, there was no escaping the fact that for a lot of the day we would be sitting with our thoughts.

Aside from *I'm hungry* (a constant thought of mine) and *Have I put enough sunscreen on?* one thought that recurred was how blooming tough it is to paddle down a river. I'd envisaged that we'd be pushed along by the current for the most part. How wrong I was...

We'd specifically chosen to do the expedition in February and March, as these are some of the drier months in Guyana and we were keen to avoid the dangers of rising water levels. The flip side of this was that the water felt like it was barely moving. Rather than floating downstream with our feet up, every stroke took a lot of effort, especially in the afternoons when the wind picked up. Safe to say that the persistent sweating didn't aid my hunger or concern about sun cream.

"This river is very slow and dry; it feels like it's moving upward!" joked Ant. It certainly felt that way.

Ant then motioned to the tree nearest us. A boa was asleep on a branch. White markings punctuated the many stunning shades of emerald green. He told us that many Brazilians try to find these snakes so they can sell them as pets.

I then caught sight of a beautiful, fuzzy-looking red-and-yellow flower near the boa. I'd seen a similar one in the jungle the previous day, so I asked Ant what it was.

"It's an anaconda's bandana," he said. "Many people say that anacondas can turn into people. When in her human form, the female anaconda puts that flower in her hair."

He went on to tell me that the flower could be a useful tool for men dealing with unrequited love.

"If a man falls in love with a woman who isn't interested, he should look at that flower, and then remind himself that she will get old and her teeth will fall out." Apparently, women shouldn't smile at the flower in case their teeth fall out.

"Then I'm buggered. Yesterday I spent a good five minutes rooting around in a bush, smiling away, trying to take a decent photo of it."

Somewhat unnervingly, Ant didn't pass comment and I felt an unexpected need to just double-check that my teeth were still securely attached. I surreptitiously turned away and gave them a quick tap. Phew! They were all present and accounted for. For now anyway. I looked back at Ant and beamed at him.

"Do you ever get stressed?" I asked him in a bid to get to know him. I was curious, as he had a pretty relaxed manner and I wondered if this was his character or the result of being on the river.

Find the pace that works best for you

"Never," he replied in a slow, leisurely way. "If I feel stressed, I just stop work. I'll go back home, go fishing or see my kids – I love them. Then I go back to work again," he said. "Don't rush the brush. If you scrub your clothes too quickly when you're washing them, you may rub your hand or make a hole in the clothes."

"I agree," said Romel, who was kayaking on the other side of me. "Take paddling, for example. You are your engine. If you need to take a rest, rest. There is no need to go fast. When you're paddling, you're moving. I really enjoy taking time over tasks, whether it's making *farine* or the kitchen I've been building for my wife."

Our conversation paused for a moment; the rhythmic, relaxing lapping of water against our paddles seemed to underline their point about being mindful.

Ant gestured to a large rock on the riverbank: etched into it were the figures of a man, a snake and a monkey. He explained that, historically, indigenous people would leave such marks to show where the best hunting areas were. We had no idea how old they were, but their presence highlighted the enormity of humanity and our small place within it.

"I went to London once for a tourism conference and saw everyone rushing around," said Ant as we paddled off.

"What did you think of it?" I enquired.

His response? "People wanted to get to work on time." As someone who used to try to arrive in a central London office for 9 a.m., I knew that I, too, was part of the "rushing around", making heroic dashes for a closing Tube door and leaping into tight corners, only to contort myself into a stranger's armpit. It wasn't the pace I wanted to move at, but I often found myself getting swept up in the melee. When everyone around you is operating at speed, it can be quite hard (not to mention daunting) to step off the merry-go-round and travel at your own pace in the opposite direction. I told Ant and Romel about my daily life back home – how writing, edits, emails, phone calls and social media would often dominate my day, and how, whenever that became too much, whenever I got stressed,

I would try to get into the woods or into nature. Ant considered this for a moment.

"Yes. You need to realize the power of nature. I think people think of the jungle as dangerous but it's a very relaxing place."

Given we were talking about Mother Earth, I shared my theory of trees being like people. I pointed out a bare one, almost like a lone twig sticking out from above the crowns of other trees.

"I like that one, for example," I said. "The quirkier, more gnarled or knobbly they are, the more interesting I find them."

"You see the world in a different way, but I understand," Ant chuckled.

"I lived in Georgetown for three years," said Romel. "Every day is about money. You need money for food, for clothes, the bus. If you have a motorbike, you need money for gas. I love the jungle because I can catch what I want, when I want. If I need fish, I go to the river. If I want meat, the jungle. I enjoy living. When I wake up, I do what needs to be done for food and when the *farine* is finished, I will go and tend to the cassava plant."

As if on cue, a large splash appeared in front of our kayaks.

"What was that?" I asked.

"A fish," Ant said, whipping out his fishing line.

I asked how the villagers in the Waî Waî community make money, beyond subsistence farming. I was told that gold mining, ranger work and occasional guiding trips like ours were the main sources of income.

"What happens when people are either too ill or old to shoot or fish?" I asked, as we waited for the fish to bite.

"The government has a pension available for the elderly and sometimes the elderly can ask the young people to catch things for them. But I'll always bring my granddad the extra fish I catch," Romel said. "We share."

After a few minutes and no sign of the fish, we cracked on. The day was going far slower than anticipated. Ironically, our paddling then came to a total halt. Ant had seen a green anaconda on a tree branch up ahead and we all crowded around to watch. The thick, stocky snake, which must have been around six metres long – on the smaller side for the snake which can grow to over 9 metres – wasn't planning on staying put. As Ness took out her camera to film it, it decided to dive out of the tree and straight into the water – we had either a camera-shy snake or a ninja on our hands. Luckily, none of us happened to be in the firing line and we watched as it splatted into the water. Its 5 minutes of fame were not meant to be today. Although I was actively trying not to rush the brush, I figured that on this particular occasion it might be prudent to paddle away from the world's heaviest snake, known for its hunting ability in water, with an element of haste. Given that anacondas can submerge for up to 10 minutes at a time, and the largest ones can swallow a human whole, I didn't fancy the idea of one swimming around under our boats or winding its way up our paddles.

Carve out time for slowness

As we quickly moved away, Ness was curious about how Ant had spotted it. Its olive-green body was relatively well camouflaged against the trees.

"Whenever I go into the forest, I like to see something. The iguana, for example, is hard to spot. I just focus on the leaves and see a little movement. Anything that moves a little has to be an animal or a bird," he explained.

I scanned the water for signs of unexpected movement. Unfortunately, the anaconda has hacked the art of not being spotted. Its eyeballs and nostrils are on the top of its head so it can watch its prey from the surface of the water, while its long body remains relatively submerged.

"Just now I spotted the anaconda because I was paddling very slowly at the front of the group. Everyone else was trying to pass me, but my eye, my brain, my vision was over there in the forest. Anacondas always stay near the water so they can hunt easier and faster. Once, I caught a labba, which is a large rodent, and I'd left it in our canoe. When I returned from the hunt, I found an anaconda in our boat trying to eat it."

I hoped this particular anaconda had eaten recently, as it takes them months to digest food. They only need to eat four or five times a year and I certainly didn't fancy being the lunch special.

After 10 minutes passed with no one being constricted to death before being swallowed whole, I began to relax.

"Can you eat anaconda?" asked Ness, as we slowly paddled close to the canopy, following Ant's advice.

"I've never seen anyone eat anaconda meat, so I don't," said Ant. "We don't eat puma or jaguar, either; the cats don't taste good. When I was in the mining area with Brazilian people, they shot a puma. It looked nice, like fatty meat, but it smelt rank."

Fun as wildlife spotting was, if we were to finish the expedition, an element of faster paddling was also going to be needed. I was beginning to sense Laura getting impatient with the speed of travel. She was desperate to see Ran and Ed, who we were due to meet, along with Charlie and cameraman Jon, in the coming week. Over the next few days, we'd have to find some sort of balance if we were going to meet them in time. For now, though, I was trying to surrender to the tranquility of the river, the shimmering brown water of the Essequibo now turning rich and radiant as the sun began to bow its head.

What are you missing out on by rushing about?

I smiled as I watched Romel head to the riverbank to check out a potential campsite for the evening. His paddling style was a living embodiment of his words: "If you're paddling, you're moving." He moved in fabulous style and his paddle strokes had almost a relaxed swagger to them, with his shoulders gently rolling, swaying from side to side as if dancing rather than paddling. In his camouflage jacket and wide-brimmed white hat, he looked like a cross between a soldier and a fisherman. A man moving on his own terms.

At various points during the day, I'd watched him and Ant put down their paddles and just lie in the kayaks, looking up at the sky as they drifted with the wind across the river's calm water. I hung back from the rest of the team who were heading to shore. After our chat about taking our time over things, I made sure to try to appreciate the day and the setting sun before beginning the routine of setting up camp. I felt the temptation to join them. The worry of being judged for not pulling my weight. Thoughts of *There are things to do to set up camp* were quietly creeping in. I pushed them away, rationalized that I would have hours ahead of me to help and took a few minutes to lie on my back, kayak at the mercy of the wind and the river. My thoughts were lost in the moving clouds above me.

As my kayak drifted toward the shore, Laura gave it a friendly shunt back toward the middle of the river. I took it as permission to spend more time relaxing, and playfully gave her both middle fingers as I floated away (I turned it into the peace sign halfway through, which made her chuckle).

As my eyes lowered from the clouds to the canopy, I let them rest on the branches overhead and I saw something move. Suddenly, just beyond the boat, about 4.5 metres up, something dropped out of a tree. I saw four limbs upturned and flailing, plummeting through the sky and ending in an unceremonious "plop". There was a hell of a splash, which somewhat ruined the peace. Like an animated flip book, I had seen it all play out, frame by comedic frame; life operating in slow motion. Falling from the sky had been a green iguana.

Instinct

(noun): the way people or animals naturally react or behave, without having to think or learn about it.

This might be a bit presumptive, but you're an animal. Deep within you, whether you're aware of it or not, lies a glorious, wild beast just waiting to roar. We might have removed ourselves from nature, but nature remains within us. We have just lost sight of the untamed and wild parts of ourselves. We often like to think that we are at the top of the food chain but being in the jungle was a stark reminder that, if you place a single human being in an unfamiliar – and possibly hostile – environment, they are probably going to be pretty useless. Yet, it also felt as though I'd tapped into a whole new superpower I'd never explored properly before – my senses came alive. I became attuned to every rustle. Every crack of a branch. I was sensitive to eyes watching me (usually caiman). We weren't plugged into headphones or glued to a screen. We became part of the environment. We became more alive.

Instinct is one of the most powerful gifts we possess as humans, yet so many of us are numb to it in urbanized life. Whether you get a sense that someone is looking at you, you pick up on someone's energy or you have a gut feeling that a situation is uncomfortable, you should tune into these moments. When I was younger, quite often I'd stay in a situation that felt off because I didn't want to offend anyone. As I started travelling more, especially when alone, I learned to trust my instincts more. Now, if a situation feels dodgy to me, I'll try to remove myself from it – no explanation required.

Despite no longer being immersed in nature, that sense – that fight-or-flight mechanism – still fires. Because of smartphones, constant connectivity and the ability to work all hours, arguably we've taken the jaguar and put it in our pockets. Every bleep, every notification, every buzz triggers us. In the jungle, when the threat goes away, we can relax, but technology enables us to be in a constantly wired state. Animals shake to release fear, yet we're zapping ourselves day in, day out with constant low-level threats – the dreaded to-do list, the feeling you haven't replied to people fast enough, that constant anxiety that there's something you should be doing but haven't.

This kind of stress appears to be a hangover from our need to survive – utterly useless, knackering and counterproductive when you don't actually need to gear your body up for an encounter with a jaguar or wild pig.

In such wired states, it's little wonder, then, that we often struggle to really listen to ourselves. Our gut reactions, "a feeling" or our dreams are often dismissed as slightly "alternative" or "woo-woo" in a tech-based, urbanized world. Yet, these are the tools that kept our ancestors alive. They're the little nudges that remind us when we've strayed off our path – both literally and figuratively. Perhaps it's time we really start listening to that inner voice and evaluating where the real threats lie. I'd hazard a guess that the first one you might want to tackle is the jaguar in your pocket...

Days on expedition: 38

Location: the Essequibo River

Status: scared out of our wits

"It's hunting you," Ant said, clutching a machete, as he shone a very bright torch on a 2-metre caiman.

"Er, hunting?!" Laura and I laughed nervously.

Ant was deadly serious. As was the caiman, whose stance at the river's rocky bank was solid and purposeful. The torchlight wasn't deterring him.

Laura and I had been washing up at the water's edge. We'd accidentally overboiled the rice and the burned, crusty remains on the bottom of the pan weren't coming off easily. I'd taken to using my fingernails to scratch what I could from the bottom of the pot. As Laura tackled the team's cutlery and cups, she was enthusing over her vegetable plot back home, trying to convince me of the benefits of gardening and what season was best for planting things. Just as she got on to the topic of chickens and foxes, we felt something was off. Laura picked up her torch and scanned it over the water. Red eyes shone back at us from the centre of the river. We watched as those same eyes deliberately sped toward us with absolute precision, torchlight picking up a worryingly long, flat, scaled tail propelling the caiman along at speed. Laura and I ditched the pans, alerted the others and ran up the riverbank to our jungle camp as fast as we could. From slightly higher ground, and in the presence of the rest of the team, I felt my body begin to relax after being scared out of my wits. I also figured there were now five of us knocking around so my chances of not being dinner were marginally better.

"It's there," said Laura, guiding Ant's torch to where we'd been washing up just moments ago. The caiman was now out of the water and peering up at us. Given that caiman attacks on humans are unusual, Ant suggested that it could be defending its territory.

"Or they like white people," added Romel, as he and Ant started throwing rocks in its direction. After a few misses, one of the missiles must have hit its mark because, without warning, the caiman moved like lightning – so fast that Ant had to scan his torch around the water again. Then it was back in exactly the same place.

More rocks rained down and, finally, it slunk back into the water. I felt deeply uncomfortable that an animal might have been hit because I raised the alarm. Yet, equally, I didn't fancy one of us becoming an evening snack.

Instincts are there for a reason

Instinct is a funny old thing. It's there to alert us to threats. Ant, who had a great flair for telling stories with his whole body, shared how scared his ancestors had been when they first came across an aeroplane.

"My great-grandfather and great-grandmother heard a plane overhead. They'd never heard one before and said to each other: 'Psst, in the hole.'"

He made a very comical movement with his arm, gesturing that they took cover. The "hole" turned out to be a nearby cave.

"They were very scared. The same thing happened when Brazilians showed them a flashlight. They shone it in their eyes. 'Psst, in the hole,' again."

I chuckled and said that if there had been a hole around when I'd first heard howler monkeys, I'd have dived into it, too.

The laughter had come as a welcome relief. In the early hours of the morning, I'd woken up from yet another nightmare. Recently, they'd been happening night after night, and they were increasingly vivid and situational. In this particular dream, my kayak was deflating rapidly – a hole in the boat was letting air out faster and faster. Reality and slumber merged, and I felt I was about to drown. I woke myself and the rest of the camp up with a scream, feeling overwhelmed by panic. I checked my watch: 2 a.m. Laura called through the darkness to check I was OK and Ness, who usually got out of the hammock once in the night for a pee, used it as an opportunity to give me a hug. Feeling the warm embrace of a friendly human was just what I needed. Her hug made me feel solid, more grounded somehow. After I reassured everybody that I was alright, we all tried to settle back to sleep.

Listen to your spirit

The truth was, I wasn't alright. I felt massively unsettled. The best way to describe how I felt was to compare it to when you're looking to rent or buy a house. There are some properties that seem to welcome you in, while others leave you feeling cold. Recently, the energy of the landscape had changed. It might sound bonkers, but it started as we paddled between massive, black boulders either side of the river. There was almost a statuesque quality to them. As we got closer, it looked like a gateway into the wild – the upcoming twists and turns of the Essequibo a mystery. Initially, the days that followed had been magical. It was as if we'd entered paradise. After a day of paddling, we'd swim together and splash each other in the clear, shallow, protected pools of glassy water that had appeared on the riverbanks. We'd lie in contented peace on large, flat rocks warmed by the heat of the day, marvelling at the sunsets and waiting for stars to skip across the sky. It was a fairy kingdom if ever there was one. Then, suddenly, with seemingly no particular trigger, the energy of the jungle felt different; it felt negative. It felt dangerous.

Sensing danger around but not finding it was making me exceptionally exhausted and wired. I tried to talk myself down and rationalize the very real, albeit unlikely, threats. I'd downloaded several podcasts onto my phone before I left the UK and I put on an old episode of BBC Radio 4's *Today* programme in the hope that familiar voices and a dose of home might help with sleep. I was experiencing another paradox of the jungle – it's simultaneously one of the most calming yet also terrifying places I've ever been. Sometimes I'd felt completely relaxed – possibly too relaxed, given that I hadn't taken my machete with me to the loo for weeks and hadn't taken it to bed with me for days. Yet I'd never been anywhere where I'd felt more on edge. For a few nights in a row I'd been on high alert. I recognized I was feeling the same stress response I would get for deadlines and work, but in an environment where, for the first time in my life, it was the appropriate reaction. Unfamiliar sounds, a sense that something was watching me and just a general feeling of unease were enough to pull me from my sleep and into fight-or-flight mode. It was as if my senses had been fine-tuned.

I wasn't the only one who'd picked up on it.

"It feels like we're in a whole different place, a whole different world, now…" said Laura when I discussed the change in mood with the group over breakfast the next morning. I knew what she meant. It felt scary, ancient and otherworldly – or perhaps, more accurately, entirely worldly and a reminder of our temporary state in it.

"I keep waiting for a dinosaur to pop out," Laura said, as she served porridge up into everyone's Tupperware. "It feels like there's a sorrow here. I feel really sad. It feels like we're on edge and like something bad is going to happen. I almost want something bad to happen so we can move on."

Maybe we were unsettled because the landscape was new to all of us and, subconsciously, we were all on high alert. It had been a very windy night, with many cracks and creaks coming from the jungle. I'd spent about 30 minutes shining my torch through the hammock to see what was lurking in the darkness. I say "shining through", but if you shine a torch out of a hammock, the beam just blinds you with the reflection as it hits the mosquito net. Not ideal when checking for threats. You either have to press it right up against the net or, better (but more terrifying), unzip it and physically pop your head out and shine the torch out. It sounds silly but I felt so much safer inside a net, although I am entirely sure this would offer as much protection against a predator as a piece of lemon meringue.

"I slept so badly," Ness said. "Just as we got into bed, I thought Laura was playing a trick on me, as I heard a voice that sounded like an elderly lady saying, 'Be careful.' You know how there are some things that are so vague it's almost like you can think you're daydreaming, but then there are other things that you *know* you've heard? There's a difference. That's why I asked Laura if she'd said something. I can remember the exact voice to this second, how it sounded, how it felt…" She trailed off, for a moment. "It was a long day so maybe we're getting powerful hallucinations?"

Romel piped up. "My spirit, our spirit, it tells you when something is around. Maybe it was a jaguar or an anaconda – you don't see it but your spirit feels it, and you're frightened, you know? During the night your spirit doesn't sleep well. I felt it before you screamed, my spirit telling me something was around. The whole night there was a sense that there was something dangerous," he continued. "The jaguar is the most dangerous in the forest. We are in their area. We don't know, maybe we are camping in their home? Last night I woke up and I heard someone crying. I thought it was Laura."

"I wasn't," Laura clarified. "We're literally going into *The Blair Witch Project*. The heebie-jeebies are around. When I went to the loo, I swear I saw a skull hovering about a metre off the ground. Almost like the Day of the Dead skulls you see in Mexico. Could it be that whole suggestive thinking thing? Have my eyes created that so that I'm a bit warier? I was staring at it, waiting for it to move."

"Hang on, you mean like hovering?" said Ness. "Dude, you need to drink more water."

"Hopefully, there aren't any uncontacted people around here," Laura replied.

"Sometimes the spirits of the animals tell you someone is dying," Ant informed us. "Back when I was mining, I heard a lone monkey crying at midnight. It's really unusual to hear. According to traditions, this means that someone will die within the month. A few days later I got a call from my wife saying her sister was ill. A week later she died.

"Sometimes you feel restless when you travel, too," he added. "Anyway, it makes it interesting. Although we miss home, and miss parents and friends, and think: *What are we doing here? It's how life goes...*"

He stopped and took a long look at Laura, who had accidentally smeared her face with soot after having picked up our large black cooking pot to wash. At some point over the last few days, it had clearly been plonked in the fire's ashes.

"Laura, what happened to your face?"

"I was born like this, I can't help it," she cackled and proceeded to rub soot over all of us. "It's warpaint. Come and get me, spirits..."

The spooky goings on were making me look forward to Charlie's arrival even more. Only when removed from physical touch do you realize how comforting it is. I was longing for a hug from Charlie, not least because I was feeling rather unwell. It felt like there was a large lump in my stomach and I couldn't stop burping.

Yet my excitement at seeing people was also tempered – partly because of the belching, but also because I began to wonder if the isolation of the jungle was playing tricks with our minds. We later shared this story with some people we met downstream. Turns out, the area we'd passed through had historically been a place of tribal warfare. We can't rationally explain it, but I do know we all felt that something was off.

After lunch we saw Ant and Romel charging at speed toward the riverbank. We assumed they'd spotted something in the bushes – and they had. It was a sign. Seeing something man-made in an area we knew to be uninhabited was very discombobulating. Here we were, thinking we were alone in the jungle, and yet two white, handwritten signs on what looked like PVC board appeared in front of us. They read:

R. Ramnarine
Lic #: 4580
D.O.L: 11.09.08

Underneath both signs, a name: Rick #21 and #20. We guessed that "D.O.L" was "Date of Landing" and perhaps something to do with mining.

"Rick, Rick, are you there?" Laura called out to the jungle.

"Wilson, Wilson," replied Ness, referring to Tom Hanks's character in *Cast Away* who, washed up on a desert island, talks to a volleyball for company.

We laughed but I could relate; when you're in a fragile state, you will use whatever psychological tool you have in your armoury *Trust yourself* that helps you to survive. Even if that meant befriending a ball.

If I could have conjured up the support of an animal, vegetable or mineral that afternoon – living or dead – I would have done. We'd hit upon a system of rapids, full of twists and turns, and some nasty-looking white water. As we clambered over rocks to assess the rapids below, I felt light-headed and utterly out of it. I felt that the sensible decision, especially after my dream, was to step back, as I didn't fancy taking them on. It seemed that my body, mind and spirit agreed on this as the best course of action. Ant kindly offered to run the rapids twice. He'd go down in his boat and then climb back up to bring my boat down for me. I thanked him, before slowly climbing down the rocks, taking care not to slip. If I'd been feeling myself, it would have only taken around 5 minutes, but I was moving like a granny.

As I sat on the rocks at the bottom of the rapid, something crept up on me – a feeling of being totally isolated, alone and vulnerable. The last few days had shown us the fragility of our existence – my nightmares, the unsettling stories, a weird mood change in the jungle. I felt a sense of rising panic.

I tried to calm my nerves by focusing on a discarded grey feather nearby. It reminded me of a seagull feather and a book my dad gave to me, one of his favourites, called *Jonathan Livingston Seagull*. For the benefit of anyone who hasn't read it, it's a beautiful children's tale about a seagull who senses he has a calling beyond just flying to catch food. Jonathan wants to perfect the art of flight and, despite opposition from his flock, sets out on his own path. I, too, love the sentiment of that story – yet, sat physically alone on my own path, with no sign of my teammates and thinking of my family, I felt very sad.

I thought back to our conversations about safety in previous days and it made me realize how isolated – and like a sitting duck– I was out on my own. So much of this experience was about getting to grips with what it meant to be human on a very fundamental level – never in my life had I experienced raw survival, and I likely never will again. It forced me to look at the way I live my own life and compare the physical responses to stress at home and in the jungle, which are the same, even though the triggers are different. I think it's this disconnect between how our bodies evolved to live and how we live now that leaves a gaping hole in our society, and why so many people feel that "something's not quite right". It's not. At least, I found that to be the case.

Like many, I no longer live in a way that's attuned to nature, yet my psyche – the thing that makes us human and allows us to survive – does not register that. I learned in the jungle that I feel safer with other people; being in a group is a form of protection, yet the majority of us lock ourselves up in overcrowded cities, feeling even more isolated from each other. When our body senses danger, the stress response kicks in. This has a real, practical use at 2 a.m. when you hear rustling around your hammock and you gear yourself up to fight for your life, but not when you're checking emails.

Sadness was soon replaced with abject fear as I realized I had only carried with me my water bottle, which was nearly empty. My life vest contained a few emergency items: rations, a knife and a small life-saving kit that Ben, my sister's boyfriend, had given me for Christmas. I had no means of communicating with the outside world and my supplies wouldn't last for long should anything happen to me. I tried to refocus my mind by staring at the beautiful seaweed-like flora that adorned the rock I was sitting on. It progressed from a rich red colour at the top, through to yellow as it neared the water's edge, to a brilliant emerald green in the water itself. It was stunning. I shifted my focus to the way the water roared over the landscape. A huge tree was growing out of a rock above me and looked like something out of *Avatar*. However, in my weakened, ill and achy state, the cacophony of white water sounded like an airplane about to take off. The isolation seemed less peaceful and more dangerous. I'd never felt like that before in nature; it was weird and unsettling. I began to cry.

I'd been waiting for about 20 minutes, and still there was no sign of anyone. Ness had watched me get to the bottom of the rocks, as I'd been feeling dizzy, but when no one appeared, I began to worry for their safety so I climbed a little way back up the rocks to see if I could see anyone. Thankfully, I spotted some bright red – the helmets worn by Ant and Romel. Never had I been more thankful to see safety gear! The ladies were all OK, too, and were lining boats around a difficult section below. I remarked to them later that it was far more stressful watching your mates plotting a course through the rapids than being on the water with them, as you could see the margin for error way more clearly.

Turns out my worrying about my teammates was unfounded; they'd been having a ball.

"It was fantastic," Ant said. "I saw a lot of waterfalls and I just wanted to do them all straight up. I was so excited to go right away, but I had to wait for you guys. I have to be together with you guys and cooperate. To give advice and make sure you are safe."

"It was like a slip and slide," said Laura. "We had an accident on it – I fell in at one point, as it was quite steep. Then Ness came up after and said, 'I saw that!'"

Listening to them talk, I was still glad I'd chosen to sit this one out.

You can feel when something is wrong

Romel's point about your spirit knowing when something is around is spot on. During our evening wash that night, I detected that something wasn't quite right. As I went about my business, ridding myself of the dirt of the day, I felt something very uncomfortable in my bum. I investigated the situation a little further and found a small, unusual lump where the pain was emanating from. I gave it a yank and something gave. Tentatively, I looked at the results. It was a tick, making a home in my orifice. Joy. Surprisingly, I managed to get it all out with one pull.

"Squish it between your nails," said Laura, as it wiggled around. "I'm surprised it managed to survive there."

When I told Ant, he was completely unfazed. "Yes, I find them very often when I go hunting. When women farm, they often find them in their groin, too."

Clean and deloused, I was feeling much better. I was hoping for a more peaceful night's sleep. Ant had other ideas. As we tucked into a pacu fish, he shared a story.

"This is an unknown area, so we have to be careful. It's why we need to camp further into the jungle. Sometimes we will camp very close to the water but only in areas we know. There are wild people in the jungle. People who are very aggressive, who could come in the night and kill you with a bow and arrow. Caimans might also see you and catch you. Even anacondas can come onto the land. This is not a stupid thing I'm telling you. It's so you can learn. You have to be careful," said Ant.

"But before bed?!" exclaimed Laura. "This is a breakfast story not a supper story."

I asked Ant how he was taught to be brave as a child and not to fear the jungle.

"My dad took me hunting with him every Saturday from when I was about eight," he said. "He taught me that even when you see the white-lipped peccary running toward you, you mustn't run. You must be brave. Don't run – stand there and shoot it. I will teach my children the same. My dad is now in Brazil so I have to do all these things alone." He paused. "I didn't go to school because there was no school in the bush, but if I can't describe something, I'll draw it. I can't write but I can do a bit of everything else – except fly a plane. I don't know how to do that. But knowing a little bit of everything, from maths to how to build a shelter, means no one can bluff you up."

I wasn't entirely convinced. I now knew a bit about the jungle and was still pretty sure I'd be terrified if I came face to face with anything charging at me. However, for better or worse, I had started operating on instinct. I had to have faith that it would continue to kick in when situations arose.

Just as I was about to get into my hammock, I noticed that dozens and dozens of spiders had spun a huge web across my tarp. Romel had told me earlier in the evening that they were friendly and batted them away. By bedtime, they'd spun an entire new village.

"Please bring your machetes with you to see me in the morning. You might have to cut me out of a spider cocoon," I said to the team.

Ness laughed. "It's funny what you get used to in the jungle," she said.

Before bed, I located the miniature bottle of El Dorado rum I'd been carrying for what were meant to be special occasions. I took a small swig. That warming burn bolstered me temporarily. I reminded myself I would control what I could and I'd work on the rest.

"I will be brave," I vowed, as I closed my eyes and waited for the night to unfold.

Conflict

(noun): a serious disagreement or argument, typically a protracted one.

When you're with the same people 24/7 (and even if you're with them for less than that), the likelihood is that there will be a few arguments. Little niggles, if not talked about, can escalate quickly, and it doesn't take much for the sore spots we've developed as a result of being human to be pressed and triggered. Yet, in the jungle, in order to stay alive, we needed to work as one, and navigate that balance between voicing our own needs and accommodating others. The jungle is often described as a "hostile" environment. For the uninitiated and underprepared it certainly can be. Just as we had to navigate our way through the jungle, we also had to navigate the murky waters of human relationships.

It's so easy to look at others and think they have things more sorted than you do. The truth is, your own emotions are probably the best indicator of how others are really feeling. No relationship will be perfect. No families are blissfully happy all the time. Other people's minds will feel inundated with problems, just like yours does at times. In the jungle, I struggled, got frustrated and became irritated, so it's no wonder my teammates did, too. I realized that this journey was not a battle of wills – prioritizing one person's want over another's. It was about finding a way for our desires to sit together – or at least voicing them so that they were heard. Arguably, we all need to find that balance between treading our own path and not disturbing others along the way.

This trip taught me it is OK, vital even, to set and stick to our boundaries, voice what's really bothering us, and learn to let go of things that are minor in the grand scheme of things. You have to be honest with yourself and those around you, because holding on to negative emotions will only eat you up. If you need to express yourself, make sure you do, but in the kindest way possible.

Days on expedition: 40

Location: the Essequibo River, just before the Kuyuwini River

Status: running behind schedule

As an utter people-pleaser (not a trait I'm necessarily fond of), over the years I have tried hard to accommodate the wishes of others. This is all well and good until you find that your path, beliefs or values inevitably rub up against others. Then it becomes a choice: sideline yourself and prioritize someone else or stand up for what you really want and believe in. Usually, I'd go for the first option, reasoning that putting others ahead of yourself is a kind and loving thing to do. But the jungle showed me the perils of consistently doing so – and how it can actually lead to festering anger and resentment.

I was so desperate to avoid conflict in the jungle that I suggested the team seek out the services of a High Performance Coach before the trip. Sandy from Peak Dynamics took us through a series of both psychometric and practical survival tests. We then completed a survival exercise. The scenario: our plane had crash-landed in the Arctic and there was no chance of rescue for weeks. Laura and Ness reckoned we should keep moving to a hut that we could see on the map and make it to a camp a few kilometres away. The reason, they argued, was that at least we were taking charge of the situation and moving.

My plan was to do nothing and just wait. I suggested we had enough shelter and food to stay put for a few weeks until help came. However, rather than stand up to the others, I went along with their plan – which, in a real situation, could have potentially killed us. My inability to speak up and engage in what should have been a discussion – but which I saw as conflict – could have been fatal. Our parting advice from Sandy was that we were to agree on a common goal for the trip before we set off. Apparently, having a focused group aim greatly reduces the chances of conflict. To further aid this, we agreed that Ness and Laura should allow me space to talk and that I should be confident enough to speak up.

However, it seemed we had all forgotten Sandy's words. Like a dugout canoe with a small hole, our team had slowly been taking on water. For the last few days, tiny cracks had appeared in the dynamic and were threatening to grow into something more sinister. We were all partly to blame.

The expression "woke up on the wrong side of the bed" has origins in the Roman belief that it was unlucky to get out of bed on the left. I am not sure if there is a jungle equivalent, but I can confirm that it's also possible to get out of the wrong side of a hammock. I'd woken up to a roundhouse kick in the head after Laura accidentally hit me from hers. Perhaps it served me right for stringing mine up so close to someone I knew was a nightly fidget. Needless to say, it didn't get my day off to the best start.

Ness, too, was in a foul mood. Partly, I think, because her foot was badly infected. The top of her ankle was full of sores and a red swelling was spreading up her leg. In the jungle she'd been using duct tape to provide ankle support, but the covering seemed to have infected her hair follicles that now looked angry and full of yellow-and-green pus. In a more light-hearted moment, I'd joked that Ness's career as a foot model might be over, but someone with a foot fetish might be into it.

"Roll up, roll up, boys," we'd shouted as we examined a particularly large, flaxen, oozy sore. Given it was so big, we decided it deserved a name and settled on calling it Boris. However, the situation was less funny now. We managed to get hold of Dave, our expedition medic, on WhatsApp and he said we'd have to watch that it didn't develop into cellulitis, as that might infect her lymph nodes. It was amazing to realize how, once again, it's the little things that can take you down in the jungle, be that a foot rubbing against sand for days on end or getting a hair follicle infected. We were going to have to keep a watchful eye out for Boris and hope it didn't get worse.

To round off the less-than-joyful team dynamic, Ant and Romel seemed irritated by our constant need for speed, and weeks of physicality with very little rest were beginning to take their toll on me, Ness and Laura.

Take a step toward what's bothering you

"I've been awake since 3 a.m.," Laura yawned, clinging unusually hard to her morning coffee after a restless night. She dipped her finger into the top of her brew and fished out a rogue bit of leaf that was floating around. She flicked it off her finger. "I thought I heard a jaguar and couldn't get back to sleep after a massive adrenaline spike."

"A jaguar wanted to attack me one time," Ant shared. It wasn't the most reassuring start to a story, least of all when you're in their territory.

Most of the tales we'd heard from our Waî Waî teammates involved jaguars being inquisitive, smelling human tracks but leaving people in peace. Ant had told us on previous occasions that he had seen over 20 jaguars in his life. Apart from one killing his dog when he went hunting, this was the first time we'd heard of a conflict.

"I was in the forest when I heard what sounded like a strong breeze coming toward me. I didn't initially see what it was, but my nervous system knew something was wrong. My whole spirit just swelled. The jaguar ran at me, jumping in front of me. I tried to attack it with my machete – I swished it from side to side." Ant gesticulated for effect. I clocked that Laura was now clutching her coffee even harder, causing her fingertips to turn white. He pressed on.

"However, the jaguar was very skillful and moved back with every step I took toward him. He tried to defend himself behind the trees. We stayed like that for a while, him just watching me, and then he walked away. He didn't catch me," Ant said, clearly proud that he'd survived the stand-off and offered up this advice. "The minute you blink or move backward, the jaguar will take advantage of it. You need to go forward: be the attacker."

Get clear on what you are – and aren't – prepared to compromise on

We didn't know it at breakfast, but that day was going to be largely about fight mode. Ant's advice to move toward the problem was something we probably all should have heeded.

His story also reminded me of an email that Ed had sent before we left, recapping our jungle training. At the time, it had made me both laugh and almost pee myself with fear.

"Jaguar: you may actually see them because Guyana is awesome and unspoiled. I very much doubt a jaguar would come close or attack but if (improbably) you get confronted by one, stand your ground and make yourself large. Put your hands in the air, and don't turn and run. The jaguar should then be intimidated and slope off. If he charges you then you may be f*cked. Your machete in hand would help. :)"

I am not sure the smiling face was entirely necessary. Yet, thinking about it, perhaps it was. As we were to discover as a team, a sense of humour can be a great tool when it comes to defusing conflict.

When you spend weeks at a time in the company of the same people, you really see all sides of them – the good and the bad. Inevitably, small annoyances that would have been manageable in a normal situation start to build up. Once our team's goal had subtly changed, this build-up was far more noticeable. When we set off, we'd agreed that the journey was not about setting a speed record but more about having fun, meandering down a river and enjoying the process. I'd foreseen that Laura might struggle to be away from her son, which is partly why I'd suggested that we see a coach before the trip. For the most part, Ness and I were able to disconnect from life at home and enjoy where we were, but the depth of Laura's pain really ate away at her. Each evening she'd be desperate to connect her phone to our portable satellite terminal and see if she'd received any updates from her family. She was, understandably, consumed by the need to return to Ran. However, knowing how close they were meant that Laura had a new goal – to reach her family as quickly as possible.

By and large, the team understood this and tried to accommodate, but Laura became obsessed with the distance we'd cover in a day – 20 kilometres, 22 kilometres, 27 kilometres – each kilometre a step closer to having her son back in her arms. As someone who likes to travel slowly through environments (much to the frustration of most people who have ever travelled with me!), I can't say I was loving the slog. While I understood why we were pushing hard, if I'm honest, I was beginning to get irritated by feeling like

Try to be productive (and adult) in your conflict

we had to rush everything. I wasn't entirely convinced that the pressure was aiding the team's performance, speed or distance but I wasn't handling my annoyance in the right way. For a start, I hadn't said anything.

A few days previously, I had noticed that my boat was slowly deflating. My kayak had a slow puncture and, at one stage, started taking on a lot of water. I really needed a pump but couldn't get the attention of either Ness or Laura, who were each carrying one but were streaks ahead, powering away. Ant and Romel were behind, nowhere to be seen. Angry that this wasn't what we'd agreed in terms of safety, I began to get crosser and crosser. I felt isolated, forgotten by the group. Annoyed that Laura's desire for speed seemed to be dominating all else. As I saw it, we were on a once-in-a-lifetime journey and yet she seemed so focused on getting home that we weren't enjoying where we were. On top of that, I seemed to be sinking. By the time I got to Laura and Ness, who were by then parked up and sunning themselves on a flat rock on the river, I was fuming and uncharacteristically blunt. I told them I'd been trying for what felt like hours to catch their attention and no one had stopped or even seemed to look back. Before we started the expedition, we'd said that we'd always keep each other within eyeshot. They both seemed pretty taken aback at my outburst.

"We did look back," said Laura. "We just didn't realize there was a problem or we would have stopped."

"Yeah, sorry, mate. A good learning for us, though," Ness said, giving my stiff, angry body a hug.

As we waited for Ant and Romel to catch up, I tried to cheer myself up by eating a piece of mango I'd saved from the Waî Waî village. Uncharacteristically, I didn't offer it around.

"We've actually had a really lovely morning just chatting away," said Laura, in what I guessed was an attempt to lighten the mood.

"Well, I am glad *you* had a nice morning," I muttered passive-aggressively and entirely unproductively.

"Did you use your whistle?" Laura asked.

I hadn't. Stupidly, I hadn't even thought about it. I was now both cross and embarrassed, especially as I was also being a hypocrite – I hadn't waited for Ant and Romel, either. Instead of just apologizing, saying that I'd perhaps overreacted and letting the event go, I held on to it. This was partly because the incident was an example of a larger problem for me that I'd failed to address – the fact that I didn't agree with the pace of the group or that it was solely dictated by one person. By holding on to my anger, I was only fanning and tending to it. I don't think I was the only one.

The embers of exasperation were stoked further that afternoon when Laura, who had been hanging back, suddenly powered past me, kayaking at speed.

I asked if she could perhaps switch boats with me at some point, to see if she could gauge whether there was anything wrong with mine. She agreed and then muttered, also passive-aggressively and entirely unproductively, that she had deliberately tried to catch up to see how long it took, and it hadn't taken that long. I felt like it was a horrible dig and I could see no purpose to it other than to make me feel even worse. The mood darkened once again. The fire inside was burning bright at that point.

Ness, however, was more wet than fiery. She, too, was feeling the strain of Laura's constant need for covering more distance. Not wanting to stop for fear of slowing everyone down, she had attempted to pee off the side of the boat. It hadn't gone so well for her, as she had ended up toppling in, phone and all.

Remember: the people who love you will weather the storm with you

Ness was frustrated. She often liked to hang at the back, alone, looking up at the canopy and staring at wildlife, but with a new goal emerging in the group, this was becoming more difficult. Of course, I wanted to see Charlie, but I didn't have the same desperate need or drive that propelled Laura. I suggested to

Ness that we ought to talk to her; there was no other word for it – she was manic.

Like most overwhelming emotions in life, sooner or later they will find a way of coming out – sometimes in harmful ways. As Ness and I rounded a river bend, we found Laura parked up on a rock, hyperventilating, seemingly in the midst of a panic attack. She was on the satellite phone, sobbing between gasping breaths. We deduced it was Ed on the other end of the line and he was trying to reassure her. Sensing she needed some space, we waited anxiously in our kayaks until she finished the conversation and then we paddled over to the rock to find out what was wrong. Ed's chat had clearly worked: she seemed calmer as she said goodbye and packed away the large phone back into its case.

"It felt like everyone around me had died. Like my heart had shattered or someone had pulled out my guts," she said, bursting into tears again as she recounted the story to us. "There's this emotional umbilical cord that connects you to your child and it felt like it had snapped. I thought something had happened to Ran. It felt like I was mourning the loss of a child."

We all gathered around her on the rock, hot from the midday sun. We tried to comfort her with hugs, words and water. We told her that Ran was absolutely fine, and that we'd see him and Ed very soon. Slowly, the tears became less frequent and the extent of her distress became clear to the rest of us.

"I also thought Ness was really pissed off and upset because she fell in the water," Laura continued. "I got myself in such a tizzy that I panicked. I haven't felt such intense emotion that I couldn't calm for a long, long time. I felt possessed like a demon."

Worryingly, she revealed that in her emotional state she'd smacked her paddle on her thighs and had been deliberately throwing up.

"It helped to calm me down and relieved a lot of angst," she told us.

Laura's revelation around using food as a means of control was worrying. We'd all been losing weight on the trip due to the sheer physicality of it, but Laura had lost more than the rest of us. Seeing her in such distress helped me to put my frustrations

Understand that everyone has their own internal battles

to one side for the moment. She needed support and I hadn't noticed. I remembered back to when Ness had had a whole Firepot for lunch one day. Laura had said, "Oooooh, daring." At the time, the comment had irritated me, as we had more than enough rations and would soon be approaching settlements. I'd pushed back and said that the food was meant for one meal, not to be spread out over two. I'd interpreted Laura's comment through the lens of my own frustration – seeing it as her desire for control – but in reality it was indicative of her struggle with food, which I'd failed to see.

Ironically, the things you react to in others are often the same you dislike in yourself. My own desire for control meant I reacted strongly to similar tendencies in Laura. Unfortunately, this battle of wills I was engaged in had prevented me from showing up for her in the way I would have wanted to. With Laura at an unhealthy breaking point, the kindest thing to do for everyone was to try to resolve the issues in the team and acknowledge the personal battles we were all going through. Romel had left his new baby, just a few days old, whose name he didn't yet know. Ness had been working through the aftermath of a break-up. Ant shared that he, too, missed his family but said that it was in God's hands.

"Even if they die," he said, "God will take care of them. Laura, you have to trust in that."

I didn't entirely share Ant's sentiment, but we could – and needed to – care for each other.

With Laura calmer, and reassured that Ran was happy and healthy at home, we resumed paddling. The group's mood had lifted but, unfortunately, the pace was still relentless. Ant led the way this time, with Laura behind. Keen to make her feel better and get some distance under our belts, I sensed we were definitely putting our all into the kayaking. However, after about an hour of Laura powering like a crazed demon, she stopped and began floating on the river. I assumed she must be stuck on a sandbank, because why else would this woman on a mission stop? Then she turned to me.

"I want to apologize. Pip, I've been trying to catch up with Ant for ages and couldn't. I felt like the faster I was paddling, the faster he was, too; it was pretty scary, so I'm sorry. I know how you must have felt now."

I really appreciated both the unexpected rest and the apology. It pretty much dissolved my bad mood immediately. Laura hadn't finished.

"I said earlier that it had been a really slow day. It hasn't been slow. I was just angry about the situation and taking things out. It was completely unjustified and I want to apologize."

Her words caught me by surprise. Laura was brave enough to be honest and vulnerable about her feelings. In hindsight, I wish I'd used the moment as an opportunity to voice my own frustrations and desires. However, keen to avoid more conflict, I took what I thought was the easier option: paper over the cracks and continue as if nothing was wrong. Although we'd made up, underlying tensions still remained unaddressed.

As I washed with Ness that evening, it appeared she'd done the same thing and was also still frustrated. She'd wanted to say something to Laura at lunch, but her meltdown had somewhat overshadowed that. As a friend, Ness had wanted to support her, so she had stayed quiet, but it didn't change how she was feeling. That evening, rather than hearing the jovial call of: "*Warwap*!" – the Waî Waî equivalent of "grub's up" – saying grace and eating together, we ate cold, leftover food at different times. Ness took herself off to bed very early, and Ant and Romel followed soon after. Everyone was clearly frazzled from the tempestuous events of the day.

I once heard a saying that holding on to anger is like holding a hot coal – the only person you're hurting is yourself. The freshness of the evening breeze brought with it a sense of perspective, as it wrapped around me. With everyone else in bed, I decided to channel my nan's advice – to never let the sun go down on an argument – and took the opportunity to express myself properly (and more productively) to **Remove high emotions from your environment** Laura. She clearly needed some support, and I had things I wanted to get off my chest. I picked up a stick and traced a pattern in the dirt as we waited for the water to boil. Once we were sure it had been vigorously boiling for a good 5 minutes, we took it off the fire and let it cool, before filling up everyone's water bottles for the following day. The sound of "Somewhere Over the Rainbow" played on Laura's phone in the background. Random flashes of lightning shone in the distance but there was no accompanying thunder, or any sign of a storm, in the starry night. I took a deep breath and tried to express myself.

I was honest with Laura and said that I'd been annoyed at her, as I felt like everything was now on her timescale and about what she wanted to do. That she hadn't been taking into account how others on the trip might feel, as a result of focusing on her situation. However, expeditions and conflict can hold a mirror to yourself and, as is the case with life, sometimes you don't always like what you see. For her part, she told me that, at times, she'd felt that I'd stared daggers at her and I'd made snippy remarks. I apologized and admitted that I wasn't good at expressing negative emotions and, instead, tended to bottle them up. I'd kept quiet because I didn't want to rock the boat but evidently my eyes had given away my annoyance at the situation. I was glad she mentioned it, and I asked her to tell me if it happened again. It was something to be aware of and served as a reminder, once again, that if something really bothered us, we needed to express what we thought and felt – even if this temporarily meant upsetting people. By not doing so, we could unintentionally make the situation worse.

Unfortunately, the beautiful scene of reconciliation was somewhat ruined because we were both quite gassy. This was not a new occurrence, for Laura at least. Indeed, Ness and I had taken to calling her Pumba, after the Disney warthog known for being somewhat flatulent. (In fairness, they had nicknamed my pubic hair "the ferret" – owing to the fact that any sort of hair removal in the jungle is asking for trouble – so I didn't feel too bad for Laura's moniker.)

"Lift your bum cheeks apart; it makes less sound," Laura advised, clearly a more seasoned pro in such matters.

I laughed. "The things you learn on expedition, hey?"

"Life lessons right there," Laura grinned back. Our friendship had been tested but I knew in that moment that we were prepared to weather the storms together. I'd seen that, if handled well, conflict offers the opportunity to cement rather than destroy a relationship. As we headed to bed, chatting away as normal, I had a funny feeling that going forward everything would be OK. Shame I was only partly right...

Try to find a common goal

Sleep had brought with it a sense of clarity and I was already feeling better about my barney with Laura. However, immediately on waking, I sensed that something was wrong. The dawn chorus of the howler monkeys had already started up. Bleary-eyed and groggy, I tried to figure out how close the noise was. Their call can carry up to 5 kilometres but, given the volume reverberating around our camp, I guessed one was much closer. They are one of the loudest creatures on the planet – their calls have been recorded at 140 decibels, which is louder than a military jet taking off (130 decibels). Over the commotion, I detected another sound: panic. My teammates were clearly in a bit of a flap.

"What's happened?" I croaked out.

"A boat is gone," someone replied.

"What colour is it?"

"Blue."

Balls. Mine was blue. I had a real sinking feeling in my stomach and my mind started to race. Did I not pull it far enough up the rock last night? Did I not tie it on properly? I had left both dry bags on it and I'd only taken out the essentials; surely that should have been heavy enough to keep it securely grounded? It turned out that my boat had stayed put and instead it was Laura's that was missing. Thankfully, she wasn't carrying the generator or the medical kit, and she had the satellite phone with her. In the worst-case scenario, the only things missing were our dehydrated meals. We packed up as fast as we could to try to find the boat. Laura temporarily hitched a lift in Ness's kayak.

Ironically, the missing boat seemed to bring us together. Laura was in much finer fettle. She'd regained her characteristic sense of humour and joked about the state of her foot, which the jungle had been taking a toll on.

"You know those mutant films where people turn into a spider or a reptile? I feel like I'm turning into a turtle," she said while waving her scaly, pink, eczema-riddled foot at me from Ness's boat.

"From South Laaandan, mate, it's X-ma," quipped Ness, suggesting it could be a good name for Laura's alter ego.

Luckily, the kayak hadn't gone far. Within 5 minutes we'd located it, pinned in place by the branches of an overhanging tree. Everything seemed to be accounted for. Just as we were pulling it out, the Garmin beeped, alerting us to a message. It was Ed telling us that they'd managed to push back their flights to Guyana. This would give us more time to get closer to Apoteri and hopefully more days with Ed, Ran and Charlie. It was fantastic, not least because everyone already seemed so much more chilled out.

"Awesome news," said Ness. "It takes a weight off our shoulders knowing we don't have to rush."

Laura smiled and rolled her eyes. "Yes, but as you know, remaining calm about time is my constant battle."

Ness delivered her reply in the form of a paddle flick, splashing Laura's face with water. In retribution, I paddled closer to their boats and tried to soak Ness but ended up covering them both. Let's just say, it didn't end well for me, either.

The day was turning out to be a good one – we'd slowed down, laughed and spent more time close to the riverbank, looking up at the canopy. At one point I paddled right under a hawk that seemed entirely unfazed by my presence. It just sat there, staring for a while, before deciding it had better things to do. We could see that Laura was still struggling with the slower pace, but she did agree that it was nice to stop, breathe and smell the roses. Or, in our case, piranha, as Romel had caught one for lunch – which we also enjoyed at a leisurely pace, before getting back on the water. Suddenly,

I could see Romel and Laura pointing and gesturing for us to go slowly. Up ahead, about 30 metres away, we saw something large basking on a rock. It was a jaguar. It was utterly majestic.

It clocked us. Wary, but in no particular hurry, the jaguar stood up and started slowly, deliberately, moving toward the jungle. The confidence in its movements, the sinews moving with such grace, the way it padded across the rock, owning each footstep and the land beneath it – it was incredible to see. I felt no fear whatsoever, although maybe that was because of my distance and the fact I didn't realize what good swimmers jaguars are.

The team were all buzzing.

"It was insane," said Laura, afterward. "I dreamed of seeing one. Prayed for it. They're so elusive that I thought it was almost impossible. Goes to show you that nothing is impossible."

Establishing (and sticking to) your boundaries can actually reduce conflict

"You were so lucky. It's by chance that you saw it," said Ant. "Jaguars are very camouflaged and if we just paddle, paddle, paddle like we've been doing, we might miss them. However, if we focus then maybe we can spot one. You are blessed, as lots of people would like to see them. It was a lucky day."

Ness took this as her opportunity to speak up about her desire to spend more time engaging with the wildlife.

"We've been paddling all day, chatting away, talking to each other. We need to balance it with time when we're quiet. We would never have seen it otherwise. We could have gone past so many animals," she said.

"I'm just a little bit scared of my own head at the moment," said Laura. "I'm scared that if I stop talking and interacting, my head will have the freedom to go off on tangents I don't want it to. I'm scared I'll go a bit crazy. It can be tiring sometimes to focus," said Laura.

"We need to do both," said Ness, voicing her needs.

The solution we came to was to focus on paddling hard for chunks of half an hour and then relaxing for a bit. This way we could achieve distance, conversation and wildlife spotting.

Ant pointed out the vultures circling in the sky. He told us that, when you see them, it's often a sign of a jaguar knocking around.

"They're nature's sanitary animals. They clean the dead away." He seemed quite taken with the beauty of the process. I shared with him a story of sky burials. During our bike trip, Charlie and I met a man in China's Sichuan province whose job it was to cut up corpses. He told us that they would be left on a mountaintop, exposed to nature and the elements. It was a final act of generosity by the deceased – offering up your flesh to those who can use it and, in doing so, continuing the cycle of life. Vultures would be the ones to usually pick it apart.

"Oh," came Ant's reply. I am still not entirely sure what he made of the concept.

At about 4 p.m., we came across a large, beautiful island in the middle of the river, quite unlike anything we'd seen before. Ant and Romel said it used to be an old gold-mining site but it had been shut in 2015. The whole island must have been the size of an old manor house. A handful of smaller trees were growing on a slightly raised mound in the centre. Surrounding them, from what I assume was the silt churned up from the dredging, was a sandy beach. It was stunning, despite the violent way it had come into being. The sand sloped into the river, giving it the feel of a holiday resort; the water seemed clear enough and perfect for swimming.

We climbed out of our kayaks and waded through the water to dry land, smiling as we did. The opportunity to camp on our own desert island seemed too good to miss. It looked idyllic, not least because the small sand dunes that had formed on one side of the beach had filled up with rainwater, creating pool after shimmering pool. As the sun set, it looked as if each mini pond had captured it – the rays reflected every which way. Occasionally, in the fading light, you'd catch glimpses of fool's gold in the sand.

Because there wasn't enough space near the trees for us all to hang our hammocks, Ant and Romel created a wooden structure so we could sleep on the beach. Large, solid branches had been cut off the trees and dug into the ground. I hung my hammock closest to the water. Sleeping out under the stars sounded blooming marvellous. Or at least it did until we went for a swim…

"Er, guys, what's this?" said Ness tentatively. Her bikini-clad body had paused before the water and she was pointing to the ground.

"A jaguar track," replied Ant after examining it. "Fresh and from today."

The discovery somewhat took the edge off the beauty of the place. The fading light meant that moving campsite wasn't an option, so we just got on with our evening routine. What was an option, however, were marshmallows. Given the stresses of the last few days, we'd decided to celebrate the fact that today had been a good day and cracked open our only pack.

A fire had been lit and logs pulled around it to function as benches, and the sunset had given way to wispy grey clouds. Stars were slowly revealing themselves to the jungle canopy. Frogs croaked in the distance, and every now and again we could hear the "plop" of a fish jumping around. I looked at my friends as we dangled our sticks over the fire, sugary blobs clinging to the bark, and I thought that if ever I had to be stranded on a deserted island, this would be it – albeit perhaps without apex predators lurking.

"This is similar to what the Atlantic is like. They're incredible," said Laura, as she stared up at the stars. "Nearly everything about today has been a highlight – definitely the jaguar, this camp spot, bathing, taking loads of photos, all of us chatting this morning. Being together. Paddling together. Stopping together. We felt like a team again."

"I always think nature has a way of knowing how to bring things back into balance. It brings perspective. It reminds you where you are," said Ness, pausing briefly to pop a perfectly toasted marshmallow in her mouth.

"When we saw the jaguar today, I felt like it was a reminder of how stunning this environment is and just how lucky we are to be in it. I think it brought back our dynamic, too. Our balance as a team."

The jaguar sighting had indeed helped to restore harmony. It also reaffirmed the need for us to work with, not against, each other. If we were going to complete the journey – and with our friendships intact – we needed to share the burden, not add to it. Our battles had to be picked, and our niggles voiced, explained and then forgotten. Turns out that friendships are not just valuable for our sanity, but in many ways our survival, too.

After dinner, Ness said she wanted an early night, as her foot was causing her more pain than before. She was now on antibiotics, as recommended by Dave, but we were all keeping a close eye on it. She could barely walk; it was more of a hobble. After saying goodnight, she teetered away slowly but returned rather more quickly.

Pick your battles wisely

"Guys, I think I heard a jaguar just a few metres away."

Ant jumped up and grabbed his torch. "What did it sound like?" he asked.

She made a low grunting noise we recognized as a jaguar call. Thinking there'd be safety in numbers, I followed Ant, Ness and Romel toward our hammocks. Laura, however, remained by the fire, gallantly watching over our toasting marshmallows. Ant shone the light in the direction Ness had indicated and there were indeed eyes staring back at us. It wasn't a jaguar, but it was perhaps equally concerning. A 3-metre-long black caiman was looking at us from the water, only about 15 metres from my hammock. Worryingly, my hammock was also closest to where we'd seen the jaguar print. After a while, the caiman seemed fed up with the torch being shone in its eyes and it sank from sight. Our seemingly perfect campsite was becoming less shiny by the minute.

Having established the source of the noise, and ensured that the threat seemed to have passed, Ness, Ant and Romel disappeared to bed. Laura and I remained. She was boiling water for us to drink the next day, and I sat writing. Ant unexpectedly reappeared, flashing his torch into the forest and across the water.

"Have you seen something?" I asked.

"No," he replied, his face unconvincing as he continued to scan with his torch.

"You have, haven't you?" I pressed.

"Be careful tonight," he warned. "There are jaguars and crocodiles all around. Make sure you put the food away and keep an ear open. If you hear anything, just call me. Keep your machete close."

It felt like the equivalent of sleeping out in the open in the African savanna, setting up camp smack bang in the middle of the Serengeti. As Laura pointed out while we reluctantly trudged to our hammocks, we didn't have much of a choice.

Turns out sleep wasn't an option anyway, as within an hour of getting into our sleeping bags, there was a hell of a wind- and rainstorm. Rain was hitting the hammocks at a sideways angle. Everything was getting drenched and the tarp threatened to blow away entirely. After we'd got out of our hammocks and retied the tarp tighter to the wooden posts, the storm seemed to pass. Exceptionally damp, tired and fed up, we climbed back into our wet sleeping bags and tried to kip once more.

The next morning, I found Romel on the beach, looking dejected. I followed his eyeline down to his T-shirt that was lying on the floor. It was covered in sand. I asked what was wrong.

"A caiman tried to steal it," he said.

I thought he was joking.

Then he showed me the animal tracks that led from the log where his T-shirt had been to where it was now, lying on the beach. I paced back from the T-shirt to our hammocks – I counted 11 steps, and I'm only 1.6 metres tall, with short legs. Had the caiman taken a shining to the three hanging cocoons just a few steps to its left, the morning might have started very differently. We shuddered to think that we may have been watched as we were out fixing the tarps, entirely consumed by the task in hand.

When we had initially pulled up to the little island, we thought it so serene. Outwardly, everything seemed perfect but the reality was very different. There was much going on beneath the surface that we hadn't realized. Apparently, even a paradise has its problems.

"Ah, well, I guess I'm wearing a ripped, soggy T-shirt today," Romel said, picking it up and shaking it off. A wet shirt wasn't worth getting into a conflict with a caiman for. Sometimes you just know when it's time to let things go and move on.

Limits

*(plural noun): the furthest extents of
one's physical or mental endurance.*

The beauty of adventure is that it pushes you to all
sides of yourself, but you also need to acknowledge
your own limits. It's like walking a tightrope; the
trick is knowing where the balance is between risk
and reward, and staying on the right side of that
line. You can achieve more than you think you can,
but you must also remember that you can't achieve
everything. It's OK to admit when you're out of your
depth. You have to be honest with yourself. For
instance, if you're craving a new challenge and you're
choosing between attempting Couch to 5K or BASE
jumping, first examine your motives. Compare what
you have to gain by pushing a limit versus what you
have to lose. Are your limits self-imposed or realistic?
Are you just scared? Do you genuinely have the skill
set for this? If it doesn't result in death or harm to
yourself or those around you then perhaps it's a risk
worth taking. What will happen if you don't? Limits
can stretch; you just have to respectfully prod at
them every now again.

Days on expedition: 46

Location: Jacobs Ladder

Status: taking on the rapids

"It's dangerous but we could take a chance," said Ant, discussing how to tackle the rapids in front of us – a series of rocky, fast-flowing pools known as Jacobs Ladder Falls. Despite his calm approach to life, it transpired he could be something of an adrenaline junkie, and he jumped at the chance of riding a waterfall. However, his assessment of these rapids didn't exactly fill me with joy, not least because in the past few days I had spent some of my time unintentionally swimming.

Romel did not appear to be keen, either. Having done his own internal audit, he decided he wasn't going to run it.

"I am frightened in the water because it's dangerous. I don't want to capsize again," he said. Then he added, "I have a little headache and am not feeling well." Romel was shaken after falling out of the kayak a few days previously. Although he didn't let it show at the time, he'd mentioned around the campfire that evening that he'd been frightened by the rapids. I gave him kudos for admitting it. My respect for him went up greatly.

You hear white water before you see it. It's a roar that heightens your senses; adrenalin floods the body. The white froth of trapped air is both taunting and inviting; a Faustian bargain – what would you risk to run me? I'd found out during training in Wales about how unrelentingly powerful water can be. I'd always given it a healthy respect, but after my experience of white water pummelling down on me, it was now even greater. Its allure was as powerful as it was dangerous.

Over the last week or so the team had slowly been growing in confidence. We'd taken on some tricky rapids and come out the other end. After one of our previous runs, Ness had said she'd enjoyed watching the rest of us come down.

Be honest about why you're pushing yourself

"Your faces just lit up like little kids'. It was like you'd had too many sweets. You were shaking!"

She, too, had had a blast riding down the white water. "The contrast between the adrenaline of the rapids, and then the calm serenity of the flat water is amazing," she said. "It's like dropping down into a giant sheet of glass. I kept expecting to feel fear, but I had so much fun."

"Yeah, they're huge adrenaline highs," agreed Laura.

The adrenaline levels had never been higher than several days previously, on the largest rapid we'd ever run. It was a roaring monstrosity of a thing. Looking down at it, there seemed to be a clear line and running it appeared possible for our level of skill. Doing so successfully, however, wasn't a given. Ness had gone first, somewhat gung-ho, and nailed it. The rest of us then had to decide if we would do it, too. I could see from Laura's face that she wasn't entirely convinced.

"I had to question whether I'd run it or not," she said afterward. "I was asking myself: 'Is there a possible line? Am I being pressured into doing it or am I actually comfortable?' I had to remember that just because everyone else had done it, it didn't mean that it suited me and my skill level. And it wasn't like you were ganging up on me, or anything, but, you know, it's just easy to feel like you should do something if everyone else is doing it."

Laura's reasoning was sound. I'd gone through the same thought process and decided I would take it on.

As I walked to the boat, I was lost in a bundle of nerves. I hid behind a rock for a pee and almost thought I was going to poo myself, too. I was so nervous. However, once I was in the zone, my entire mental state changed. As I paddled toward the rapid, I was just looking for the line, visualizing how I was going to get through it by trying to steer the boat in the vague direction we'd planned and then hoping for the best.

It was an absolute blast. Waves crashed over the boat. For a brief moment it felt like I was on the high seas, the kayak bobbing and soaring, and sheets of water pushing me along. I was on such a high afterward, buzzing for ages. I'd never experienced adrenaline like it – I had so much excitement pumping through my system that I felt like I needed to stop and rest. I needed to centre myself somehow. We all recognized that the thrill we got from it was not necessarily a good thing in such a remote area. In Wales we were with experienced kayakers and help was accessible, as were good medical facilities. Here, we were 24–48 hours away from medical help, depending on what time of day we called the helicopter – and that was if it could even land.

Have you bitten off more than you can chew?

As a team, there had been plenty of times when we'd had to be realistic about our abilities. On a particularly steep, rock-laden, fast-flowing rapid we decided we'd have to attach the rope to the kayaks and individually lower them down from the riverbank. It was a good job we didn't run the thing, as we watched the boats get churned and mashed up at the bottom of one of the rapids. The sound was immense. It was amazing to think how quickly things could have gone wrong, due to inexperience and overconfidence. The force of the water was so strong that I ended up slipping on the rocks as I tried to hold the rope firmly. Ant leaned over to help me catch it, stopping me from slipping into the rapids in the process. Despite his help, the rope still flew out of my hands and I watched my kayak tumble away, untethered, over white water. Thankfully, we recovered the boat and we were in one piece. The reality was that we were lucky.

That wasn't the end of our run-ins with the rapids. We'd come a cropper on a complex cascading system of rapids, too. It was difficult enough to navigate as it was, seeing as there were so many rocks and weeds, but to make matters worse, on this occasion I ended up having to improvise my route midway down.

Ant, who had gone first, had got stuck on a rock in an eddy, a sort of calm parking place in the water. The rest of us had followed too closely. There was no room to stop. Ness made it into the eddy, but Laura, ahead of me, had nowhere to go.

The fear of coming up to an eddy, realizing that we weren't going to be able to fit, and then knowing we would have to career down white water on a line we hadn't assessed sent my adrenaline through the roof in a bad way. I watched as Laura's boat turned and she got sucked backward into the flow. Fear widened her eyes. Weirdly, it snapped my brain into a place of utter clarity. I knew I wasn't going to fit into the eddy, and that I had no choice but to take on a raging drop and whirlpool of water below, with no forward planning. From her vantage point in the eddy, Ness shouted to Laura that it was OK – the line was good.

"I'm with you," I called to Laura.

Thankfully, she managed to turn her boat around and we all made it down safely. I was shaking like a leaf when we got to the end, body coursing with nerves, euphoria, fear and adrenaline.

Ant was terribly upset when we all regrouped at the bottom and felt so bad for getting stuck. We told him that it was our fault for following too quickly behind him, and that we should have allowed for problems with the person in front. It was a wake-up call for the team: even if something looked doable, we couldn't afford to be complacent. There were no second chances in this environment.

"My highlight was not dying on that waterfall," Laura said that evening when I asked the team for their favourite moments of the day.

It turned out that this wasn't going to be the only time on the journey when Laura thought she was about to die on a rapid – however, the second time she was in no danger whatsoever. Just

Don't be afraid to back off

before a tiny rapid, Ant's helmet had fallen out of his boat. Laura was up ahead and closest to it. To try to alert her to it, Romel screamed for her to wait, just as she was approaching the rapid. We watched as Laura then started paddling like a lunatic away from the flow, panic on her face.

"I was wondering: was there a waterfall? Was I about to die because I didn't wait?" she recounted later. "Then I saw everyone pointing to a helmet. I was like, for goodness' sake, I thought I was about to die for a helmet." It tickled the rest of us greatly.

Apart from Ant – Mr "When I See Waterfalls I Must Go" – the rest of us weren't so convinced about taking on Jacobs Ladder Falls. Thankfully, he'd also spotted a small opening in the forest near the rapids. As we approached, it almost looked like a curtain to the jungle; it was a well-established portage route – complete with branches laid on the floor, presumably to help roll the dugout canoes. It was also the first sign we had come across that we were nearing people.

Rather than sending the kayaks down the rapids on ropes and climbing down the rocks, we opted for the longer but safer option: we would hike around the rapids. Ant capitulated, conceding that the portage would be good exercise and that he needed to cooperate because the falls were too large. As a line had already been cut through the jungle, I rather enjoyed the sweaty hike, back under the canopy once again, with monkeys darting around overhead. It was also a reminder that my trench foot hadn't healed properly. I'd noticed that morning that the small, itchy holes were beginning to turn black in places.

For 30 minutes we carted as much kit as we could physically carry through the jungle, until we came to a beautiful, mossy wood-like area that opened on to a steep slope, revealing a sandy beach that led to the river once again. As we approached the opening, we saw to our right a raging, cascading waterfall. We'd heard the roar of white water before we saw it, and the torrent that we eventually saw reaffirmed that we had definitely made the right choice to walk! We weren't the only ones to have made this call. Marked on a tree at the top was a stick figure and a date – 2018. Along the portage route we'd seen other old marks cut into trees, too. Romel explained that you leave these cuttings when you travel so that others can see that people have been this way before.

As we slowly descended back to the river, Ness slipped, aggravating an old hip injury, and so she limped the remaining distance to the beach. Unable to walk properly, we told her to stay put and dose herself up on Tramadol while the rest of us walked back to fetch the remaining boats and dry bags. Since we were going to have to make at least another two journeys, Laura wasn't overjoyed at the prospect. We expected it to take at least a couple of hours.

"I hate this sort of task. It's both monotonous and tedious," she said as we trudged through the jungle alternating between balancing the kayak on our shoulders and holding it in front of us, as muscle burn set in. We'd specifically chosen the NRS Outlaw kayak for this purpose. Weighing in at just under 12 kilograms, they are incredibly light for the class of boat, although we still worked up a hell of a sweat with dry bags and life vests also in tow.

We did get a temporary reprieve when a massive thorn went through my jungle boot.

"Do you want to pull it out?" Laura asked, quickly followed up with: "*Christ*."

The next thing I knew she'd put the boat on the floor, jumped into it and was screaming as if overtaken by madness.

"Ah, ah, ah. It's got me in the eye," she said as she slapped her arms and legs with wild abandon. I couldn't work out what the hell was going on; I thought she'd lost the plot. "Get into the boat, Pip! They're all over you, too; we've stopped on an ant trail."

The scent, or pheromones, that ants leave to trace their way back from a food source to their colony had been unintentionally disturbed as a result of our portaging, and they were now in defence mode. The biting started and I, too, knew what Laura meant. It must have looked hilarious, the two of us, standing on an inflatable kayak, leaping about, whooping and walloping various body parts. You may well ask why we didn't immediately vacate the area but when you're being bitten by hundreds of ants, it's hard to think straight. Handily, though, the boat offered a temporary refuge: a) for me to remove the thorn from my shoe and b) for us to assess where the ant trail was and how to avoid it. I also made a mental note to check that specific kayak for punctures. (We had learned that fixing punctures on the river wasn't the most fun task, after Romel had accidentally left a loose fishing hook in his boat!)

Laura and I finally emerged from the gap in the jungle canopy to see Ness sipping on a protein shake, seemingly in better spirits as the drugs had kicked in. Unfortunately, we knew she couldn't chill out for too long, because coming just a few kilometres further down the river was King William IV Falls.

This was the last waterfall we were expecting before meeting up with Charlie, Ed and the rest of the team.

Not long after we'd got back in our kayaks, we came across a beastly sounding drop – rocks that looked almost silver lined the fall. Water poured over them, battering them with a torrent of froth and rapturous energy. We'd reached King William IV Falls.

We gazed down at the only possible route, which plunged straight into a churning torrent of white water. It was far too steep to run.

"I'm guessing we're lining the boats down?" I asked Laura.

"Well, I'm not in the mood to commit suicide," she said.

Ant and Romel began lining the kayaks, while Laura, Ness and I ferried any other bags that were loose.

We began our dangerous descent down the silver rocks. White water raged next to us, a very sensory warning of where we'd end up if we messed up. Despite saying she was OK to continue and that the pain had subsided, Ness seemed to be really struggling with her hip. Laura and I had taken the weight of the bags off her, but even so a clamber over the slippiest, albeit most beautiful, rocks we had yet to encounter wasn't ideal. I thought to myself that it was funny how, after a while, things become normal. If you'd have told me at the start of the trip that I'd be carrying a heavy camera bag across slippery rocks above a torrent of white water, stepping over holes covered with spiderwebs and putting my feet in dark water while hoping for the best, I'm not sure I'd have believed you. While Laura and I shuttled the bags down the rocks, Ant and Romel worked together to guide the kayaks down the rapids, using a combination of ropes and heavy lifting. After around an hour of manoeuvring boats down the rapid, as well as ourselves, we had all, thankfully, made it in one piece.

Bizarrely, as we paddled away from the falls and into flatter water, I saw a bird that looked like a duck, swimming around.

The perceived familiarity of it, the juxtaposition of remoteness and familiarity, startled me so much that I choked up. I'm not sure what the bird was but watching it glide on the water – rather than flying through the sky like the numerous macaws, parrots, herons and swallows we'd seen – jolted me back to a world that seemed so far away.

A few hours later, just after 4 p.m., we came to another set of rapids. Having had an exhausting day, I suggested we set up camp for the evening. Laura, knowing Ed was close, had just sent a message to ask what the terrain was like further down.

"I can see a canoe. Two canoes. Three canoes," Ness shouted.

I had wondered earlier in the day if the guys would surprise us. Indeed, 10 minutes earlier, Ant, who has the hearing of a bat, had said that he could hear an engine in the distance; I'd heard bugger all, apart from the sounds of the jungle.

Seeing boats appear on the horizon was so bizarre. We'd spent the past few weeks in isolation, so meeting people for the first time, and in such an unexpected way, was both exhilarating and unsettling. I scanned the boats, desperately trying to find Charlie. I knew Laura was doing the same for Ran and Ed. Our cameraman, Jon, would be in there somewhere, too.

I finally spotted Charlie standing on one of the boats, wearing a blue shirt and baseball cap, waving with such vigour it looked like his hands might fly off. Before we could be reunited, there was the small matter of the rapids in front of us. But they were only small. I pointed my kayak in Charlie's direction and paddled as hard as I could. In my excitement I nearly wedged myself on a rock. In this instance, the risk was worth the reward. As our kayaks approached their boats, Charlie leaned down, hugged me and told me how proud he was. Tears streamed down both our faces. A similar scene was happening with Laura. We'd been so excited to see them. We hadn't anticipated how emotional it would be. My best friend, my partner in crime, had finally arrived.

Connection

(noun): a relationship in which a person or thing is linked or associated with something else.

The beauty of travel is that it connects us to the world around us, other people and ourselves. Over the course of the expedition I realized, firstly, how much humans crave genuine connection and, secondly, how important it is that this isn't just surface level.

Connection, in all its forms, was the glue of the expedition, the thing that held it (and me) together. Our relationships, our friendships – these are the core of life. Those we choose to spend time with, and how they treat us (and how we treat them), matter. True friendships and connections should be positive and respectful of the other's needs, and enable us to grow in a positive way.

It's not always easy, especially when you take people for granted or assume they'll always be there. Genuine connection takes work, energy and attention. But the upside? It's so much more rewarding when you're fully present. In an age where we are seemingly more connected than ever before, technology has allowed us to disconnect in unhealthy ways. We can have a coffee with a friend while texting someone else. Instead of connecting with ourselves while relaxing in the bath, we're swiping through apps, or we're updating social media while in bed. Or we can be in beautiful virgin rainforest feeling jealous about someone else's life. The contrast between how I felt on the days when I'd connected online versus the days where I'd spent most of the time engaging with people face to face (or boat to boat) was huge. Although I am introverted by nature, it made me realize how important genuine connection is – nothing beats it. So, nourish the relationship with the people you cherish and show up for them when they need it (and even when they don't). Give them your time, love and full attention. And never, ever underestimate the power of a hug.

Days on expedition: 46

Location: Nearing King William Adventures Lodge

Status: reunions

Never have I been so pleased to see Charlie. Not least because he came bearing sugar. Charlie and Ed had brought with them supplies of sweets and a box of Cadbury Creme Eggs as a gift from Chris, our kayak instructor. Sweet tooth aside, seeing him was just the boost I needed. Laura looked so much more relaxed with Ran in her arms and Ed next to her; it was almost as if the stresses of the last few weeks hadn't taken place at all. It was so good to see the tension dissipate from her face as we ate dinner together. I watched as she threw Ran up in the air, his little giggles a welcome addition to the sounds of the river.

It had been a delightful first evening. We had set up camp pretty much immediately after seeing each other, and food had been taken care of by Fay James, the owner of a tourist fishing lodge further downstream, who had organized us a feast. She'd heard about our journey and wanted to meet us. Her dad, Campbell, was one of the two boat drivers who had brought the team to find us. Fay had suggested we recuperate for a few days at her lodge – King William Adventures fishing lodge – which was a few days' paddling away. After this brief catch-up, Ran and Ed would be heading back there, and the rest of us would be joining them as soon as possible. It sounded like heaven – as did a change to our diet. On the menu that evening was a hearty fish and tomato spaghetti dish and Guyanese "bake" – essentially, a delicious fried bread that is typical of the region. Having someone cook for us felt like such a luxury. We rounded the evening off with a ton of Laura's favourites – Haribo.

"I've been going to HA meetings for a while now," she said, her face stuffed full of them, clearly so much happier to have seen her family.

"HA?" I replied.

"Haribo Anonymous."

It had been good to get to know Jon a bit better over dinner, too. We'd spoken to him on Skype, after he got in touch over social media when we put out a call for a cameraperson, and had instantly warmed to him. However, spending a month with someone you've never even met is a gamble – on both sides. Although, thinking about it, perhaps Jon got the raw end of the bargain, as he was joining a group of kayakers slowly pickling in a smell of vinegar that seemed to be emanating from their armpits. He'd also arrived as we were approaching the more urbanized part of our paddle. Thankfully, Jon not only seemed to cope with the smell, but he also turned out to be a great videographer and awesome fun to have around. I had already heard him chatting football to Ant and extolling the virtues of supporting Liverpool.

Nurture connections with people who help you grow

With a full stomach, I cuddled up to Charlie as we sat next to the fire, stars gracing the sky. Smoke curled out of the fire and seemed intent on wrapping itself around Fay. I watched as she tried to withstand the smoky haze filling her nostrils and making her eyes water. From our brief interaction I could tell she was a lively, can-do character. She told us she was a single mother of two, with a passion for – and unrivalled knowledge of – fish that I'd never witnessed before and doubt I am ever likely to again. She shared with us that she often called herself Jungle Jane, and took her 29-year-old self and her dogs into the jungle alone to spend the night. She was a badass. I warmed to her immediately.

Fay put up with the smoky haze for as long as she could, before getting up and moving around the fire. "My grandmother said you should never move spots when you're eating, as your partner will get up and walk away," she said, unfazed, taking her food with her.

"When I was little, my grandmother would say that if the smoke followed you, it meant you have a lot of boyfriends or girlfriends," Ant said.

"One is enough," replied Laura, smiling happily, re-energized by having seen her family.

I leaned into Charlie and slightly zoned out of the conversation. I thought how nice it was that he was finally here. Like most relationships, ours isn't perfect. It wasn't a "love at first sight" fairy tale; we were friends who became something more. We have had our ups and downs and no doubt will continue to. But above everything, he's my best friend and the person I will continue to show up for – whatever life throws at us. Spending months looking at trees, away from him, also got me thinking about my favourite quote about love. I read it in the book *Captain Corelli's Mandolin*, where Louis de Bernières compares love not to the blossom in the tree but to the moment when you realize that your roots are so entwined with one another that you are one tree, not two. There's a realness to the idea, an earthiness that speaks to something deeper. It's a rawness that suggests love can be found in the dirt: a strength rooted in understanding the darkest parts of ourselves and of those we love. It sparked an idea for a poem.

Fall in love

Fall in love with those
who see beauty in a raindrop,
who appreciate a wilting rose
knowing it has lived,
who do not condemn the storms
but embrace them as life.

Fall in love with those
who ask hard questions
and will wait for raw answers,
who compliment kind eyes
not beautiful ones,
who ask what they can give
not what they can get.

Fall in love with those
who judge value by values,
who see the dark in others
yet focus on the light,
who tend to the embers
when lust has burned up.

So if you must fall in love,
first fall in love,
then fall in love with souls
who will stand in love with yours.

I turned my attention back to the team and watched the fire's shadows dancing around Fay's face. It seemed I had tuned back into the conversation at an alarming point, as she was delivering a warning about how important it is to connect with and understand your environment.

"You've got to be careful as you go further downstream. Caimans are more used to seeing humans, so they know their weaknesses. We've watched our dogs being taken, right in front of our eyes. We had 24 dogs but now we only have five. Now if we see caimans, we usually climb. Take a long stick with you, too, because caimans think it's a bow and they know what that is. If you hold a machete, they will go straight for your hands." I squeezed Charlie's hand a bit tighter. Fay seemed unperturbed by the wide-eyed reactions.

"I've been watching how we set up camp tonight," Fay continued. "We need to light the fire away from the water, further into the forest, as it gives you more protection from predators."

Then she pointed to the water. "Hunters have been bitten by caimans, too. One boy was eaten and his body has never been found. The last time his mum saw him was in the middle of the river and the caiman had him in his mouth, but they never found the body or bones. The village killed about twelve or thirteen caimans and cut them up to try to find the body. Once the caimans taste something, they always come back."

Disconnect to reconnect

Fay stared at the flames before speaking again. "That's why I'm worried all the time. I really worry that my son bathes without his grandmother who looks after him when I'm working. We can't go to the loo alone. It's nothing to be ashamed of."

"I don't know about you guys, but I thought as we were approaching people, we'd be safer," said Laura, looking increasingly concerned.

Fay's story had deeply unsettled me. From the sounds of it, the more caimans interacted with humans, the less afraid they became. Ironically, the more we've tried to dominate the landscape, the more it's come back to bite us. I began to realize how disconnected we can be from nature.

The day after we'd met, Charlie, who had turned off data on his phone entirely since arriving in Guyana, snapped a photo of me, Laura and Ness sat around a noisy generator, huddled close to the BGAN, typing away and uploading things to social media. We looked like zombies illuminated in blue light. It was something I'd been struggling with on this trip – finding the balance between sending messages to family, fulfilling social media obligations to sponsors and keeping interested followers updated, while not letting the experience of our journey pass us by. To compromise I'd started to write emails or posts in advance and hitting send when online, as well as trying not to disappear down the rabbit warren of other people's lives. There was something deeply sad about being sat on a rock, in a beautiful rainforest, comparing filtered images of curated lives against my own and coming away feeling like I was the one missing out. The more I could limit that, the better. Proof, if ever I needed it, that however amazing things are for you, connecting with what doesn't nourish you isn't good for the soul.

"Be careful," said Charlie that night as I lowered my foot into a bag of talcum powder he was holding open for me. It's fair to say it wasn't just the environment, natural or digital, that we needed to be careful of; our self-care had been somewhat lacking. We'd been paddling for 18 days straight before we'd met the others. Ness, Laura and I had all said our periods were late. It hurt to move our hands, especially our thumbs. Despite wearing gloves, a large blister had appeared in the centre of my hand. My glands were swollen and big snotty sneezes kept escaping. Then there were our feet: Ness had a boil and Laura's were covered in what looked like a bad case of eczema. My trench foot hadn't improved; if anything, it was getting worse.

When I'd shown Ed, he'd taken a photo of it and sent it to our fixers Sophia and Anders to see what they recommended. Almost instantly, we received a message on the Garmin, saying they were trying to source treatment and that I needed to keep my feet as dry as possible, put them near the fire at night, wear cotton socks and use as much powder as I could. I was told that if the holes got any worse – turning black, blue or green – I would: "Need to get out!!!" If untreated, trench foot can go gangrenous and, in the worst case, result in amputation. Alarmingly, the little black dots that had appeared a few days earlier were still there. I hoped the powder might turn the tide.

Not one for grand romantic gestures, Charlie's help was his love in action. Being cared for by him, who diligently helped to cover my feet night after night while he was with us, made me realize how blasé Ness, Laura and I had become in many respects. We'd become so used to mosquito worms, ticks in the groin, arse rashes and other jungle ailments.

Connecting to your surroundings helps you to appreciate them

I attempted to crawl into Charlie's hammock that evening for a cuddle, but it was so small it felt like I was trying to re-enter the womb. I told him I felt safer and more at peace when he was around.

"I wouldn't," he said. "I'm a complete foreigner in this environment."

A day after Ran and Ed had left, I'd woken at around 3 a.m. to see Charlie's face illuminated by his phone. I could tell he was wired – a man on edge.

"You OK, Charlie?" I whispered.

"I'm pretty sure something was just sniffing around us. I felt something underneath the hammock," he said.

He's an insomniac at the best of times and the chorus of howler monkeys going berserk probably didn't help matters. I tried to reassure him that I'd felt super on-edge for my first few nights in the jungle, too.

"It's likely just the usual night-time comings and goings of rodents and frogs," I said. "Try to go back to sleep."

How wrong I was. Two hours later, at 5 a.m., Charlie's instincts were proven spot on. A loud shout broke through the darkness. Distinctly human. It was Campbell. A jaguar had roamed right past his hammock and he had sprung into action, waving his torch and shouting to chase it away.

"I knew I felt something," Charlie said over breakfast. It was certainly a hell of an induction to the jungle. Given how knackered we were physically and mentally, arriving at Fay's lodge that evening couldn't have come soon enough.

Reconnecting with loved ones was amazing – for two of us at least. Romel shared that, while he really enjoyed hanging out with everyone, he was also sad, as it made him think about his own family – sentiments echoed by Ness and Ant. It reminded me that it's so easy to take for granted the people we see day in, day out, yet they are the threads that we weave our lives around.

Fay's lodge was built high into the riverbank, looking down on sweeping vistas of the Essequibo. An expanse of grass led from the edge of the escarpment to the beautiful wooden cabins. We climbed the steps leading up to it, and Ed and Ran were there to welcome us. It marked the start of a few days off in far too long. We couldn't wait. It was a chance to breathe, to reconnect and to focus on each other, not just the task ahead of us. Ed had brought a bottle of red wine out with him, which he cracked open and shared around. I'd love to comment on how nice it was, but I managed to knock over my glass, so I'm not entirely sure. As I watched liquid grapes sinking into the wooden floor of the cabin's balcony, Mother Nature roared.

From the safety of our perch high above the Essequibo, we watched a storm dance over the river. Rain beat down, the light casting an orange glow and making the green of Fay's grass seem all the brighter. We all danced and ran through the warm rain, lifted by the joy of connection. In that moment everything felt as it should. In the distance, a rainbow – a beautifully pregnant arch – stretched out across the river.

"A full rainbow means the rainfall will be short," bet Romel. It was. As quickly as it had appeared, the rain left, its departing droplets gifted to the grass now shimmering in the evening sun. If only the rest of our stay had been that perfect.

Rest

(verb): ceasing work or movement in order to relax, sleep or recover strength.

How often do we give ourselves permission to rest? To look after ourselves? To take time to get off the treadmill and to consider where it is that we're running to – and why? It's ironic that it's usually during holidays that we get sick, when our bodies and minds heave a sigh of relief that finally we're starting to listen to them. It's almost as if they suddenly realize, "Phew, I've been running on empty for a while." It shows us that the pace at which we've been going has been possible, yes, but healthy? Not so much. Rest allows us to remember balance, as well as the need to stop, to take stock, to re-evaluate. It is that pause that often allows us to make the most of life and its opportunities.

Days on expedition: 50

Location: King William Adventures lodge

Status: sickness hits

Ness's eyes rolled to the back of her head, before she fell to the ground with a thump and then started convulsing. Laura held her in her arms and, in a calm, rhythmic voice, encouraged her to take a big breath in and a big breath out, putting her hypnobirthing practice to good use.

"I'll get help," I yelled, leaving Ness with Laura and Jon, as I charged from the riverbed up the slope to find the others and the satellite phone.

"It's Ness! She's collapsed," I shouted when I saw Ed and Charlie. They raced down the bank while I located the phone to call the medic. Seeing a friend in a bad way, in such a remote location, was terrifying.

Earlier that day we'd had a giggle when Laura appeared for breakfast, wearing a nappy.

"Just in case," she said. "I thought I'd farted earlier but it turns out it wasn't a fart."

"I think the correct term for that is sharted," said Jon, evidently on hand not only to help with filming, but also with all things lexical.

We'd laughed at the time, chuckling when Ness said she too had a dodgy tummy and had managed to block the loo. We'd shared tips on using buckets of water to clear it and what foods are useful to plug up. But it didn't seem so funny now, with our friend on the floor and being unsure as to why. I searched Laura and Ed's room – the satellite phone was missing.

Ed and Charlie, both men nearly 2 metres tall, had Ness draped over their shoulders, unconscious and hanging like a doll, as they slowly climbed the bank to the lodge. We took Ness to her room, laid her down and she slowly began to come to. We found the satellite phone on her bed and Ed tried to get hold of the expedition medics he uses when he films in remote locations. Eventually, he got through to Dave, who suggested giving her more antibiotics and, crucially, days of rest.

Take time to do things that nourish you

The prescribed rest was welcomed in many ways. We'd pushed ourselves to the point of burnout. Stopping gave our bodies a chance to recover. Having mocked Ness and Laura that morning, I too found myself rushing to the loo every hour or so. In our small wooden cabin, where the bathroom was right next to the bedroom, Charlie and I certainly weren't having the romantic catch-up we'd hoped for. On the plus side, not being on the water every day was greatly aiding the recovery of my trench foot.

Unable to travel far, we spent the next few days chatting, and getting to know Fay and her lodge. One of her dogs had had puppies a few days previously and we often played with them. Despite being newborns, they'd already been bitten by vampire bats, but that was the least of their worries, according to Fay.

"My grandfather told me to comb puppies with piranha teeth for the security of the dogs," she said. "Apparently, the jaguar doesn't like it."

Fay then handed us a brochure for the lodge, telling us she'd spent ages on it. Fay is originally from Apoteri but received a scholarship to study agriculture. After leaving her village, she went further upriver, purchased the piece of land we were sitting on and turned it into a lodge. Her mum now looks after her two children in Apoteri, where they go to school, and Fay shuttles between the lodge and the village to see them. This takes about four days, if paddling, or around 2 hours for a heavy boat with a 15 horsepower engine.

"Everything I do, I do it with passion," she said. "If I want something, I do it and complete it." We believed it. Fay ran her lodge with enthusiasm and confidence. "I am a cook. I know a bit of financing. I can do every single thing," Fay said, as I examined the leaflet. "When it comes to meals and menus, I know what to buy so I don't overbuy. We have different menus here; for example, menus for Americans and Japanese. I don't make unnecessary trips for things that cost a dollar but will that cost two hundred dollars in fuel. To me it's just common sense. You ask what people need and share transportation costs."

The brochure contained pictures of an absolutely huge fish. One shot showed three men struggling to hold the thing up, as it was so large.

"What do you think this country needs?" Charlie asked Fay, who was nursing a coffee.

"It needs good management," she said, as she took a sip. She explained that she visited a lot of areas through her work and so heard what people in different villages desired in terms of tourism.

"In the communities I visit, I'm often asked lots of questions about what they can market," she said. Apparently, people in government sometimes picked her brains on how to develop the region, especially the river.

"When there's mining and logging interests in the area, is ecotourism really a viable way of earning money here?" I asked.

"That is exactly what I talk to the government about," she said. "I have travelled the country – this is the last pristine forest that we have. I ask them: would you like it to be destroyed like every other part of Guyana? The government recognizes that it's the last land.

"I think money and jobs have changed the culture. We used to share a lot more. I feel some people are jealous of me being a successful woman. Anyway…" She paused, changing the subject. "I once paddled to Georgetown with my brother. I've got an inflatable kayak, too."

An idea started to hatch in my mind. Laura had initially wanted this trip to have an all-female team. However, when she looked deeper into the logistics, she was told she wouldn't be able to find any local women to join. I ran my thinking past Laura and Ness, who were both on board. That afternoon, as we played with the puppies, we asked Fay if she'd like to complete the journey with us.

"Are you serious?" she said. "I'd love to."

And that was that. After calling her mum and clearing childcare duties, Fay became the latest member of our team. We just had to get better first.

The period of rest did us all good. Days stretched out ahead with nothing for us to do but build up reserves once again. It was an opportunity to get off the treadmill and refocus on where we were running to. To talk at leisure. To cuddle baby Ran and watch him squeal with glee as his parents played with him. To read. To journal. To do the things that we'd wanted to do but never made time for on the river. Charlie and I discussed *ikigai*, the Japanese concept of finding your true purpose in life. Ant and Romel used the unexpected stop as a chance to visit their friends in Apoteri. Slowly, over the days we were there, Ness got better. We never did establish what was wrong. Given that we'd been there longer than anticipated, we were all keen to crack on. Deep down I knew I could have done with another few days, but my desire not to let the team down meant that I, too, agreed to leave. I wish I'd listened to my body.

Our setting off once again marked the end of one chapter and the beginning of a new one. It was time to wave goodbye to Ed and Ran. A boat had come from Apoteri to pick them up. We loaded their luggage into it and gave them a final round of hugs before the rest of us stepped away to let Laura say a proper goodbye to her family. As Ed carried Ran into the boat, his podgy hands wrapped around his daddy, and Ness and I put our arms around Laura. We waved them off, Laura sobbing until they were just a speck on the horizon.

"Playing with Ran is perhaps the happiest I've ever been in my life," she said as we shared a group hug. "He was laughing loads when I threw him in the air. It made me so happy." She smiled at the memory.

"You're a tough cookie, Miss Bingham," I replied as we returned to the lodge to pack up the rest of our gear and get going.

Charlie was joining us for a few more days, until we hit Apoteri, where he was going to get an outboard to Fairview, the largest settlement in the area. Good job, too, as, although the others had recovered, my stomach had other ideas. It was miserable. We had dismantled my double-ended paddle to form two single canoe-like blades, so that Charlie could sit with me on the kayak and help to propel me forward for a while.

I sensed that he was starting to get fidgety.

"God, this is dull," he said, putting his paddle down temporarily and stretching his back out across the dry bags in the middle of the kayak. "How do you cope with the monotony?"

Nature needs rest, too

"Focus on other things. The canopy, for example," I replied, throwing him a sweet.

"It's amazing what you can see when you start looking for things, or question why things are the way they are," I shared, nibbling on one of the Sour Squirms sweets that Charlie and Ed had brought out for the team. "Take deforestation, for example. Did you know, it will take around four thousand years for the forest to grow back to a native state, but secondary rainforest can regenerate in around sixty-five years?"

"I did not know that," Charlie replied, still struggling to get his long limbs comfortable in the kayak. "I feel like we've been paddling for about sixty-five years." I laughed, glad of his company and dry humour.

I told him that, on one section of the river, Ant and Romel had pointed out the site of an old village. Initially, I couldn't see what they were talking about. The trees were similar heights to those around them. However, on closer inspection, there was a lack of vines, trunks and dead wood in the area, making the canopy look leafier than the patches of virgin rainforest around it. Apparently, the village had been populated from 1991 to 1999 but everyone had left because of a malaria outbreak. When we'd gone to have a look, we discovered that no structures remained. Everything had been taken. Everything, it seemed, apart from a sunken dugout canoe and a broken white enamel kitchen sink embedded in the riverbank. With the people gone, the forest had had a chance to catch breath and was beginning to return to its natural state.

Unfortunately, it was around this time that I alerted Charlie to the fact that my bowels were behaving most unnaturally.

"In any other setting, having you help me paddle might be quite romantic. Like a gondola in Venice," I moaned, as Charlie helped me to quickly direct the kayak toward some large boulders, where I could jump out. We made it in the nick of time.

Once we regrouped for lunch, it turned out that my adventures on the river had nothing on Romel's. After eating, he disappeared into the jungle. We thought nothing of it, until he reappeared looking slightly shaken and somewhat on edge. Fay's warnings about going to the loo in pairs as we went downstream had been accurate.

"Er, a jaguar has been staring at me for about five minutes," he said quite matter-of-factly. "I wasn't really scared."

The rest of us looked at him, aghast.

"It was a big one," he continued, stretching out his hands. "Must have been two and a half metres from head to tail. I went to the toilet and I heard it walking slowly. I tried walking toward it but it still came toward me. I whistled first, and then called Ant's and Jon's name. Ant heard me and as he approached, the jaguar started to walk back slowly."

"The jaguar was frightened of me," Ant said with certainty. "When I was small, my daddy burned bamboo and put ash on my face. Whenever a jaguar sees me, it just walks away from me."

"Fair play, Romel, your loo story makes mine feel positively trivial in comparison," I said, as we set off toward Apoteri, hoping the only trouble my bowels would get me in would be finding a suitable place to stop. The combination of Charlie about to leave, Romel's jaguar encounter, dodgy stomach and trench foot that was finally healing served a real wake-up call that I had to start looking after myself properly.

I held Charlie extra tight when it came to saying goodbye at Apoteri. Seeing him had been wonderful and buoyed me in so many ways. Yet seeing his concern had also been a reminder that we needed to be less blasé about looking after ourselves. This was not an environment in which to be complacent. Whatever the context, the stresses and strains of daily life add up if we don't pay attention to them. We have to check in with ourselves every now and again. To accept that sometimes it is OK to say we've had enough and are overwhelmed. That we need to stop.

Take time to look after yourself

That evening I had a night terror. It was as real and situational as if it were happening in front of my eyes. A baby jaguar had pawed at my hammock, cute at first, but then the mother appeared from behind the tree, angry and foreboding. In my dream, I tried to wake the camp but no one was stirring. I woke, sweating, my heart pumping.

Fay had said that if you tell trees your bad dreams, they won't happen. I took a deep breath, thinking about what I wouldn't have given for a hug from Charlie at that moment. Exhaling, I offered up my unfiltered terror, as I whispered my nightmare to something more rooted than me. *Please*, I willed, *let us rest under the embrace of your branches.* Goodness knows, I needed it.

Happiness

(noun): a state of well-being and contentment.

This trip taught me three things about happiness. Firstly, don't look for it. Master the art of acceptance instead. Despite the spectrum of human emotion, we put so much emphasis on just one feeling. It strikes me as bizarre that happiness is pushed down our throats, as if it's the only one worth striving for. That gap between expectation and reality leaves us feeling less than happy. Maybe if we observed the feelings that came up each day and embraced them as part of being human, we'd be able to focus more on the experience of life rather than on one elusive, albeit pleasant, emotion. If everything in life was perfect and joyous, arguably the journey wouldn't be as rich, character-building or memorable. Food after a long day of sweating and heaving always tastes better, and the laughs, when they finally come (and they will, even if it doesn't feel like it at times), are all the heartier. If you are feeling anything other than happy, you are arguably experiencing part of what it means to be human.

Secondly, acknowledge the dark in yourself but focus on the light. There's an adage about facing problems: you can either change the situation or, if you can't, you have to accept it. This advice applies to learning the art of self-acceptance, too. As humans, we all have rich and deep interior worlds. When you become introspective, you start to acquaint yourself with your shadows – the parts we seek to hide from the world. Like many people, I've had points in life when I've struggled to accept these parts of myself. We all have them, but we shouldn't be ashamed of them. They don't make us worthless or inconsequential; they make us human. Just as we shouldn't be afraid to let our light shine, we shouldn't shy away from the elements of ourselves that make us feel uncomfortable. We should make friends with them and have the humility to try to change our behaviours if they're impacting negatively on ourselves or others. In the jungle, the forest floor is mainly shadow – it only receives about 2 per cent of sunlight – yet, it is precisely because of the shade that decomposition can take place, recycling what has died to provide new growth. The rainforest wouldn't function without it. The trick for us is in trawling through the lows and celebrating the good that can come from that dirt; your darker parts can help you grow.

Finally, seek fulfilment by looking outside of yourself. Very often I have found the greatest happiness there – when I've bypassed my ego and am helping other people. If you want to be happier, stop focusing on yourself.

Ironically, by doing these things and not chasing after the feeling, you might – just might – find a glimmer of the elusive state we call happiness.

Days on expedition: 59

Location: the Essequibo River

Status: logging on

It was while assuming the squat position, pants around my ankles, that I first heard it. A buzzing noise close to me. It sounded like a massive bee. I gripped my machete a little tighter. Within seconds I was face to face with it. My heart leaped – but not out of fear. It was pumping joy. Arse out, exposed to the world, I was eyeball to eyeball with one of the smallest birds in the world – a majestic, iridescent hummingbird. It seemed suspended around my face, hovering to the left and then to the right of me, wings beating so fast they blurred. Deciding no nectar was to be found on this particular flower, it buggered off back into the jungle.

As exciting as it was to see, the bird brought with it a sense of trepidation. After one flew close to the canoe, Jackson had told us that seeing a hummingbird meant that news was coming. "Perhaps when you turn on your Wi-Fi, you will find out if it is good or bad," he had said.

As I pulled up my trousers, (after first checking that nothing had crawled in while I was distracted with the hummingbird), I felt unusually **Acknowledge** anxious. I was right to be. That day was **the shadows** one of many when I wished I hadn't **in yourself** bothered removing myself from real life to connect with a virtual one. You know those moments that hit you out of the blue and send you into a complete tailspin? Mine came in the form of a private Twitter message.

"What you're doing is remarkable, not least because the optics of the trip are at best neo-colonial and at worst racist."

The message was perfectly timed. I'd been in a weird mood for days, barely sleeping and spending a fair amount of time navel-gazing. Having hours alone on the water to think brought me face to face with my own ego, and I wasn't liking what I saw. I'd been spending far too much time in my head, consumed with thoughts of myself. A few days prior to this message I'd jumped out of bed determined to make other people's lives better and not to be so self-obsessed. As I looked up at the trees full of birds, I apologized, resolving then and there to try to be a better, more selfless person. It had been an incredibly weird journey, an unexpected awakening of sorts. The message reaffirmed what I'd been worrying about.

A wave of shame came over me. Even though I didn't know the sender personally, they were someone whose work and opinion I admire. We'd received hundreds of positive messages of support about the trip, but this was the one I still remember practically word for word.

I felt sick. Through my work I have tried to foster understanding and connection, so to think that what I was putting out in the world could be racist was mortifying. Journeys are multifaceted – a dive into the people, nature and the self. I felt like I'd got this balance wrong often on this trip. The Twitter user was right. Ego and narcissism, the desire to put up selfie after selfie, had led to a portrayal of the trip online that was entirely different to the journey we were having. It wasn't my intention, but by making myself the story, I'd failed to give enough credit to my Guyanese teammates. I share this tale not to try to centre myself once again, but in the hope that others with the privilege to travel might learn from my mistake. The author of the message should not have had to send it, but it was a much-needed wake-up call and I am so grateful they did.

Initially, my reaction was one of shock, upset, embarrassment and tears – an entirely unhelpful, unproductive response. Yet, once I sat with the notion, and got beyond my own ego and the idea that people might see me, or my actions, as racist, I began to understand the comment. As a white, privileged writer and traveller from the global North with a platform (however small), by only sharing my image and my thoughts I was neglecting the voices of the citizens we encountered. The impact of this over time is that the way a country and its culture are viewed is shaped not by the people who live there, but solely by those passing through. Writing it off as "just a selfie" or "that's just social media for you!" fails to acknowledge that this practice perpetuates a system of oppression and sidelining of communities that have suffered at the hands of colonization and racism for centuries. For that I am genuinely sorry.

Fay clocked that I was being more introspective than usual. "You OK, Pip?" she asked, prodding the side of my kayak with her paddle. I explained the situation. She thought for a while before responding.

"There is a lot of racism toward Amerindian people. I've experienced it a lot of times. I used to play international football for Guyana and we'd travel around the country a lot. If we didn't have cash on us, we'd ask people for water. Some people would refuse to help, or watch me like a dog; others would say if you want water, go to a shop," she paused, her eyes meeting mine.

"Even today, I notice every kind little thing people do for me. If you make a mistake today, just make sure you don't make it tomorrow. Go past the negatives and be positive. Make sure you go further."

It is advice I'll never forget.

Receiving that message was the lowest point of our trip, but looking back with the benefit of time, learning and love, I wouldn't change it. The hummingbird certainly brought news that day. At the time

Appreciate your capacity for growth

I thought it was bad news. Now, I'm not so sure. The comment sparked a change in my path, a journey of learning that when you fail to acknowledge your privilege and use it positively, you can be well-intentioned but still unintentionally hurt those around you.

When you think about it, travel (and travel writing) brings with it a wave of ethical questions. Who has the ability to travel and where are they going? What are the photos that are taken and what do they say about a place? Who is benefitting financially? Is tourism even appreciated in some places? Should I even be writing this book or attempting a world-first expedition in a country that's not my own? I'm embarrassed to admit it, but as someone who travels (and is also privileged, British and white) I'd never really thought as hard as I should have done about the intersection of history, power and race, and the implication of my presence in a country.

Indeed, the very river we were paddling is reportedly named after Juan de Esquivel, a European who encountered the Essequibo with his ship in 1498. (Interestingly, the Spaniard was the deputy of Christopher Columbus's son, Diego.) Travel is brilliant in so many ways but it's equally problematic. Knowing what I do now, there is much about my previous work and how I've conducted myself during my travels that I would change if I could. There is likely much I am still getting wrong and a failure to acknowledge otherwise is only perpetuating the problem.

As I reread the message, I knew I had cocked up. Starting from the next day, I vowed to take Fay's advice. Like the other 7.8 billion people going to sleep that evening, a new day ushered in a chance to go further. An opportunity to get outside of ourselves and, in doing so, to maybe catch a glimpse of happiness along the way.

You may be wondering what this has to do with happiness, and the reality is that, deep down, I knew that **Get** focusing on myself – whether that was being **outside** wrapped up in my own thoughts or constructing **of** an image on social media – wasn't nourishing in **yourself** any sense. There was something hollow about a purely inner focus. Intuitively, it didn't sit right. Why take a selfie when you can take a snapshot of what's really going on around you? Photos of friends, old and new, of landscapes, of things that make your heart sing. Indeed – why the need to document it at all? Perhaps, sometimes, the answer is just to notice, to store the feeling away and treasure it or relive it at a later point. Or yet again, another approach could be sharing things that may be of interest or use to others. I've felt happier when using social media to amplify voices and ideas that aren't my own.

It wasn't just me that struggled on this journey. Our extended periods of paddling had brought up issues and reflections for the whole team – relationship problems and breakdowns, eating disorders, guilt, grief, anger, fear, irritability, greed, narcissism and shame. We were all imperfect humans just trying to make our way down a river in one piece. Yet, as we snaked down the Essequibo, it would occasionally touch us: happiness's gentle kiss. It had been in the belly laugh that came from Jackson styling his hair into a bright blue soapy mohawk. It had been in the hilarity that followed my attempt to demonstrate yoga moves with only one functioning eye, which ended with an unexpected face full of sand. We'd found it in the water fights, the dancing and when running around the sandbanks together in the rain, marvelling at the rainbows that followed. It appeared in the songs we sang in both English and Waî Waî. We heard it in the giggle of a baby. We saw it in the shining eyes and the satisfied smiles of Ant, Fay and Romel when they caught and admired a fish. When I asked the team for highlights each night, again and again, the stories people shared about what made them happy involved interacting with something other than themselves.

Romel told me he was happy spending the day "gaffing" to his best mate, Ant. Nigel had found happiness in travelling with us all. Laura found she was happiest when she had a part to play: getting involved, lighting a fire or giving me a brightly coloured feather because she could see it brought me joy. Huddled around a fire we had worked to build, sat on bags on the jungle floor, eating simple food, smelling

Don't look for happiness – it will find you

of river and being surrounded by a team who had worked hard to make that happen made our hearts sing at times; it was community, it was connection, it was working together for a common goal.

That's the thing about happiness: we try to seek it out but it often creeps up on us and gives us an unexpected tap on the shoulder to let us know it's arrived. I thought back to one of our happiest days on the river: Mother's Day. At this point I should apologize to my own mum. I'd texted her that morning to wish her a "Happy Mother's Day" and she'd replied, saying that it had made her day to hear from me, since she'd been feeling a bit down. A wave of guilt rushed over me; I knew that whenever I was away she struggled with worry, and I could understand why.

"Dad says he's just seen the photo of a caiman you posted."
Oh balls, I thought. *That would really freak her out.*

"It's cute," I typed back.

"It doesn't look cute," came the response...

Laura, too, had been worrying about being apart from Ran on Mother's Day but it unexpectedly turned into one of our best days in the jungle.

Around 3 p.m., just as the sky turned to a magical orange hue, it felt like we'd reached paradise. High in the sky, a golden light was competing with threatening grey storm clouds and, lower on the horizon, blue sky was freckled with fluffy white clouds. We pulled up to a resplendent, sandy beach where small black boulders were covered with beautiful trees peppered along, and behind these were larger black-and-red boulders. It was stunning, truly stunning. The guys suggested we wash there, and what a spot it was! A shallow beach with beautiful little fish swimming around the unusually warm water.

"*Ppffffff.*" A jet of water hit me square in the face. I turned to see that Laura was spraying river water out of her mouth.

"You're so grim," I said, lying on my back and kicking water in her direction.

Ness was her next target. Unfortunately for Laura, as I was splashing her, Ness had clocked what she was up to. Pockets of water were loaded up in Ness's cheeks – a cute-looking human guinea pig – and Laura found herself drenched.

Sensing danger, Ant and Romel tried to move out of the firing zone. It was too late. A full-on water fight ensued; dunking, squirting, kicking and splashing meant that not a single one of us didn't resemble a drowned rat. We were giddy with laughter.

As the silliness slowed, we all gathered together in the water to take a snap with Laura's phone, handily housed in a waterproof case. Just as Laura took the picture, I felt something distinctly hand-shaped on my bottom.

"Who has their hand on my bum?" I enquired.

A little squeeze was the reply. Ness giggled.

The hand then moved to the other cheek and gave another squeeze. Again, a chuckle from Ness.

At this point, her guffaws gave the game away and the culprit was accurately identified, although not before a parting two-handed squeeze finale. Right there in the middle of the Amazon jungle, in one of the most beautiful sites I've ever seen, my mosquito-bitten bottom was getting a bit of loving. Ness's wheezing laughter was just too funny not to respond in kind, and all hell broke loose. A moment of pure joy, connection (more than I bargained for on my part) and hilarity – our uncontrollable, side-splitting belly laughs were captured on camera. They are photos that I treasure and ones that will forever make me smile.

"It's nice on Mother's Day to have laughed so much," said Laura as we waded back to our kayaks. "It could have been more of a sad day, but it's been a fun one."

"Yeah, everyone seems happy," said Ant, clean and smiling, holding the soap.

Ness fished her towel off her kayak and flung it around her. "Yep, it's definitely been a good day," she agreed. "I've enjoyed being present. I think that's a recipe for happiness. Or in my case, happy Ness."

It was one of those days that just seem to work. Where friends laughed and mucked about, nature was kind and we had all we could ever need. Our joy had been wonderfully unexpected. It was a day to cherish for precisely that reason.

With more settlements on the horizon, it was beginning to feel like our stint in the wilderness was slowly ebbing away. The Twitter message had been a reminder of our interconnectedness as humans, the importance of understanding how we interact with the world and where we choose to put our focus. There would be more good days to come, and there would also be bad ones. Perhaps only hindsight would tell us which was which.

Sustainability

(noun): avoidance of the depletion of natural resources, in order to maintain an ecological balance.

My first encounter with the rainforest was filming a documentary with Reza Pakravan, which looked at how deforestation impacts the people who call the rainforest home. Before that trip I'd never really thought about what I consumed – or why. Yet, seeing first-hand the devastating slash-and-burn impact of cattle ranching, soya plantations, timber and gold mining, I began to realize that my life choices were directly impacting a global system that needed more regulation and transparency. Returning to the Amazon biome, this time by water, only cemented this.

As a consumer, I am still far from perfect. Indeed, as I write this, I am surrounded by "things" that are "wants" and not "needs". Our habits have become unsustainable; we've come to think we require more than we really do and often the things we buy aren't designed to last. It's likely that there's no such thing as a "model consumer" – the term is an oxymoron. Trying to be one is a sure-fire route to guilt and self-flagellation. Yet, we can aim to be *better* and more mindful consumers. Websites like The Good Shopping Guide and Ethical Consumer are good places to start if you're interested in looking at where products are sourced and how ethically. There is power in your purse and even small changes can add up.

Maybe it is time that our politicians, our businesses and we as consumers stop focusing on "growth" and ask instead what it is we are growing for the long term. Could wealth be considered beyond purely financial terms? Can we think more creatively about how we're living? What about being time-rich, having an abundance of nature or enjoying the luxury of health? Rewarding businesses that ensure they're not ravaging the environment? Making that tree worth more when it's alive than when it's dead? I have more questions than I do answers, but when you're trying to find solutions, they're the only place to start.

Days on expedition: 60

Location: the Essequibo River, approaching Fairview

Status: colliding with society

For the two months we'd been together, Ness, Laura and I had fallen into a routine in the forest. We'd found a rhythm, a peace, to being outside. We hadn't picked up our wallets, looked in a mirror or engaged in new social situations. Now, though, we were approaching a settlement called Fairview. The village was formerly a hub for trading in gummy latex, known as balata, and cattle rearing. These days it is home to around 200 families, mainly of indigenous people, and it's a jumping-off point for many tourists to the Iwokrama Forest, its canopy walkways and a butterfly farm. Unfortunately, our schedule meant we didn't have time to get a bird's-eye view of the jungle. We had to press on; Laura needed to get back as soon as possible, as Ed was due to shoot his next TV series. Honestly, we were all a little nervous and uncomfortable about seeing other people more regularly. Someone had described my hair as "borderline feral", which was a pretty good description of how I was feeling generally – feral but feeling great for it. My usual standards of hygiene had gone out the window. My clothes stank, due to a mixture of damp and sweat. If I clocked a few dead bugs in my porridge, I'd eat them anyway and wouldn't think twice about gulping down water speckled with floating mosquitoes. Our time in the wild came with no judgment, no expectations, no "shoulds" or "ought tos". It was about waking up, moving and surviving. In some respects, what we expected of ourselves had been wonderfully simple.

I largely enjoy meeting new people but, like many, I sometimes find large social gatherings exceptionally awkward. Knowing we were about to encounter people en masse made me especially melancholy because it meant that we were at the end of our stint in true wilderness. It was fitting that our re-entry back into society was on April Fool's Day.

We knew we were approaching other humans long before we reached Fairview; we could see a campfire with a tail of smoke that lashed the sky above. As we drew closer, however, we noticed that it wasn't a campfire that was burning.

Knowing how quickly blazes can spread, we decided to check on the situation and pulled our kayaks onto the bank. As we approached, we saw that a termite's nest was on fire. The flames were threatening to burn the tree, too. Fay started prodding the nest with a large stick and the burning bundle fell to the ground, where we stomped the fire out with our shoes and then covered it with sand. She was livid.

"Someone must have burned them. I have no idea why anyone would do that. It makes me so angry. I saw human tracks leading to here."

I stared down at the charred remains smouldering at my feet. I wondered if there was a reason why the nest had been set alight, whether there were crops or settlements nearby that needed protecting. On the map it looked like we were still a kilometre or so away from Fairview, so there were no homes at risk. I looked around at the trees, which had thinned out at this point, dotted between rocks with sand leading to each one; there didn't seem to be any obvious reason. From what I could see, and following Fay's reaction, it appeared that the nest had been burned for fun. The incident only added to my discomfort about seeing people again, but I tried to focus on the positives, as we returned to our kayaks to paddle the final stretch to the village.

Despite our inauspicious introduction, a part of me was also looking forward to reaching Fairview.

We stopped to restock food supplies at the small shop we'd *You* *adapt* *to what* *you have* been told was at Iwokrama River Lodge and Research Centre – a popular destination for tourists as well as scientists studying the rainforest. The Iwokrama Forest, in central Guyana, is of particular interest to biologists, as it's the point where the flora and fauna of the Amazon give way to those of the Guiana Shield. Romel had already alerted me to the different bird calls we'd been hearing for the last few days.

We'd also received word from our fixer, Sophia, that three ladies from the village wanted to paddle with us for a bit. Apparently, they had borrowed a three-seat kayak from a friend who worked in Guyana's adventure industry. Having pretty much cleared out the small shop of every dried good they had, we went back to the river to meet the ladies, who were waiting with their kayak.

We warmed to the oldest one in the group immediately. Leonie had a boisterous, fun, contagious energy. After introducing herself, she clocked Jon with his camera by his side and flashed him a cheeky smile.

"I have been in many documentaries now," her eyes twinkled. "I am a movie star."

Leonie made me chuckle as we went to get in the kayaks. She was wearing a beautiful pink dress, which she suddenly took off to reveal a tank top and camo cycling shorts, which she then paired with a shorter blue skirt. She clearly meant business.

She told me that her ten-year-old son panicked that morning because she'd put so many clothes on and he thought she wasn't coming back. She'd promised him that she wouldn't be gone from home for long. "Otherwise I'd have come with you all the way to Georgetown," she said.

Leonie's sister hitched her multicoloured dress over her knees to take her place in the middle seat of the kayak and one of the ladies from the lodge also hopped aboard. It was Leonie's birthday as well and we all sang to her as we paddled off.

It was fascinating talking to Leonie and her friends as we travelled, and also a welcome distraction from our painful and calloused hands. Leonie had been working on the village council, and spoke with passion and confidence.

She shared that she thought the key to happiness was being self-contained, and she questioned the benefits of connectivity. In her opinion it was a shame that in 1992 Fairview was connected to the Linden-Lethem road that gave easier access to the capital, Georgetown. She said it had changed the culture. She also described how, since the arrival of the internet, the younger generation were always on their phones.

"Previously, they would have been learning how to scrape cassava and making food, but now they just type."

Her main point was that there was great joy to be had in living sustainably – surviving off the land, spending time with your family and not constantly working on things that didn't bear fruit, so to speak. Although I knew that living the sort of self-contained life she described was not going to be possible for the vast majority of people and that, despite its downsides, connectivity has had so many economic and social benefits, I agreed with much of what she said. As a guest in the jungle, I saw for myself that there was much to be gained from reconnecting with nature and living more sustainably – in whatever form that took for an individual and their circumstances.

We spent the afternoon paddling and swapping stories. Despite my initial reluctance, it was wonderful to have the opportunity to talk to people outside of our little kayaking bubble.

"It is a difficult journey you're on," Leonie commented as we said goodbye on a large sand strip. A storm cloud was looming in the sky above, and a gentleman from the village had brought a speedboat to pick them up and take them home.

In so many ways the expedition had been tough, yet there had been a great poetry to life on the river. We'd been travelling on what is a life source for so many beings, each life just seeing a small fraction of a much larger force – the notion of "home" shifted like the riverbanks. The mighty Essequibo was a thread connecting the natural world to the urbanized one, and travelling down it had been a challenge like no other. We'd faced many threats up to that point and overcome innumerable difficulties – but we knew that what lay ahead, in the coming weeks, was perhaps going to be the most difficult challenge of them all: seeing how our life choices impact the environment.

We were due to stay the night in a guest house. The owner and her daughter had welcomed us warmly to their establishment but said space was limited, as it was Easter Sunday. We were told the Rupununi Ranchers' Rodeo had just taken place in Lethem, a nearby town, and so rooms were in short supply. There was, however, one room free, as well as a place outside where we could hang our hammocks. We opted to keep together and all sleep in the garden area. I was happy about the decision, as I was beginning to feel about my hammock the same way most people do about their bed – there's nowhere quite like it.

An inquisitive young lad offered to show us where to store the kayaks for the night and he hopped aboard my boat. I gave him my life vest, with the warning that my paddling was so bad he definitely needed to put it on. He must have believed me, as he later passed the message on to his young female cousins. The two little girls looked about four and seven, and it was amusing to explain to them what we were doing. Their eyes widened when it sank in. It made me feel happy that we could share a small part of the story with these young women.

We were then shown to an open concrete structure with a metal roof and numerous hammock hooks screwed into the edges – our accommodation for the night. Under usual circumstances, I would have found the place fun and one I'd enjoy staying in, but my heart wasn't really in it.

Unbeknown to the rest of us, Fay had slipped away and kindly bought the team a room inside for the night, so we had somewhere to store the camera equipment.

"I don't trust it will be safe otherwise," she said.

It was ironic that, for weeks, we'd been pulling boats up high onto the beach to prevent the caimans from nicking our stuff, but now we were purchasing hotel rooms to safeguard our belongings against other humans. I wondered whether it really was necessary to protect our equipment or if being in unfamiliar environments exaggerated our sense of danger.

The room also offered us the added benefit of a shower, which felt like a real luxury because we had not washed properly since leaving Fay's.

Freshly washed, we headed to the open-air restaurant area, and we each had what was meant to be a celebratory packet of spicy cheese crisps and a 250 ml, 4.3% bottle of GT: "Genuine lager beer, made in Georgetown". For months we'd been hankering after, discussing in detail and practically salivating over snacks we couldn't have. Now they were literally in our grasp – but we weren't any happier.

What you think you want won't always make you happy

"I miss the wilderness already," Ness said. "I will stare any jaguar in the face but the thing I fear most is humans. I prefer the sound of jaguar to a loud noisy truck."

"I miss the safety of the jungle," Laura replied. "Here we have to take our bags everywhere and we can't just pull up on the landing."

The irony of the sentiment was not lost on us.

"It's a whole different danger," Ant replied. "Instead of the danger of jaguar we have the danger of men."

"When was the last time you saw a car before today?" Laura asked him.

"Last year, when I went to Georgetown. For us, it's a huge noise which is not really good. It's not nice."

I withdrew into myself, unwilling to make conversation, and left the others to go for a short walk. I was feeling totally overwhelmed by noise. It was an assault on the senses. Music, the roar of idling engines – I was repelled. A huge telecommunications pylon rose up above the jungle. Having become so accustomed to seeing large trees, I found it an eyesore and a jolt back to urban reality.

What are you choosing to value? Value or values?

As night drew in in Fairview, so too did the punters to the guest house. Those who had enjoyed watching the bareback bronc, calf and sheep roping, and bull riding were beginning to arrive. A large family group set up a picnic spot next to our hammocks. Francis, the 79-year-old grandfather, invited us to join them for supper.

"We've brought a lot of food with us," he said. "We've extra fried chicken, if you fancy it?"

We gratefully accepted his offer and he passed us each a picnic plate full of perfectly cooked, succulent chicken. It was delicious. As we ate, Francis shared some of his story with us. He told us he was Guyanese but of Indian descent.

"The British brought us over as slaves, you know, around 160 years ago," he said.

Francis was referring to the indentured labour system that was introduced after Britain's abolition of slavery in the 1830s. Indentured immigrants were brought over to what was then known as British Guiana to work on various colonial estates, but particularly on sugar plantations. The system essentially meant that workers, mainly from India, China and the Pacific nations, signed a contract that said they would work abroad for a set period. In return they'd usually receive wages, a small amount of land and, in some cases, a return ticket home. However, the reality of life abroad turned out very differently. Despite the initial voluntary aspect, testimonies from former slaves indicated that these indentured workers had been treated the same way that they had been under slavery. From 1838 to 1917 it's estimated that over 500 ships bringing 238,909 people came to Guyana from India. Only around 76,000 of these indentured immigrants or their children returned.

Francis continued: "I feel British in a way. I used to live in London, working in the wood industry. Near Regent Street and Madame Tussauds."

Later, as families slunk off to bed, the night owls came to face down the dawn. Having said goodnight to Francis, our team had regrouped in the restaurant area to discuss plans for the coming days. Thumping dance music, usually the type I'd embrace, started up from one of the cars parked near our hammocks. The boot was open and a souped-up sound system seemed to have been fitted into it, complete with large subwoofers delivering a juggernaut of bass through our bodies. People were definitely in the mood to continue the party.

"This would be noisy at the best of times, even coming from a city," Jon bellowed over the bass. "I can't imagine what it's like after two months in the jungle."

A group of men in their twenties and thirties – the people behind the music – came over to say hello. We played cards for a while and shared some whisky. The evening was pleasant enough but, even though I wasn't sleepy, I made my excuses and went to bed. Ness and Laura were still drinking but I knew I needed some time in my own head, even if I felt like a party pooper. Fay remarked that Ant and Romel were finding it tough, too – the Waî Waî's culture doesn't encourage drinking and the current vibe was very different compared to the tranquility of their village.

Our journey had heightened my appreciation of wild places, but it had also increased my disdain for much of urbanized living, namely consumption. I couldn't help but feel uneasy at our pile of discarded plates, the general rubbish, the beer bottles and the empty plastic wrappers. Even the rusty nails screwed into the wood where we were hanging up our hammocks served as a reminder that we were consuming in the short term without thinking of the long term. Nature lasts, nature renews, but we constantly take.

Ant came to say goodnight. "You OK, Pip?" he asked.

"No, I feel like I've collided with the human world and I don't like it. I miss the jungle."

"Me too. It is too noisy here," said Ant.

I think we were both comforted that someone else had their head in the wilderness. My hammock felt like a refuge, save for the smell of sick that kept wafting over from under a nearby swinging bed. I lay there, enveloped by that warm whisky glow, music thumping in the background, drunk people laughing, the peep of an occasional car horn. My heart sank; it was such a weird, uncomfortable feeling. Charlie had sent me a message when he was staying here, saying he missed me, and I felt exactly the same. This stay reminded me that nothing in this world – money, accolades, "stuff" – compared to the value of time spent with loved ones.

I felt battered by the urbanized world; it was familiar, yet I felt so changed. The fear I'd felt in the jungle, whether it was caused by the territorial growl of a caiman or the purr of the jaguar, was visceral, innate. In contrast, spicy cheese crisps, cards, fried chicken, booze – what many of us use as a way to give life meaning (or to escape from it) – felt hollow. Time in the wilderness had shown me the fragility of life and the benefit of keeping things simple. I felt like the modern house of cards I had built around myself had fallen in a way it had never done before, and I found myself wanting to run back to the jungle. I couldn't help but feel that on April Fool's Day, the joke was on us.

Hope

(noun): an optimistic state of mind based on the expectation of positive outcomes.

When you're confronted with something tough in life, it's perhaps too simplistic to say, "Just focus on the positives." A situation can often feel so much bigger than you and too overwhelming. Sometimes, as hard as we look, perhaps there aren't any positive perspectives to be found. However, if we travel too far down this road, a sense of despair or apathy can set in. This is where I think hope becomes useful – hope that things can get better, even if it doesn't always feel that way at the time. Hope is the thing we can reach out for to help us take action, however small, to improve the circumstances we find ourselves in.

Throughout our journey – and since our return home – there have been points when I have nearly given up on the concept of hope. Often a problem can seem so large that it's hard to see why you should even bother trying to deal with it. In these moments, I remind myself of the people I've met who have found solutions to cope with or overcome even the direst situations. Sometimes, just envisioning that a better path might exist has helped to give me the courage and strength to move toward it.

Days on expedition: 72

Location: Sloth Island nature resort

Status: digging into gold mining

"Just so we're all on the same page with this, we're not sex workers," said Ness emphatically.

I'm not sure the clarification was necessary, but the exchange made me chuckle. It was our first day off in weeks and we were somewhere we'd been looking forward to visiting ever since leaving Fairview, which was now hundreds of kilometres away. We were at Sloth Island nature resort and our host, Michael, was showing us around the grounds. We had the day off, so Ant and Romel had caught a boat across the river to a town called Bartica. Fay, Ness, Laura and I were on a mini tour with Michael. As he was a former miner, we'd got chatting about why he left that job to work in tourism. We'd also shared with him some of our encounters with miners over the past few weeks. By and large, they'd been cordial, with the only exception of being given the stink eye by some ladies we'd met when buying supplies of water and rice from one site. Michael had dug a little further into the story and suggested that they were likely sex workers.

"To be blunt," Michael said, "you ladies passing through probably looked competitive."

"Well, even if we said we were working, I doubt anyone would believe us," Laura piped up. "They'd just have to smell us."

Michael nodded and chuckled, before showing us a pineapple growing in the ground. When looking directly down at it, the way the leaves were growing made it appear as if an eye was peering out at me from within them. Michael continued his story.

"There are prostitutes in every mine – local Guyanese women, as well as women from other countries. They do it for the money and the gold. People even come across illegally." He paused. "Sometimes they don't go back home because they don't find gold – or they're dead."

I shuddered, recalling some of the heartbreaking stories I'd heard, about murders, rapes and sickness, when reporting on the mining industry across the continent.

Something moved in the tree above us, catching our attention.

"A sloth." Michael pointed at a small one hanging off a branch. We watched the stunning animal hang there. Apparently, they'd beat any human in a pull-up competition, as they're around three times as strong as the average person – from the minute they're born they can use one arm to lift their entire body weight. Their amazing grip is especially handy when it comes to withstanding the force of a jaguar trying to rip them out of trees. The arrangement of their tendons means that their hands and feet lock into place, which is why they can also fall asleep upside down. Incredible when you think about it; when pitted against jaguars, they are a real-life version of David and Goliath.

Even when the chance of success seems slim, there is always hope

"Why did you leave the mines, Michael?" I asked, the sloth clearly not in the mood to move.

"Because there is too much sickness, malaria especially – mosquitos breed in the big pools of water in the mines. The last time I mined was in Region 9, a place called Marudi Mountain. There was a lot of gold but also a lot of malaria. Unfortunately, I've had it about twenty times."

Michael explained that he had been mining manually, by himself, and making good money – apparently around 25 per cent of artisanal miners find gold, which is a draw for many people. However, every two weeks there would be a case of malaria, and attacks and robberies on those who struck gold weren't uncommon. For Michael, the balance between health and wealth wasn't paying off. He looked up at the hanging sloth, before showing us his hands.

"By the end, my hands were stiff, I couldn't move and I was pale, with no blood. I was so ill, and in total pain – muscle aches and headaches. I thought, 'Either someone will burn me and I'll die here or I'll go home.' It was better that I condemned the pit. I packed it up that afternoon and went straight home. I sent for a doctor and they found that I had dengue, typhoid and pretty much every strain of malaria. It took me around five months to really recover."

Michael gestured for us to move on and took us to visit the forest walkway that the lodge had built for tourists. We climbed up wooden steps leading to a bridge that wound through the jungle, stopping at various lookouts perfect for peering into the world beneath our feet. It was a strange perspective for us, as we had become accustomed to life on the jungle floor. I wasn't paying too much attention to the various plants and ferns that were being pointed out. My head was still with Michael's story. Given his energy, zeal and obvious love of nature, it was hard to imagine him as a shell of a man.

Michael's illnesses presented an example of the very human impact of mining. Since leaving Fairview, and over the hundreds of kilometres we'd covered, we'd also witnessed its environmental ramifications. The river had naturally split into a complex network of pathways and island systems that were a nightmare to navigate. Thankfully, we had Fay on hand to help advise us on what route she'd heard was the safest. In many ways, it was like being handed a plate of spaghetti and we just had to pick a strand.

These winding waterways also provided the perfect opportunity for independent mining prospectors. Despite having a low overall deforestation record, according to Guyana's Forestry Commission, 85 per cent of forest loss is due to illegal mining, mainly gold.

I shared with Fay how in Brazil and Peru, Reza and I had reported on the devastating impact of mining (especially unregulated mines) and deforestation up close. We'd seen how there wasn't just the environmental cost to consider – there was a human one, too. Mercury is often used to extract gold but can contaminate the fish that people eat and, during filming, the team and I had heard heartbreaking stories about deaths caused by mercury poisoning. We'd also listened to tales involving drug and alcohol abuse, sex work, health issues, poor working conditions, long hours, robbery and murder. Fay nodded. This wasn't news to her.

"We will need to be careful about washing near dredging areas, too," said Fay, as we paddled closer. "My friend lived near one, and was covered in open and itchy sores. She said she thought it was because of the mining."

From here on in, we knew we would have to change how we interacted with the landscape. Fishing wasn't an appealing option and nor was drinking the water. The river that had sustained us over the last two months suddenly seemed less hospitable. To see the change was a hard pill to swallow. I had to remind myself that I was getting a very granular view of the situation. Guyana is one of the greenest countries on Earth, with around 85 per cent of its rainforest still intact and some of the lowest levels of deforestation in the tropics. In many ways, it is a model of how to keep forests.

This is partly why the first dredger we saw came as a bit of a shock. We'd picked a small side channel to paddle down and it had faster-flowing water – enough to push us along but not forceful enough to put us in any danger. We bobbed along in single file, rocks lining either side of this breakaway channel and trees growing overhead. It felt like the sort of place Center Parcs might have modelled a log flume on, and it had been an afternoon of light-hearted fun. When we rejoined a larger section of the river, we heard something unfamiliar. Sound ricocheted off the water's surface, an aural bullet to the ear. Up ahead, in the middle of the waterway, was a dredger. It looked like a mini, floating two-storey house, with cranes sticking out at either end. We paddled closer, careful not to get in the way of the steel-wire levers that were manoeuvring a 20-metre-long pipe used to suck up the drilled gravel from the riverbed. On the end of the pipe was a cutter head that looked like a pineapple. It appeared that this was what had been making the noise as it cut through the riverbed below. We later found out that those drill bits can bore down to around 61 metres and that miners often go through them very quickly at a cost of thousands of dollars a day.

As the river water wasn't clean enough to drink, we had to rely on the kindness of people we met on the way. We waved at the crew, trying to seem approachable, and gestured to ask if it was OK for us to board. They waved back and beckoned for us to come over. As we approached, they helped us tie our kayaks to the side of the metal barge. No one spoke English but we quickly established that they were from Brazil. Ant, who spoke some Portuguese, translated that the crew had been there for seven months.

The man in charge had a kind, open, bearded face. He proudly offered to show us around. Downstairs was where most of the machinery was kept. Motors, pumps, generators, winches and pipes that seemed to have been rewelded recently – they all sounded like they were working hard to suck up and process the river floor. Our host plonked himself down on a large seat next to some hydraulic controls – various buttons, levers and pressure monitors suggested this was the heart of the operation. A cup of half-finished coffee rested on the metal dashboard. Behind us, water from the river was being pumped up the pipe and spat out into a series of angled trays on different levels, in what is known as a sluice box. A carpet-like material lined the various trays. Apparently, the force of the water traps the heavier gold in the carpet, while the lighter sediment flows away. Any gold caught at the top is then shaken out and collected – a more industrial version of panning for gold. Next to the control panel, a bright light illuminated one such pan covered with a sieve-like meshing: this was where the gold would be finally collected.

"You can barely hear yourself think," yelled Ness over the noise.

"Apparently, it operates for forty hours at a time," bellowed back Ant.

"Don't stand in front of the fan," I shouted. "I just got a faceful of unbelievable heat."

"What was that, Pip? You want something to eat?" Ness hollered.

I gave up trying to explain. Although, it wasn't a bad guess on Ness's part. I could always eat.

Turns out that the only woman on board, the boat's chef, was on my wavelength. She was an older lady, wearing a red T-shirt and glasses, and she told Ant that we should come upstairs to sample her freshly baked pineapple cake and sweet Brazilian coffee.

"We need to take our shoes off," said Ant, pointing to the pile neatly lined up at the bottom of the stairs. The team clearly took pride in their dredger. Upstairs was incredibly clean and tidy. There was a chest press and a kitchen so well stocked with eggs, biscuits, oil and flour that it looked like a small shop. A shower and some bedrooms led off from the kitchen area – small box rooms but with enough space for a bed and some privacy. Or at least that was the intention. One of the miners had just sauntered out of the shower and nearly dropped his towel in surprise at seeing a gaggle of smelly kayakers being shown around his living quarters.

In some ways, boarding the dredger was a welcome break, but in a very visceral way it was hard to forget where we were. Having finished my cake, but still working my way through the coffee, I went to the balcony to get a better view of the mining operation. Leaving the carpeted kitchen was an error. The metal balcony floor was burningly hot. I almost felt my bare feet sizzle against it. Not ideal at the best of times, and especially not when you've got trench foot. The whole experience of being on a barge was a sensory one – there was heat and noise, and the vibrations reverberated through our bodies, as the barge not only moved through the landscape but sliced through it.

The miners had been exceptionally kind, both offering us food and ensuring we could continue the journey. They refilled our individual bottles, as well as three big containers that we'd been carrying since our stay at Fay's. This was the first time we would be paddling with such weight. Ness offered to be the first to do it and the miners helped to lower the heavy load into the middle of her kayak. As we were waved off, we were told to watch out for typhoid in areas with stagnant water and to beware the 3–5-metre waves as we reached Georgetown.

"Those people where very kind to us; they treated us with respect," Ant commented as we paddled away, the call of the jungle once again replacing the dredger's noise.

"What's weird is that we turn the corner and we're back in beautiful rainforest again," said Jon. "It's quite strange."

It really was. Going from the tranquility of being your own engine to literally standing on one had been bizarre. In many ways it was hard to reconcile the destructive nature of what was taking place beneath the dredger with the kindness shown by the people on it. Our encounter pointed to a deeper, more complex story about the industry, and a need to try to understand each other's actions and motivations. If we took the time to do this, perhaps we would be more likely to find a better path for us all.

Seek to fully understand a situation, in order to find a way out

It reminded me of a fable that Ant had shared about the anaconda people – anacondas that can take on human form. The tale was as follows:

A young man was looking for a wife and he went to the shaman of the village.

"Shaman, I want a wife," he said.

"OK, who do you want as your wife?" came the reply.

"I want an anaconda girl."

"I'll see what I can do."

The shaman set about building a wall of leaves, which he then crossed in order to speak to the chief of the anaconda village. It was agreed that a beautiful wife would be found for the young man from the human village. The shaman passed back through the wall of leaves and found the man.

"I have found you a beautiful wife. All you need to do is go through, touch her and then she will talk to you."

The man was very excited and went through the wall of leaves, expecting to find a stunning wife in her human form. Waiting for him , though, he found a huge, curled-up anaconda. He was terrified and dived back through the wall.

"What's wrong? Did you touch her as agreed? Did you talk to her?" enquired the shaman.

"She was terrifying," came the reply.

"Let me see what I can do," the shaman said and went back to the anaconda world. He found the female anaconda upset and crying.

"He was terrifying. I can't do this," she said and she slipped away into a nearby river.

Ant told us that the man never did get married.

It's a story I've thought about a lot since that day; it reminds me that we need to respect and try to understand each other, rather than immediately assume the worst, and to be prepared to look at things from a different perspective. Over the coming weeks I began to see that my own narrative around mining had always focused on the negatives of the industry. While this expedition didn't entirely change that perception, it helped me to understand the nuances and context of mining, and, in turn, it sparked a sense of hope for a better future. Over the course of hundreds of kilometres, we would encounter many more dredgers (although none as well kept as that first one). Rather than approaching the miners from a position of judgment, I tried to observe from a position of understanding.

On one particular barge, the custodian said he didn't believe the accusation that mining was damaging to the environment because there were still plenty of fish around. Then there was Terrence, a miner, who explained he did it because he felt he had no other option.

"I'm fifty-nine and you're sat on my pension. This barge is all the money I have in the world," he said.

Most of the miners we met on the river were small-scale operators like Terrence. It's estimated that there are around 20,000 in Guyana alone. The people we came across made me realize that, in order to find workable solutions to global environmental problems, we can't just see things as we want them to be; we first have to acknowledge them as they are. As

Ant put it, the miners we'd encountered were doing the best they could in their individual situations.

"Miners… That is their living," he said as we paddled side by side. "They need to work. They need to find a way to maintain their family."

Ant, like many of the men from Masakenari, had done some work in the mines. I asked him what he made of the industry.

"I don't think we can stop it but perhaps it can be done in a proper way? Same for logging. It's big in Guyana. This part of the river is already polluted," he said. "However, I don't think there should be any big-scale mining or logging at the head of the Essequibo. We have to be strict on that. There will be no virgin forest otherwise."

Having got to the end of the spaghetti section of the river, the waterway had once again got larger. We saw first-hand what Ant meant by big-scale mining – up ahead of us was South America's second-largest open-pit mine.

For the last 130 years, Omai has had some sort of mining operation. It hit global headlines back in 1995 after waste containing cyanide leaked into the Essequibo. An 80-kilometre stretch of the river was declared an environmental disaster zone and, for seven years afterward, those who relied on the river for water had to use alternative sources.

Before we even reached it, the mountains of soil piled up in the river hinted at what was ahead. Over the last few weeks we'd come to associate large areas of sandbanks with mining. They'd progressively become more of a feature of – and hindrance to – our paddling. Increasingly, we'd found ourselves beached on them, as the water had become more and more shallow. The sandbanks threw up a few other problems, too. Very often they'd force us into the centre of the river, away from the shade of the canopy, so we were getting hotter when paddling. I'd also noticed more insects knocking around, especially sandflies that seemed particularly active at dawn and dusk. They were one of the critters on Laura's extensive risk assessment, as they are known to carry something called leishmaniasis, a flesh-eating disease which sounded particularly unpleasant.

It wasn't just the piles of sand that alerted us to Omai's presence. In parts, huge swaths of riverbank had entirely collapsed, leaving lonely-looking trees and a troop of capuchin monkeys clinging on for life. It was hard not to feel emotional.

"It's not sand; it's scars; the river has been turned upside down," said Ness as we paddled past a massive mound protruding out of the water. She pointed at the monkeys. "They're clinging on to the last bit of wilderness they have."

"Originally, I was like, 'Why is everyone banging on about gold? It's just a few extra sandbanks'," said Laura. "But even as someone who makes jokes out of everything, I can see it's just not very funny. Now I understand."

"I think I can see someone," said Romel, pointing to a gated entrance.

"We're running low on water; it's a good opportunity to ask," ventured Fay.

Reluctantly, we paddled over to the official-looking entrance. Two security guards were looking after the area and waved back at us as we approached. They introduced themselves as Joseph and George. After we shook hands and explained what we were doing, they offered us a ride on their quad bikes to show us the mine. Ness, Laura and I squished onto the seat behind Joseph, and Fay and Jon hitched a lift with George. Ant and Romel volunteered to stay with the boats.

Given the mine's turbulent history, I was surprised when we reached the top. From our viewpoint, we could see two massive pits below – one was full of a beautiful turquoise body of water, which I presumed must have been rainwater, as the mine wasn't in use. Deep, angled steps were cut into the sides of the crater that stretched before us, almost like an amphitheatre for giants. Far, far in the distance, we could see the rainforest.

We could hear a generator blaring away but we couldn't see it. Presumably, some work was taking place near or in the second pit.

"What got you into the mining industry?" Ness asked Joseph, as we took in the view.

"Gold. It makes you rich overnight. I want to be a millionaire," he replied, surveying the massive pits below.

We could understand his reasoning – and the global appeal of mining. Gold is now one of Guyana's primary exports which, in turn, helps to drive development.

I listened to Joseph as we surveyed the scale of the operation and I pondered what global economic development should look like going forward. I thought back to a question that a miner in Brazil once asked me: how many primary forests are left in the UK? At the time I didn't have the answer. Having looked it up since, I now know that ancient woodland covers around 2.5 per cent of the country. We plundered our own natural resources – and those of the countries in the British Empire – during the Industrial Revolution in the mid-eighteenth century. You can understand why developed nations can look hypocritical. On the other hand, the tricky issue with rainforests is that they are a massive carbon sink, the lungs of the planet, and the whole world relies on them. One solution is paying for preservation. In 2009 Guyana and Norway signed a five-year deal where the former agreed to keep deforestation rates below 0.275 per cent, per year. In return Norway agreed to pay US$250 million as a way of offsetting its own carbon emissions. The scheme has both its supporters and critics but at least it attempted to find a solution. There's no getting away from the fact that preserving a country's natural resources has to come at a cost.

"It's such a massive issue to get your head around, isn't it?" said Ness as we walked back to the quad bike to return to the river.

"Yep, it's a complicated global web of politics, power and money, that's for sure," I replied. "There are just so many factors to weigh up. You've got the issues of supply and demand. If consumers keep buying products, they're going to keep being made. Then you've got a nation's right to self-determination to use their resources versus the global impact that environmental damage can cause. Climate change doesn't have borders, but countries do. Oh guys, I'm so confused," I sighed, briefly pausing for breath. "Somehow we need to make a global business case out of conservation. Compensate countries with resources that can impact the future of the planet? Make a tree worth more alive than dead? That's got to be the hope. Where's Greta Thunberg when you need her? I could do with some help articulating all this. Along with: 'Is a Jaffa Cake even a cake?' these are the big questions of our time."

Feel hopeless? Find role models who inspire you

My diatribe over, Ness put her smelly armpit over my shoulder and gave me a squeeze. "It's been a hell of journey, huh?"

"And here we were, thinking we were just paddling down a river…" Laura prodded me, trying to lighten the mood.

The sloth in the tree at the nature resort moved, bringing me back to the present moment and snapping me out of my thoughts of the last few weeks.

"It's so sweet," Laura commented, as the shaggy sloth finally decided it was probably time to have a quick stretch. We were lucky to see it move, as these animals are usually asleep for around 15 hours during the day.

"I still get delighted by them," Michael smiled, as it lumbered along the branch. "I don't think I'd ever leave tourism," he continued. "Mining sounds simple, easy, fast – if you are lucky. If you're not, you could work for years, barely scraping something together. With tourism you can have a steadier income and can see the beauty of nature. It's something we need to love. I hold workshops to encourage other miners to see this," he added.

The sloth came to a standstill once again, clearly having done its exercise for the day. It was a sloth after my own heart. *Move and rest, move and rest, I hear you buddy*, I thought. The way it clung on, upside down, its shaggy coat dangling, reminded me of the way a child's hair hangs when they're on a climbing frame. I wondered what the sloth was seeing, and how much of its topsy-turvy view it could make out with its poor vision. I fished around in my back pocket and pulled out my phone to snap a shot. Sunlight glistened off the screen, hinting at the gold inside. Pure gold doesn't tarnish, but having seen the impact of it up close, it had definitely lost its lustre for me. We stared at the sloth for a while, transfixed. *Maybe it was us who were seeing the world the wrong way round?* I wondered to myself.

"It's mad to think that little dude could defeat a jaguar. On the face of it, it seems impossible," I mused to the group before we headed back inside for a spot of lunch. The sloth's sighting had been a welcome one. It was hard not to feel that the end of the world was probably already here, and that there was no use trying to puzzle out moral dilemmas. I might as well just eat all the Jaffa Cakes without bothering to decide whether they were biscuits or cakes. But the encounter reminded me that, if a sloth could hold on when confronted with something as powerful as an apex predator, perhaps, if humanity took action, we could find solutions to protect and preserve the environment. *There is always hope*, I thought – and Greta.

Gratitude

(noun): the quality of being thankful; readiness to show appreciation for and to return kindness.

Our team faced discomfort on this journey, but it was discomfort we had the privilege to sign up for and I'm grateful for that. Arguably, if you lead a relatively comfortable life – you have a support system in the state, family or friends who have your back, your health, food on the table and a roof over your head – you have reasons to be grateful. The journey not only illustrated the importance of being grateful for things like this, but also of the act of showing gratitude.

Our journey down the Essequibo would not have happened without a wider support network. I am grateful to Laura for having had the idea, for asking me and Ness to be part of her team, and for getting the expedition off the ground in the first place. However, we couldn't have done it alone.

The expedition was made possible by the support of our kayak teachers, the kayaking community, our sponsors, our patrons, our fixers in Guyana, the Waî Waî, our teammates, our cameraman, the people we encountered along the journey, our social media followers, our family, our friends and our partners. To mix my environmental metaphors again, the team that completed the trip was the tip of the iceberg. The support network below the water not only shared in our success, but they also enabled it. Anyone who has achieved something as a team will know what I mean when I say that seeing a shared goal reflected back at you in someone else's eyes is so much sweeter than looking out alone.

Days on expedition: 76

Location: the Atlantic Ocean, the mouth of the Essequibo

Status: reaching the finish

Smack. Another wave hit the kayak. We were only 15 kilometres away from the finish, yet with a strong headwind and huge waves – a result of the river becoming the ocean – it may as well have been a lifetime. Over the last few days the water had been getting increasingly choppy. We thought the finish was in the bag, but the Essequibo had other ideas. A bright pink building had been on our right, taunting and demoralizing us, for what seemed like hours. Progress was slow, painful and hard to achieve. I was so exhausted, I cried at one point. We'd nicknamed this the "endurance section". As the river became the sea, the water beneath was both the beginning and end of something.

"At least the footage looks really dramatic," Jon yelled across the crashing waves. He, too, was working hard, trying to juggle filming among the waves and rain, while trying not to get the camera too wet. At one point I watched as he wrapped a waterproof over his head like a shroud, leaving only the camera lens and his feet sticking out from underneath it. I would have found the scene comical if my *Take nothing for granted* shoulders and arms hadn't felt like they were on fire from the paddling. It was the final push, and we had the fatigue to go with it. Weeks of paddling had taken their toll on all of us.

A massive, rusting ship was overturned on the bank – a stark reminder of the might of the ocean.

"It looks like you're battling to get to the beach – and with shipwrecks on the side, it looks cool," came the now muffled shout.

"I'm not sure about 'looks like', Jon," I bellowed back. "We are bloody battling."

Despite the tiredness, I found that some conversation – albeit snatched over the wind – was quite useful to lift the spirits. There had been points over the last few days where I would silently sob when I focused too much on the exhaustion or pain, often made worse by the worry that perhaps we wouldn't make it to the end. Despite coming through so much together, the ferocity of the wind and waves made it seemed possible that we might not finish. In a funny way, seeing how much everyone else was struggling, too, kept me sane.

"When I sleep, I'm still paddling in my dreams. I don't know why," Romel hollered.

"Do you even like paddling?" I called back.

"I think I enjoy it," came the not-entirely-convinced reply. I winced as his kayak rode straight into a large wave. He was soaked. Recovering, he cracked on. "But this last couple of days, my fingers have been getting cramp in the night. When I wake, I have to slowly move my hands to loosen them up again. I've also never been in waves this big before. My boat is very heavy, as it's so full of water. It's quite frightening."

It was frightening and must have been especially so for Romel. He had switched kayaks with Fay and, unlike ours, hers wasn't self-bailing. Despite his concerns, he was doing a gallant job of manoeuvring her old, cumbersome boat through the mighty Atlantic Ocean.

With the exception of Fay, none of us had paddled on an ocean before. The rolling, relentless nature of the waves offered us opportunity to practise the best way to take them on. It became a constant game of judging which bit of the wave to aim for and where the wind was coming from. As our kayaks rose and fell with each swell, we had to try to remember not to cling too hard to our paddles. Being tense didn't aid the process. The style of our strokes was likely atrocious but at this point it was a case of doing whatever worked to stay upright and in the boat.

Laura, bless her socks, was also struggling. Her bum was unbelievably sore, as she'd developed some large, painful, oozing abscesses. I'd had the dubious pleasure of checking these out the day before, as she'd asked if I could investigate the cause of the pain. Feeling somewhat like a midwife, I'd found bulbous boils splattered across her behind. The skin around them was red, raw and angry-looking. Walking was clearly agony for her and she remarked that, when she did, it looked like she'd pooed herself. She wasn't wrong.

"My bum really hurts and it genuinely almost feels like I've given birth again," Laura cried over to me from her boat. She grimaced, clearly trying to deflect the pain into the paddle she was now jabbing aggressively into the ocean. "I can't wait to finish 'cause my groin is basically disintegrating. I'm so excited to not be sat in this effing water."

It turned out that the majority of us were suffering with some sort of groin issue – although it was hardly surprising, seeing as we were spending most of our days doused in murky brown waves. We could no longer see our bright orange paddles as we pushed them through the water. I'd go as far as to say that the viscosity of the liquid had changed – it seemed almost thick.

A particular lowlight had been a lunch stop on a grubby-looking mound of mud in one of the side channels leading to the mouth of the river. The tide was out and the soggy, clay-like bank seemed like a suitably flat surface for us to eat lunch in our kayaks. However, as we ate, the bank began to be reclaimed by the incoming tide. When we tried to get moving, Fay and I got our kayaks stuck in the quaggy sludge. I made the mistake of getting out of the boat to try to push Fay off, but instead I got my leg sucked into the sopping sediment. Rather than freeing her, I'd now turned her boat sideways onto an incoming wave. She got drenched. To prevent both of my legs being lost to the ooze, I tried to haul myself back into my kayak, flinging brown gunk all over the place as I finally squelched free. Eventually, after some shoving and thrusting of kayak paddles against the slowly disappearing mudbank, we freed ourselves. It didn't feel like a victory. Fay cracked and sobbed.

"I can't take it any more," she said. "That ugly wave! It was so dirty – and itchy. My skin is so sore, and it just burns and itches." She gestured to her wet kayak. "It's like being sat in a pigpen and then being sick into it. I can almost feel worms on my skin. This is not something I'll ever forget."

I knew what she meant about the itch. My nether regions didn't feel entirely healthy, either. One time, we stopped for a pee near a logging site and, as I pulled my pants down, a boat passed, seemingly having come from nowhere. Apparently, the passengers were looking, and my arse appeared like a shiny beacon. Laura, who was about 20 metres away, said that she could see my bright white spotty bum from where she was. The news hadn't come as a shock to me. One of the wonderful benefits of being with a partner for over a decade is the unfiltered truth that can come with it. Charlie's look of amusement and shock was not quite the reaction I was expecting after revealing my naked bottom to him after weeks of being apart.

"What?" I asked.

"Nothing," he replied, a slow smile trying hard not to escape any further across his face.

"No, really," I cajoled. "I know you well, mister. Tell me what you're thinking."

Charlie took the deep breath characteristic of someone trying not to laugh. "OK, but remember you asked me to tell you... Your bottom reminds me of a teenage boy's face. It's still great, though," he reassured me between fits of laughter, recognizing that the chance of any future intimacy might be ebbing away by the second.

Contorting my body into an angle I'd never attempted before, I snapped a pic. Let's just say my incredibly spotty and bite-ridden bum wouldn't be appearing on social media accompanied by the word #peachy.

Ness wasn't faring much better, as she'd burned herself a few days previously with boiling water and her skin had blistered up terribly. It had since popped but it looked pretty infected. Boris the foot boil had improved since the antibiotics, but we didn't want to risk reinfection.

I don't think any of us had anticipated that the final leg of the journey would be this physically hard. In many ways, given how much we'd been through, we thought the worst parts of our journey were behind us. There was one bright spot when, for all of an hour, I thought I might be in luck. We'd spent a few days navigating around the vast island system that was forming toward the mouth of the river. As we left Parika the day before, the outgoing tide pushed us quickly down a narrow channel toward Georgetown. For once, all I had to do was sit still and move – a rarity on this river! *Finally*, I thought, *this is what I signed up for.* I may not have had a piña colada in hand, but my dream of floating down the river with my feet up was happening. Predictably, the wind soon picked up, which meant my paddle had to be, too, and any gains we'd made by going with the tide were soon counteracted. Once again, the Essequibo would not let us rest on our laurels – or, in our case, our palm leaves.

The villagers of Parika had been exceptionally kind to us. We'd found out about this little village from a fisherman we'd met on the river as we were looking for somewhere to camp. He suggested it might be worth a short detour down a small side channel, in order to find fresh water. The first thing we saw of the waterside community was a white wooden church next to the river. The pastor offered us food and a place to stay for the night, and invited us to church. We had a great time messing around on the river with the children, ferrying them up and down on our kayaks, which they used as a bouncy springboard for diving in the water and then clambering back on. Yet, part of me was sad that we'd been staying with people rather than in the wild.

Find gratitude in your journey

The following morning we'd woken up to a hell of a downpour. It was strange hearing the sound of rain on the tin roof overhead rather than the sound it makes in the jungle. We still had a way to go, but wilderness was firmly behind us.

As we began our paddle toward Georgetown and the finish, I started to feel quite melancholy that I hadn't got to say a proper goodbye to the rainforest. I had thought there may be more opportunities to embrace the wilderness, but human life had crept up on us sooner than expected.

As I was thinking this, I spotted something in a tree right next to me. Large, with thick browny-red fur, something was clinging to one of the limited trees as we neared the city. I pointed it out to Fay, who said it was a howler monkey. I didn't quite believe it – it had been one of the most elusive monkeys to spot in the rainforest. For the entire trip I had to have things pointed out to me. Most of the time I had missed them, but this time I had been the one to see. There were three monkeys, one with a baby, all unbelievably close and incredible to watch. The creature that had struck the fear of god into me the first time I heard it in the jungle was metres from me, but now – as I watched it hold ground in its shrinking territory – I could see that it was far from terrifying. It was beautiful and graceful, and it moved me to tears. The perception shift, the poetry of it all, wasn't lost on me. I felt it was a farewell from the jungle.

"I feel like that, too," said Ant, as I shared my thoughts with him. We left the monkeys to it and paddled toward the looming city.

"It makes me feel sad, the pollution," Ant said, as our kayaks splashed along side by side. A plastic bottle floated by and we tried to scoop it up with our paddles. "When you go up in the source, it's an amazing place – no bottles, no pollution. The river isn't a good place any more; it's already polluted. We're not drinking fresh water; we can't camp out as we used to. I can't do anything, so we just have to adapt to people here. The thing I don't think people understand is that the Waî Waî people are protecting the whole of Guyana."

In many ways, the river no longer felt like a river. It had become so wide that we couldn't see both riverbanks at the same time, so we chose to stick to the one closest to Georgetown. At its widest, the distance from one side to the other was 32 kilometres, with islands and silty banks peppered in between. The river was also becoming increasingly busy. Boats ferried up and down, transporting goods and people from one side to the other. Soon after we had left the monkeys, a boatman passed Laura up ahead.

"Are you frightened?" he shouted from the deck, gesturing to her small, loaded inflatable kayak and the waves ahead. It was perhaps a blessing we didn't know exactly what we were paddling into.

I couldn't hear her reply, but hazarded a guess that her answer would have been similar to mine: "No, not any more." We had come a long way.

Then, suddenly, a familiar scent floated around us, filling our nostrils with nostalgia. Mingled with the aroma of the river was the whiff of rotting wood. Hundreds of trees were stacked on the riverbank, where a processing plant was grinding and whirring in the background. The ends of the trunks were marked with blood-red paint. We wondered if any of these were the logs we'd seen along our journey.

"Laura, that smell… It's like being back near the source. F-ing obstacles!" I shouted, remembering Jackson's waggish riposte on Valentine's Day.

Be grateful for the people who help and enable your journey through life

Laura passed this message on to Ness, who burst into tears. I think the enormity of the trip was suddenly hitting us all.

As we approached the closing stages of the journey, I found myself trying to process the expedition, both reliving and savouring the incredible experiences. With such limited time remaining with my teammates, I felt an urgency to be especially present in our conversations. Romel, too, was reflective. The night we stayed in Parika I asked him what he'd made of the journey.

"I've enjoyed it very much. It's been interesting to see how the river has changed," he replied, smiling. "Sometimes, on the river you ask me if I'm alright. So often, I'm just thinking: *is this real that I'm paddling all this way without an engine or am I dreaming?* We have paddled past a lot of people who think we are crazy; the Brazilians on the mining boat called us *doido*, which means crazy in Portuguese. One old man we met said there are too many waterfalls and that it couldn't be done. In some ways, I honestly don't know how we're nearly at Georgetown."

We talked about his near miss with the jaguar. How we'd both been frightened at points in the jungle. He also shared his sadness. Earlier in the trip, Laura had received a message that his granddad had died, and since then he had often been crying alone when he paddled. His granddad had raised him, as his father was in Brazil.

"I didn't tell anyone how I felt," he said. "It's hard when you're away and paddling. My granddad said that you must enjoy the travelling. I've thought about my family a lot on this trip: what they are doing, what they are eating. I'm looking forward to seeing my son. I left him when he was so little. He will be very different now," he said.

Romel had been so stoic, so we'd had no idea he'd been so upset. In so many ways I wished he'd opened up to us sooner, but I was glad he had at least been sharing with his best mate, Ant. I, too, was grateful we were (vaguely) in one piece.

"I'm excited to finish," said Ant. "I'm proud of myself. I can tell people I know the area. You can't bluff me up: I'll paddle all the way to the river's junction. Partnership, Pip. This has been a good trip. I think it is about teamwork. Especially on the waterfalls *Whose shoulders are you standing on? Tell them; thank them.* and rapids – working out which route is doable. When we cooperated with one head, it worked out very well."

It's an interesting analogy about teamwork: our little group was standing on the shoulders of giants, only able to look outward because of so many people holding us up. As we approached the end, we needed to lift each other more than ever.

"You guys are the best thing that's happened to me. It's made me want this trip to last longer," said Fay. "I've never laughed so much in my life. Laughing silly helped me push through the exhaustion, and made me move and move. I've never had friends like you. You helped me find happiness."

"I don't want to leave you, either," said Laura. "I want you to come home."

I, too, was grateful for the friends I'd made on the journey and, as my will to paddle faded – as my hands, my arms, my back and my shoulders screeched to a stop – I mentally namechecked everyone in my life who had meant something to me or had influenced me in some way. It was incredible to realize how many people had, and it made me so thankful for what I was doing. They gave me strength.

When this high inevitably faded, Laura was on hand with another boost. Together we sang "Fight Song" with gusto as we stared out at the wide-open ocean to our left. To our right, the city's low-rise skyline. When that wore off, I shared my own battle cry with the ocean and screamed as hard as I could: "Hear me roar." This seemed to make everyone chuckle and, once again, we'd found that bit of extra energy.

Finally, I settled on a mantra: "You can do this. You are doing this." I repeated it with every paddle stroke. Each one was a movement getting us closer to our goal. And then, there it was. After months on the river, up ahead there was the nondescript, sloping concrete bank that represented our finish line.

By this point, we had packed down Fay's kayak and Romel had hopped into Ant's boat for the final push. As we approached the bank, I made a weird sound – somewhere between a cry and a laugh. To be honest, by that point I wasn't entirely sure which emotion was trying to escape. It was so bizarre and I could see the others looking at me, amusement on their faces.

It wasn't the most salubrious finish. The water smelled of poo and was also tinged with a powerful fish smell. Turns out we'd arrived in front of a shrimp-processing area, which explained the fish smell at least.

Some journalists were lined up behind the sea wall with their cameras; a few fish sellers and small children were kicking around as well. Our fixer, Sophia, had kindly gone to the trouble of finding us a ribbon to cross. Unfortunately, it had been a paper one and so it had disintegrated into the sea. She did, however, present us with some champagne.

Seeing the media, I tried to play it cool, but my body had other ideas. Clumsy to the last, instead of stepping from the kayak onto the sloping wall, I managed to miss and found myself balancing on a submerged groyne. I slipped and subsequently fell into the sea. My paddle flew into the air, before clonking me on the head, and my sunglasses fell halfway down my face – and Jon caught the whole thing on camera. In so many ways, it was a fitting finish for my personal journey – I was tired, battered and humbled, but still had a smile on my face and a twinkle in the eye. I'm amused it happened that way; further proof that special skills, talent and coordination aren't prerequisites for achievement. All you need is the right mindset, and an ability to get back up and laugh at yourself.

In the media interviews that followed, Fay shared something very heartfelt: the trip had changed her life and given her new friends.

"I went to their school and they came to mine," she said.

As the entire team celebrated, a group hug ensued; for a moment, we were one matted, bedraggled being that smelled of sweat, tears, the Essequibo and shaken champagne, competing with the smell of shrimp farming in the air. Wedged under jumping, cysty armpits, I looked at the individuals I now called friends. Together we had done it. We had bloody done it.

Love

(noun): an intense feeling of deep affection.

Do you operate from a place of love or fear? Both are primal emotions, and my time in the jungle really brought them to the surface. They both have their uses, but I learned that trying to approach people – and life – from a place of love will make you feel so much better about yourself and the world around you. If I'm honest with myself, the times I have bitched about others, or felt smug when hearing of the suffering of someone, are those when I've been unhappiest within myself. Bullies are often coping with their own insecurities. When I'm operating from a place of love, not only do I feel better about myself, but my own capacity for joy is also magnified by genuinely celebrating the good fortune and blessings of those around me. So, notice your thoughts and conversations about other people – then dig a bit deeper and ask yourself what that's really saying about you.

Unfortunately, love can also require a certain amount of discomfort and vulnerability. Try to get over the awkward experience of sharing how you feel, and don't believe the notion that it's somehow cringeworthy to express affection and positive emotions. The worst thing that can happen when trying to be positive is that you may feel a bit embarrassed if someone doesn't react how you imagined. In the grand scheme of things, is that really so bad? Love hard. Let it shine through your eyes and see it reflected back at you. Open your heart to the people around you, and yours will be filled tenfold. Compassion is the most powerful force I know.

Finally – and this can be the hardest thing of all – extend that compassion to yourself. Like everyone else on the planet, you're flawed but, every now and again, try to remind yourself that you're also bloody brilliant.

Days on expedition: 79

Location: Georgetown

Status: knackered

In my head, I'd imagined we'd have a night of joyous celebration about what we'd achieved. However, as with most things in life, it's that gap between expectation and reality that can lead to disappointment. The tone for the evening was set as I squished into a taxi, wedged in the back seat between a soggy Ant and Romel, with the kayaks deflated, folded and stuffed in the back of various vehicles. Fay hopped in the front and our driver, Clyde, took us back to the hotel in Georgetown where it had all begun.

The last time I'd been in a taxi was on the way to the airport before flying to Masakenari. I recalled the mixture of excitement and trepidation I had felt as we told our driver what we were attempting to do. He'd laughed when I snapped a picture of a rainbow out the window, remarking that we'd see plenty of those where we were going, and warned us of flash floods that can quickly rise to the level of his car. As we said goodbye, he extended his hand and shook mine. He'd asked if I had gloves, as my hands were exceptionally soft and smooth, and commented that he'd like to shake them again when we got back. That conversation felt like a lifetime ago. I looked down at my hard, calloused hands and resisted the urge to pick the peeling skin.

I felt so proud of what we'd achieved but, in a sense, I felt no personal glory. As I commented to Ant and Romel, without our Waî Waî guides I'd likely be dead in the jungle somewhere. Without my teammates, I wouldn't be in such good spirits. We'd belly laughed at least once a day. We'd weathered so much; the grit, and the physical and emotional energy it had taken to achieve our goal were mammoth. However, in some ways I was less sure of myself than when we'd set out; I had a head full of questions about myself and the world around me, but no answers. I realized that this was perhaps part of the Faustian bargain that came with setting a goal – you needed to be clear on why

The world looks better when viewed with love

exactly you were pursuing it. To quote John Candy's character in *Cool Runnings* when he talks about winning a gold medal at the Olympics: "If you weren't enough without it, you'll never be enough with it."

Being in a car again was bizarre; the world moved at such speed around us. Billboards flashed large on the side of the road, and I found them perplexing and hard to take in. The taxi paused in traffic, coming to a stop beside an oversized ad. A cemetery was also next to us, full of concrete slabs to commemorate those that had gone before. Many were cracked, caved in on themselves and in total disrepair. Adding to the eerie air of abandonment was the fact that it was flooded, following heavy rainfall, and many of the graves were swimming in water. It was a good reminder of the brevity of life and it made me appreciate the day even more. Journalists had already begun to ask one of my least favourite questions – the phrase that always tries to wrench you from the moment – "What's next?"

In our case the answer was easy: a shower.

The question reminded me that the highs, perhaps inevitably, would be temporary. The exhilaration of achievement would likely fade over that night, the years and the decades to come. It made me all the more eager to celebrate the seconds and savour the minutes.

However, it's fair to say that our evening celebrations didn't go well. We were ravenous, knackered and looking forward to a hearty meal in the hotel but, unfortunately, the waitress who took the order went home without doing anything about it. When it became apparent that the chefs had left and we weren't going to get any food, one of the waitresses took us to the breakfast room where she made us up peanut butter and jam sandwiches. It was better than nothing.

"I literally feel so broken," Laura said. "Half from the pain in my cyst – it's so sore to touch – and my whole right-hand side is in agony. I keep holding my back to walk around. Maybe I pulled a muscle in the wind today? My body's probably like, 'You're resting now, so I can allow you to feel pain again.'"

I knew what she meant; I felt like I'd been hit by a bus. My entire body hurt to move and everything ached, especially my core. I guessed I'd never had to work it so hard before!

In a rock-and-roll end to the expedition, we were all in bed by 10 p.m. Ironically, having dreamed of a bed for so long, I found sleeping in one to be an uncomfortable experience, as I had got used to the sway of the hammock. Bad karaoke from the floor below was our soundtrack to sleep.

The following morning, instead of waking up and dismantling camp, I rolled over and checked my phone. It was incredible to read all the messages of support from people on Instagram. Bleary-eyed, I saw we'd even received a message of congratulations from Bear Grylls – I couldn't quite believe it. What we'd done was still sinking in and it was massively humbling to be so inundated by support and well wishes. To me, it still felt like the most normal thing in the world to get up, pack up camp and paddle day after day. The idea of going into an office from 9 a.m. to 5 p.m. every day felt so much harder.

Connect, don't disconnect

Although our dinner of chicken and rice was an upgrade on the peanut butter sandwiches the night before, everyone seemed frazzled from the events of the day. Laura and I had been trying to withdraw money so we could take cash back to the village to pay for the remainder of the guiding fees. Figuring out how much we could withdraw on whose card and over how many days was a headache. We'd also been buying parts for the Waî Waî's outboard, including a fuel cap to replace the one we'd lost on the way to the source. Ant and Romel had been dashing from shop to shop around the city, too, hunting for soap, clothing and food to take back home.

The presence of fully charged phones on the table that evening, and things to do on them, was off-putting. Turning on our devices had been necessary but, arguably, not healthy for any of us. Ness said she felt like she was dealing with email overload. Jon had spent the day busily backing up our footage, and Fay was also dealing with admin and life tasks. A barrage of bleeps and pings on our phones over supper wasn't helping anyone's stress levels.

Life on the river had been simple; we had had one goal – to paddle and survive. The many stressors of a tech-filled life had been removed, so reaching Georgetown and reintroducing them was a hard pill to swallow. It was a battle for me to remind myself of the lessons of the jungle. I felt so sad at dinner, seeing phones on the table or people tapping away, visually disconnecting from the world in front of them. I, too, was guilty of it.

Ness and I were going to fly back to the Waî Waî village in two days, but Laura wouldn't be joining us. She'd booked the first available flight home, which unfortunately was on that same day. Ant and Romel had flown home the day before.

"I'm really excited to see Ran," she said. "I'm desperate to get back to him. But, in a weird way, I'm also scared to be away from you guys. I'm worried about you not being right there. I'm so used to calling you and you being around."

She came to wave us off before her own flight. "I'll miss that face of yours," she said.

As she left, I held her tight, sobbing – the kind of crying where you can feel two bodies vibrating together. I told her I loved her. Ness, too, was in pieces. This trip had bonded us all. There were times when we had irritated each other beyond belief and there were near bust-ups, but we left as family. I am often asked what it was like travelling with other women, which is a bizarre question if you think about it. There had been such power in the sisterhood; the support of Ness and Laura, and later Fay, uplifted me on the down days. But our male teammates did, too.

On the flight back to the Waî Waî, this time we were kindly shown to the VIP waiting room. Looking at the map in the lounge made me well up. We'd travelled the entire country. When we first set off, the names on the map were unfamiliar, remote – meaningless to me in my ignorance. Now, when I looked at the map it was full of colour. The stories, the people, the river breathed into life.

I hate small aircrafts, but sitting in this one, waiting to take off, felt like the end of the journey for me. The full circle. The Essequibo River had opened us, broken us and churned us around in a way we never saw coming. Yet in so many ways, we left the Essequibo stronger and more self-aware. It changed the flow of my life.

Nature is a powerful force if we stop and listen to its lessons, and I wanted to make sure I heard what the Essequibo had been telling me. It reflected my flaws back at me – my ego, the insecurities. I had desperately wanted to be brave but ended up accepting that at times I was weak. At times I crumbled. At times I needed help. But these lows gave me the opportunity to be vulnerable – to receive the help I didn't even know I needed – and the chance to grow. I felt so full of drive to become a better human, to change myself in the best ways possible and to shape my small corner of the world.

The plane whirred into life. The runway markers on the ground below began to blur and then fade – and we were off. Despite gripping my seat tightly as we hit our first bit of turbulence, I turned and grinned at Ness. No words were needed. We just watched as concrete turned to jungle.

It was bizarre seeing the river from above again, with its twists and turns. It had taken us close to three months to get here, yet it would be a three-hour flight back. We'd gone from the fish-eye to the bird's-eye view. I missed being among the canopy, the noise, the life. From above, it looked so serene, and it didn't tell the story of the thriving chaos below. As we neared Masakenari, we saw two beautiful rainbows spring up and then disappear. It seemed a fitting farewell.

As we touched down, we saw Jackson and Nereus waiting for us at the airstrip with quad bikes. It was incredible to see them again. Ness literally bounced out of the plane and ran for Jackson. We didn't have long; nightfall loomed and if the gathering thunderclouds brought rain, the earthen runway would become slippery, making take-off impossible. We couldn't afford for the plane to be grounded overnight – every hour on the ground was costing us US$450. It would also mean we'd miss our flight back to the UK the next day. We

Open up to others and they might open up to you

hopped on the quad bike for the ten-minute journey to the village meeting place. Unfortunately, the 3-kilometre track had become so wet and muddy due to a previous rain shower that we arrived at this spectacular structure caked in mud.

We found Nigel inside, sitting on one of the benches that lined the walls. He seemed to be working on a laptop.

"Nigel," I screamed.

He barely looked up from the screen, pretending he hadn't seen us. When he did lift his head in our direction, quite deadpan, he said something along the lines of: "I'm busy doing something." Ever Mr Smooth.

I chuckled and gave him a hug anyway. He looked pleased to see us.

"What have you been up to?" I asked.

"Nothing… Playing football," he said. "Oh, and making a video for the village."

He showed us some videos from our time in the jungle. It touched me that it had impacted him as much as it had us. Going through something together, whether it's an expedition or a seismic life event, bonds you. You develop a form of respect and understanding that you can't find any other way. Seeing so many familiar faces, the warmth of our welcome, was overwhelming in the best possible way.

"Nigel?"

"Yes, Miss?"

"What do you think makes people happy in life?"

"It's up to them. I don't know what your futures are," he said. "What makes *me* happy is when I see my friends coming back again." His words had a sincerity to them that caught in his throat momentarily, giving them a husky timbre. "Oh, I don't know what to say, but I think I can say this: I really miss you guys, you know? When I see my friends, that makes me happy. My mind reminds me of all the things I've been through. Every single thing."

I asked him what had been his favourite thing about the expedition.

"Seeing your faces in the morning. I missed you all when I came back."

I told him I had missed our jungle team, too, and that I'd talked about him daily. Jon confirmed this.

"She said you're really cool," he told Nigel.

I gave him my sunglasses, solar charger and a survival book that my dad had given me before we'd set out. Nigel recognized it as the one I used to flick through when not writing in my hammock at night.

"The book from your dad, right?" he said. "Won't he be mad?"

"No," I replied. "It reminds me of you. You taught me more about the jungle than any book."

The Toshao asked us to say a few words to the people gathered in the hall. Ness made a wonderful speech about friendship and collaboration. I said that we were leaving our hearts in the village and that the Waî Waî had meant so much to us.

Deli, Cemci's wife and our surrogate mum while we were prepping for the expedition, sent me over the edge as we were saying our goodbyes. Once again, I asked what she thought made people happy in life.

"By meeting each other, getting to know each other and showing love to each other. What do you think?"

"I couldn't agree more," I replied as we hugged. "You have shown us so much love, so, truly, from the bottom of our hearts, thank you."

Deli smiled. "Thank you, too. Your love is now. You went away and you came back to see us – that's the love you show us. That's the love." Her lip began to wobble, as did mine. "The love in me is just flowing; tears are coming out," she said. We were both in pieces, but it was time to leave.

We had to speed walk back to the airstrip, as the quad bikes were nowhere to be seen. Nigel helped us carry the carved traditional wooden paddles that I'd commissioned before we left. True to form, I slipped in the mud, jarring my back, and further covering my trousers and shoes in mud.

"I reckon you're stronger than me now," Nigel joked. "I wasn't sure you were going to make it."

I knew one thing for sure: without the team I wouldn't have.

As we walked up the path, we spotted a familiar roll and loll of the shoulders. It was Romel, with a woven basket on his back. He was with his wife and the rest of his family.

"Meet Ray," Romel said proudly as he introduced us to his little baby. We all hugged goodbye; I said that we would miss him, and that I loved his honesty and his soul. He looked peaceful; the quiet contentment of a man at home.

Thankfully, after about 10 minutes of walking, one of the quad bikes approached and we all hopped on. We also happened to see Ant approaching us on a quad bike, heading in the opposite direction. We had a brief chat and asked if he was coming to see us off.

"No," he said.

I thought he was joking, but he never arrived – or if he did, it was after we had left. I can't quite remember what I said, but I had thought I'd see him shortly so didn't give him a proper farewell. The only sad note to the day.

We loaded up the hold with various items that people in the village had asked us to deliver to their loved ones in Georgetown. The pilot motioned that it was time to go. We hugged our teammates for the last time. Their friendship had meant everything to us in the jungle.

"I guess this is a final goodbye, not a see you soon," Nigel said as he waved us off. "Forever in my mind," he told us.

"Forever in the jungle of my mind," I replied.

"I feel at peace now," Ness said on the flight back to Georgetown, as we watched the sun shine off the Essequibo for the last hours of the day. It looked like shimmering silver below us. "Our journey feels like it's whole."

I couldn't agree more. We both left with full hearts and memories that would last forever. We were fortunate to have seen one of the world's remaining truly wild places. Modern exploration is not about planting flags. It is not even about travel. It's about seeing the world you're in with new eyes. It is, at its core, about seeing life with love. We'd achieved what we'd set out to do. I was ready to return to Charlie, my own version of home.

As we touched down in Georgetown, sunbeams were coming through the clouds and the river was lit up like a snake crawling through the landscape below. Goosebumps marked my body as dark, threatening clouds were offset against the evening's brilliant orange and misty glow. The sun glinted off the river in places, radiating far beyond where it hit, almost like a wink. It was spellbinding. It was goodbye.

Death and Life

(noun): the end of life; (noun): yours to define.

Life isn't lived in the grand moments. It's in the touch of hands, a hug, the flicker of a candle and the joy of a child's squeal. It's found in a cup of tea and the steam that dances in the cool air – the beautiful, often overlooked, simplicity of our everyday life. World-firsts, accolades, big adventures – these moments can form special parts of a life, but they don't make it special.

Our journey through Guyana's rainforest shook me more than any I'd done previously or am ever likely to do. I am still reflecting on the lessons it taught me. I sat with (and nearly on, in the case of the snake) the concept of death more often than I would have liked. I watched as nature absorbed, reclaimed and spawned life – that ever-evolving, connected cycle of which we are but a moment.

What do I hope you'll take from this final chapter? Grab life with two hands and understand that our adventures, however big, have more to do with mindset than anything else. We can explore right now, from where we are. On the duvet days, the can't-be-arsed-days, the bleak days, the memorable days, the cherish-forever days, life is happening all around us – we just have to notice.

Days at home: two months

Location: the Hospital for Tropical Diseases, London

Status: on a drip

"Your blood tests show that you have glandular fever," said the doctor as I sat in his room in London's Hospital for Tropical Diseases. The clinic was a place I was beginning to know well, after having been in for various tests over the last few weeks.

Well, that explains why I've been unusually knackered and lacking my usual zest for life, I thought to myself.

"However, I am going to refer you to my colleague, consultant dermatologist Dr Steve Walker, to further investigate the bite on your neck."

This isn't a good sign, Scared Brain piped up, having spent far too long on Google in recent weeks.

Search engines are never your friend when it comes to investigating symptoms. This is particularly true if what you're looking up involves a crusty scab that's formed over a particular insect bite. (Apologies if you're eating while reading this.) I was sporting one such delight on my jugular. Imagine, if you will, the mark that might appear after a vampire has given an overly ambitious love bite. At first, it hadn't bothered me, as it didn't hurt or itch. But then the bite began to grow, scabbing over and, in a particularly attractive turn of events, becoming a pussing ulcer. The crater underneath, left exposed when the crust fell off, also seemed to be getting deeper. My research into what it could be had left me feeling very unsettled.

Whatever the cause, it had slowly been expanding its home on my neck ever since we'd returned from the jungle.

Uninvited guests can be trying at the best of times, but a particular lowlight of whatever was on my neck was the horrible stench that occasionally accompanied it. One morning I'd woken up to a particularly pungent smell. After unsuccessfully blaming Charlie, we started sniffing around the bed. Let's face it, this is never a good idea. My nose, fine-tuned after months in the jungle, led us to the real culprit: my pillow. Or, should I say, a patch on my pillow where the wound had seeped, before drying and becoming especially malodorous.

For a few weeks my scab had been engaged in this merry dance of falling off and regrowing. The upside of sporting such a look so prominently on my neck was that I had never been given so much space on the Tube. I had hoped that the doctor would say it was nothing to worry about and to be on my merry way. Instead he talked about "watching and waiting" and mentioned a word that Google had also thrown up: leishmaniasis. In layman's terms, it's a flesh-eating parasite. In a cruel twist of events, given how much I've come to use it, it's also a word I find fiendish difficult to spell.

Leishmaniasis is not just nasty, but also devasting. Caused by the bite of a female sandfly, my research had told me that there are three strains of the disease – a trio destined to give you nightmares. In first position, the most fatal form of the disease: visceral leishmaniasis. It will attack your internal organs and, if untreated, kill you within two years. It is the second-biggest parasitic killer after malaria.

The silver medalist, in the podium of unpleasantness, is mucocutaneous leishmaniasis. This strain has a particular liking for mucous membranes – especially eating away at the throat, nose and mouth. The pictures shown on Google of children and adults suffering with it were shocking.

Finally, bronze medalist, the most common form, but still nasty: cutaneous leishmaniasis. This bad boy of diseases causes deep lesions across the skin and can spread, leading to permanent scarring. Sometimes they can heal on their accord but in the worst cases they can lead to disability. Quite often these lesions present on the face and, in many parts of the world, this disfigurement can lead to social stigma. Depending on the strain and position – and if you're particularly unlucky – it can decide to sneak into the mucous membranes to see what all the fuss is about.

To be honest, none of these seemed particularly attractive options. More worryingly, the lesions shown in the pictures I found online looked exactly like my own crusty papule.

Like so many things in life, it is often only after they're taken away that we realize how much we valued or relied on them. Looking in the mirror, I suddenly noticed how much I liked my nose. I'd not considered it before, but it turns out I was also fond of my face. Yes, it had the odd line, wrinkle and wonk, but it was a face that had grown *Appreciate what you have* old with me – it wasn't perfect, but it was mine. I couldn't see how it would be improved by chunks of flesh being consumed from it. Likewise, life – with all its ups and downs, heartaches and worries, love and loss – turns out to be bloody brilliant when you really think about it.

So there we were: a few weeks after seeing the first doctor, Charlie and I were sitting in a waiting room, doing just that. Waiting. Waiting for news that could change my life, delivered not by a hummingbird but by a doctor. A handful of people sitting there were hooked up to IVs, passing the time reading or playing with their phones, as drugs silently seeped into their arms. Machines beeped every so often, warning staff that the concoctions were coming to an end. I sat there with Charlie by my side; I was the patient with the hole in her neck, wondering what my future was about to look like.

"Pip Stewart," called Dr Walker. "Please follow me."

Dr Walker is likely to be the walking personification of the type of doctor everybody would like to be seen by. Calm, with the kindest eyes and most reassuring manner, he had a demeanour that suggested he knew exactly what he was talking about. It was the sort of gravitas you want when confronted with potentially the most unexpected and shocking diagnosis of your life.

Dr Walker reiterated that we'd waited to see what was happening with my neck because the lesion was in a delicate area, prone to scarring, and if a biopsy could be avoided, that would be the best option. I'm no medic, but apparently there are things in your neck you don't want to accidentally nick. Having examined it, he broke the news and it was the last thing I wanted to hear: a biopsy was necessary.

"I'll see if we can book you in," he said.

I have a massive fear of needles, and the idea of someone taking a scalpel to my neck to slice a bit out didn't exactly fill me with joy. Dr Walker clearly noticed the panic in my face, my sweaty palms or the fact that I was about to burst into tears and told me to wait for a second. He disappeared and when he returned around 10 minutes later, he said he'd rejigged a few things in his diary and would do the procedure himself. It would have been entirely inappropriate to do so, but in that moment I wanted to give him the biggest cuddle I could. If someone had to hold a sharp blade to my neck, I wanted it to be him.

"Now?" I asked.

"Yes, now."

Like so many things we build up, the procedure was nowhere near as bad as my mind had made it out to be (although, I won't be in a rush to do it again). I was unbelievably grateful to Dr Walker for his time and reassuring presence. I hadn't realized then, but the hardest part mentally would turn out to be waiting for the results. My mind went to every conceivable outcome. Anyone who has faced health trouble, or who has loved ones who have, knows that it's like having a question mark hanging over you and your existence. In reality that question mark is always there, but we just don't always have cause to notice it.

In the jungle, I'd had a conversation with Nigel about death. I told him that I think about it a lot. I offered up that, when I was 18 and left school, I wrote in my yearbook that when I was older, I wanted smile lines around my eyes. Now I had them, I wished I hadn't asked for that.

"Age will destroy your face; it does to everyone," he said. A part of me knew that, but I just hadn't anticipated a flesh-eating parasite might aid this process. "Anyway, don't worry about death," Nigel had advised. "In the same way you make your plans for tomorrow, and then tomorrow comes and you feel ill or feel like doing something different, you never know really what's going to happen. I put my faith in God."

I told him that I put my faith in humanity, as wherever I'd been I'd realized how amazing most humans are.

"We think the same on this," was the vague conclusion he drew.

That conversation seemed a world away now – as did my results.

A few weeks later, I took a seat on the blue wipeable chairs you so often see in hospitals. Dr Walker calmly broke the news that the biopsy showed I had cutaneous leishmaniasis. He told me that, unfortunately, *Seek out* it was also a strain of the Viannia species, *gratitude* which meant it also brought with it a risk of developing into mucocutaneous leishmaniasis, attacking my throat, nose and mouth. I tried to take in the news.

Essentially (and these are my words, not Dr Walker's), a flesh-eating parasite was lunching on my neck and if I didn't undergo an aggressive treatment for it there was a risk it might make my face a dessert.

I closed my eyes. I could almost remember the spot where I had been bitten. We'd slept close to the riverbank, and the ground was particularly wet and squelchy. I'd been slow to hang up my hammock, as I was distracted by a cute, tiny baby caiman – the same one my mum was so worried about when she saw it on social media. I'd stayed with it for ages, fascinated by it in the same way it seemed to be mesmerized by me. Both of us were just staring, watching each other. As dusk threw its arms around the day, I thought I ought to put my hammock up. While I flung the straps around the trunk of the tree, flies appeared, as if from nowhere. The skin not covered by my shirt was bitten many times, including just above the collar. Apart from *ow*, I thought nothing of it at the time.

I hadn't connected the dots to realize that they might be sandflies or that they could be carrying leishmaniasis, which is often the case in environments that have been impacted by deforestation and urbanization. It was just another discomfort of jungle life. Although why they decided to feast on my neck rather than at a less sweaty establishment is anyone's guess.

I fidgeted on my chair in the hospital, my bum making that awkward squeaking noise that occasionally happens on that vinyl PVC-type material. We both pretended not to notice. Dr Walker ran me through what he thought was the best treatment option. I'd done some googling in the run-up to this meeting, throwing up words like "chemotherapy", "cardiotoxicity" and "drug resistance". The more I looked into it, the more I discovered that treatment options are not only highly toxic and aggressive, but also old-fashioned, dating back to the 1940s. Despite nearly a million new cases annually, and nearly one billion people in 98 countries around the world at risk from the disease, it seems there is little capital incentive for drugs companies to invest in better treatment and research into the disease. This is down to the grubby matter of money – the majority of people who need the treatment don't have enough of it. The disease impacts some of the world's poorest and most remote populations, who have little access to media, let alone treatment options suited to where they live. This will only change if governments, manufactures or those with large pockets dig into them to help subsidize it.

Apparently, those cheesy Valentine's Day cards were nearly right for me – turns out I wasn't one *in* a million, but one *of* a million. Yet, unlike the majority of those diagnosed each year, I was sitting opposite one of the world's leading experts on tropical skin diseases, discussing the free treatment plan I would undergo over the next few months. However invasive, however outdated, I was receiving help.

In this case "help" was going to be another tongue-twister: sodium stibogluconate. It's a medicine that contains antimony – an element often used to make kohl, as well as semiconductors and flame-retardant material. It's also used in the drug that was administered into my veins every day for three weeks. First, however, was the small matter of inserting a long intravenous tube that would remain in the large vein in my upper arm for the duration of the treatment. There was great solace for me in reframing my treatment (with the help of Charlie – my endless source of inspiration) from: "I have to go through this" to "I get to go through this". As someone who loves the power of words, I found this really useful.

Do you "have to" or do you "get to"?

On the plus side, this insertion gave Charlie a birthday to remember (not a phrase I ever thought I'd find myself writing).

Having warned the nurse that I don't deal well with injections at the best of times, let alone the idea of a small, hollow tube working its way up the vein, Charlie was allowed to sit in with me while it was slipped in. This was permitted on the proviso that at a certain point, when she told him to, he would turn away. Apparently, blood can spurt out and, to an untrained professional, this seems more alarming than it really is. Not one to follow orders, Charlie did look. Given how pale his face went, the nurse suggested it was perhaps best for him to sit down.

"Happy birthday, Charlie," I said, grinning from my reclined position on the hospital bed, as colour slowly returned to his face. The procedure was complete and a piece of dangling tube hung out of the crook of my arm. He looked pretty queasy. "You're so lucky you get to go through this," I reminded him.

Never underestimate the power of cheesy music and a good old boogie

Days began to blur after that. Like in the jungle, humour helped me through these tricky times. Each morning, before I left the flat to go to the hospital, I'd crank up our tried-and-tested jungle tune of "Fight Song" and that well-known motivational music – the soundtrack to *Moana*. When energy allowed, this would mean boxing moves in the kitchen, as I imagined kicking the parasite's arse. According to our neighbours downstairs, it sounded like a herd of elephants were coming through their ceiling. Perhaps not great for the floorboards, but necessary for my spirits.

Doctor Walker had left me under no illusion, so I knew that this would not be a fun drug to be on and the side effects would be severe. Its benefit was that it might kill the parasite. The downsides were that it also might damage my heart and liver. As well as being attached to a drip for nearly an hour a day, I had regular blood tests to check my liver function and an electrocardiogram to check that my heart was still working as it should. I was also warned that my veins might close up. On the plus side, if the nurses were making a cup of tea for themselves, they'd always bring me one, too. I felt very looked after. If I imagined hard enough, it was sort of like being in a spa. Only in this case, instead of waiting for moisturizer to sink into the skin, I was waiting for a bottle marked with a skull and crossbones, and the word TOXIC emblazoned across it, to get to work.

For the first half of the treatment, I couldn't see what all the fuss was about; I felt fine. If anything, it was a great excuse to put my feet up, drink numerous cups of tea and enjoy the sympathy. As much as I hated getting to the hospital, I rather enjoyed myself once I was there. It's a fascinating branch of medicine and I loved hearing the travel stories of the doctors, nurses, receptionists and other patients in the waiting room. For the hours I was there, I travelled vicariously as the drugs got to work.

However, as the days turned into weeks, the muscle aches took hold. Even the most scintillating travel tales couldn't distract me from the discomfort. My body seized up and even the slightest manoeuvre hurt. Charlie took to calling me "Crocodile Dundee", as I opted to sleep on the floor rather than our bed. I figured I was less likely to move on a flat surface. Each morning it would genuinely be a feat of Herculean proportions just to get myself from horizontal to vertical. The good news was that the treatment appeared to be working: the hole in my neck was slowly beginning to close up.

Service and purpose are more fulfilling than individual goals

One morning, after I'd been hooked up to the drip, I sent Fay a Facebook message, asking her about leishmaniasis and what her community does about it in Apoteri. She also received a hot pic of my neck scab. Lucky woman.

"Do you remember the scars I showed you on my leg? It's the same thing," she replied.

I did recall them: five silvery marks peppered across her shin. I asked her how she treated them.

"I poured burning cow fat on them," came the shocking response.

Beep, beep. My thoughts were interrupted by the machine administering the drugs alerting the nurses that it was done for the day. I watched as the nurse carefully disconnected me from it, sealed my dangly tube back up and discharged me for the day.

"See you tomorrow, Pip," the receptionist said as I shuffled off. I waved, before disappearing back into the anonymous city to begin the journey home. I paused briefly outside, next to the silver sign at the hospital's entrance. An office worker, having a fag opposite, clocked my bandaged elbow and smiled sympathetically at me. I smiled back before typing a question back to Fay. To this day, I think it is up there with one of my more stupid ones.

"Did it hurt?" I asked.

"Yes, Pip. It felt like I'd been fried," came the immediate and blunt reply.

Over the following days we messaged back and forth. I asked her why she burned herself rather than going to hospital. She said she could have done but it would have meant five to six weeks away from home, which wasn't going to be practical for her because of her children.

I'd also messaged Cemci's son, Philip, asking what the people in Masakenari did to treat leishmaniasis. He told me they crush turtle shell into the lesions as it's "faster than getting a whole month of injections".

After conversations with medics, chats with people on social media and speaking to my friends in Guyana, I began to understand the scale and nature of the problem. In a game of "would you rather" I am not sure "applying burning cow fat" and "intense, outdated toxic chemotherapy" are brilliant choices. The turtle shell sounds like a winner to me and, like the cow fat, may well be effective at healing the lesions. However, there's been very little research into whether these local treatments prevent the parasite popping up again further down the line. I'm not one to tell the scientific and medical community what to do, but I reckon the disease could do with a rebrand. (Admittedly, I have nicked this idea from the World Health Organization who say that hard-to-pronounce names also contribute to why many tropical diseases are neglected.) So, here's my thinking. Leishmaniasis was named in 1901 after the Glaswegian doctor and army medic, William Leishman, who identified the parasite during his work in India. If you ask me, we should just go with William. Saying "I've got a bad case of William" or "William has been nibbling at my neck again" would be so much simpler than explaining "leish-ma-whats-its-chops-again". Alternatively, if he was feeling particularly generous, Prince William could always change his name to Prince Leishmaniasis, and the world's press would be all over it like a rash – or a hungry parasite.

You only get one shot at life, so make the most of it

It was an emotional day for me when it came to having my IV removed and saying goodbye to the people who had helped me on my latest journey. This time Charlie was sitting down, his face firmly turned away from the procedure. Weak, aching but with a hole in my neck that seemed to have closed, I held my arm out to the nurse in preparation for the removal of the tube.

I thought back to the interconnected nature of the Essequibo River, to all the people we met along it. It struck me that so many of my worries in the jungle were flawed. I'd been so concerned about what *could* happen that I'd overlooked what *is* happening right now – arguably the biggest threat of all. Global healthcare inequality is far more terrifying than anything we encountered in the jungle. It wasn't just the parasite that got under my skin: it was the injustice of it. These are not problems of the poor; these are problems for humanity.

Within seconds the IV was out. I'd hardly felt it. The long tube that had been in my arm, was curled up like a snake and sitting in a tub, ready for medical disposal. I contemplated all the things I could do in the coming weeks, as my strength returned. I'd be able to wash both arms. I would be able to go for a proper walk and lie in bed. It was amazing what I'd previously taken for granted. I was now free. At least, sort of. I'd still have to visit Dr Walker over the next year as he monitored me for any signs the parasite may have returned.

As I sat up on the hospital bed and swung my legs to one side to dismount, I felt grateful and unbelievably lucky.

"You know, your scar sort of looks like a love bite," the nurse said to me.

I stroked the increasingly flat skin of the wound and grinned. I rather liked the idea. A visual symbol of love and what can be achieved when we start from a place of compassion.

I went to the front desk – not to pay, but to leave a card and a carrot cake that Charlie had made to say thank you. These people didn't know me a month ago, but they cared for me, made me smile and helped me overcome a phobia or two. They reminded me that however bleak the world can seem at times, incredible humans exist within it. They gave me hope that if enough good people care, leishmaniasis and other neglected tropical diseases don't have to remain neglected for too much longer. That evening, I was far too achy to move and, in the spirit of compassion, I decided to extend some to my overly frisky parasite. In a mad moment, I wrote it a poem.

A love letter to a flesh-eating parasite

You ate away at me,
or tried to at least.
Piece by piece
you tore my flesh for lunch
and considered my nose
and soft palate
a potential light snack.
Something for later, perhaps.

An unusual choice of feast
British meat, a rarity,
I wouldn't say delicacy, though,
although delicate indeed
what lies beneath all of us
flesh, bones,
the beating fear
of silence.

Yet somehow we found each other
entwined over a poorly laid spread.
You were rude if I'm honest,
turned up unannounced.
I hadn't got much in,
except my neck,
and that was pretty unwashed.
Salty mind,

it was the best I could do
at such short notice.

You didn't really introduce yourself
properly either,
leishmaniasis,
I'm still not sure I'm saying it right.
I guess sometimes,
in the heat of the moment names don't matter.
I know you don't know mine.

For what it's worth,
I'm sorry it ended so badly,
I mean the scalpel to the neck
was probably more painful to me than you.
But the drugs,
those slow-aching three weeks,
21 days picking apart the damage
like an old woman
struggling with a zip.
That, I'm sure, wasn't fun for you.

I know your break-ups aren't usually so aggressive,
but I figured a decisive ending was for the best.
I've heard from others that sometimes
you disappear of your own accord,
I'd say ghosting but given the circumstances
that doesn't seem appropriate.
I couldn't risk you coming back,
I wanted a clean break, you see,
I hope you don't mind.
My friend said she burned you,

boiling cow fat
searing into her skin
seemed like a more painful option.
She didn't have a choice.

I did think about you, you know,
toward the end.
I cried tears so salty
I thought they could pickle you.
They even monitored my heart
because of you.
It didn't break,
but if I think about you hard enough
it might.
I thought about you as my blood flowed,
analyzed to see how far you'd
got under my skin.
Drugs threatened to close my veins
to you as I could no longer
close my mind.

You've gone,
at least we think so.
You never really know, though, do you,
with lovers that really bury deep.
They have a strange habit of turning
up again unannounced.

I still think about you,
every day, in fact.
I see your mark in the mirror,
that random love bite,

a mark of compassion
for I know you got under my skin,
and will get under others' too,
one billion potentially,
I know I'm not special to you.
Although, please, next time,
if you fancy a munch
do call before you pop over for lunch.

I'm often asked, was it worth it? Would you do the trip again? It's a hard one to answer, as I feel very different to the woman who set off on the journey. Perhaps it's best explained by asking you a question. Would you give up the best moments of your life if it meant you never experienced the worst?

Focus on the what-nows, not the what-ifs

Undoubtedly, it was the adventure of a lifetime and there is much I would do differently. But like with most things in life, there's little point in regret. Our knocks, our setbacks, may leave little bruises and sore spots along the way. In some ways they make us more fragile. Yet this fragility is also our source of strength: knowing that we got up, we fought on and we're ultimately stronger for it. As Dr Walker told me, we need to take things step by step. I've personally found that ruminating on the what-ifs leads me down a dark pit. I feel most comfort by focusing on the what-nows. Leishmaniasis left me with many things, my favourite being a sense of purpose. It is an opportunity to shine a light on an issue that sorely needs sunshine.

Unfortunately, there is no test to see if the parasite has gone for good. You just have to keep a beady eye out for any signs it's returned for a binge of skin. As fate would have it, while I was putting the finishing touches to this book, I noticed some weird lumps at the back of my throat. Thankfully, I got them checked and it appears they are fine, but they will be re-examined again in six months, as there is always a chance the parasite may spread. I wish I could give you that "happily ever after" ending, with loose ends and questions tied up neatly in a bow but, as you've probably gathered by now, that's not how life works.

"So, the strain of parasite you had can turn into mucocutaneous leishmaniasis?" Charlie asked when I told him about the weird lumps. "Is that what they found in the autopsy last time?"

We both broke into a fit of laughter as we realized his error.

"I think the word you're looking for, Charlie, is *biopsy*," I said in between gasping for breath. "I'm not dead yet."

It's true. I'm not dead yet, and neither are you. Yes, there are still days when life feels overwhelming, when we're delivered news that makes us want to fall apart. However, if the expedition has taught me anything, it's that we're capable of more than we think.

Three years on, as I've been writing this book, Guyana, too, has undergone much change. The country now has one of the fastest-growing economies in the world. In 2015, a gigantic oil discovery offshore in the Atlantic Ocean was one of the largest finds of the decade. Production began in earnest in 2020. The oil has the potential to transform the fortunes of the nation. How the country will navigate the economic, political and environmental issues this throws up remains to be seen.

And my teammates? Thankfully, they've been doing well. Laura's bum is now boil-free. Far from being put off by family life in the jungle, Laura, Ed and Ran decided to live off-grid on an Indonesian Island for a month, filming a TV show for Discovery Channel: *Man Woman Child Wild*. After sadly miscarrying twin girls, they found out that Laura was pregnant again – with twins. Molly and Milly have now been welcomed into the world.

Ness found a wonderful man, Jake, and they've bought a farm in Yorkshire. Remarkably, raising hogs is part of the plan. Jon got married and lives in Germany with his wife and their little girl, Liv. Fay's met someone and is pregnant, and her lodge and fishing business are going from strength to strength. Ant and Nigel tell me our Waî Waî teammates are keeping well. Romel is still loving hanging out with his not-so-baby Ray.

As for me, I started the most challenging and rewarding adventure of my life; Charlie and I are now parents to little Willow. Willow, the wonderfully effervescent soul she is, has put life into perspective even further. Becoming a parent has made me want to be so much better than I am – and leave her and her generation a planet where nature still sings.

The jungle has not left me and it's unlikely it ever will. The spirit of the river still runs through my veins. My mind often walks with my teammates, reliving our adventures as we paddled our way through the canopy. As for my body, it carries its own unique scar from the rainforest, an unusual sort of love bite. It has become a constant reminder, perhaps the only lesson we ever really need: life is beautiful, and life is fragile – embrace it.

Kit List

Essequibo River kit and sponsors

Our expedition partners:
Transglobe Expedition Trust
Canon
Kayak
Nuzest
Mooncup
NRS
Craghoppers (Pip only)

Kit sponsors:
Vivobarefoot
Powertraveller
Altberg
DD Hammocks
Firepot
Inmarsat

General kit

On the water

- NRS Outlaw Inflatable Kayak
- NRS Chinook OS Fishing Personal Floatation Device
- NRS Ripple Kayak Paddle
- NRS Pro Rescue Throw Bag
- NRS 110L Heavy-Duty Bill's Bag
- NRS 65L Heavy-Duty Bill's Bag
- NRS Watershed Dry Duffle
- NRS 1" HD Tie-Down Straps
- NRS Women's Boater's Gloves – Closeout
- WRSI Current Helmet
- River knives (including NRS Co-Pilot Knife)
- A compact handpump (NRS K-Pump 20)

- A hose pump (NRS Super High Pressure Pump)
- NRS rope and carabiners
- NRS inflatable repair kit
- 24 hours of emergency food each
- Waterproof phone case

Footwear:

- Vivobarefoot Ultra III (Ness and Laura's kayaking shoes)
- Vivobarefoot Primus Trail SG (Pip's kayaking shoes)
- Altberg Jungle Boot Microlite MoD Brown (trekking shoes)

Sleeping:

- DD Frontline Hammock
- DD Whoopie Suspension Kit
- DD SuperLight Tarp
- DD Paracord (25m) (for use as a tarp ridgeline etc.)
- Sleeping bag liner
- Travel pillowcase
- Rab Neutrino Endurance 600 Sleeping Bag

Food (to supplement fish we caught)

- Firepot dehydrated meals
- Rice
- Oats
- Sugar

- Cinnamon
- Nuts
- Raisins
- Lentils
- Coffee
- Tea
- Milk powder
- Tofu chunks
- Garlic seasoning
- Mixed herb seasoning
- Granola
- M&Ms
- Milky Way bars
- Peanut butter
- Sweets
- Cookies
- Small bottle of El Dorado rum each

Cooking

- Letherman (multi-tool)
- Clipper Lighter
- Thin strips of bike inner tube for lighting fires
- Emergency fire starter kit
- Light My Fire Spork
- LocknLock Box
- Nalgene 1L Water Bottle
- ThermoCafé Desk Mug
- Nuzest Clean Lean Protein (powdered protein)
- Nuzest Good Green Stuff (powdered nutrients)

- 12-in. fishing hooks
- Four-piece cooking-pot set (lids double as frying pans)

Electrical

- Sealey G1000I Generator Inverter
- Plug adaptors
- Solar panels and battery packs (Powertraveller Solargorilla and Extreme)
- Inmarsat BGAN
- Inmarsat IsatPhone
- iPhones
- Cables
- Athlete's foot cream and antifungal powder
- Talcum powder
- General antibiotics
- Vaseline
- Extensive medical and trauma kit
- "Foo foo" bag (a bag you fill with talcum powder that's big enough to fit your foot in. You administer before bed and it helps prevent trench foot.)
- Dettol Soap in small LocknLock
- Toothbrush
- Toothpaste
- Compact deodorant
- Avalon Organics Shampoo
- Handbook on medicine in remote areas

Pip's personal kit

- Craghoppers NosiLife Sydney Womens Hooded Top
- Barmah Hat — 1064 Foldaway Cooler Suede Hickory
- Craghoppers NosiLife socks
- Craghoppers NosiLife Adventure II Long-Sleeved Shirt
- Craghoppers NosiLife Pro II Trousers
- Craghoppers Apex Waterproof Jacket
- Craghoppers Voyager Hybrid Jacket
- Lululemon Yoga Pants
- Sunglasses
- Pants
- Bandana
- Loose top
- Petzl Head Torch
- Packet of emergency Sour Squirms Jelly Sweets (The Natural Confectionary Company) given to me by Charlie for a "bad day"
- Picture of me and Charlie dancing
- Moisturizer and eye cream
- *Jungle Survival (Air Ministry Survival Guide)*

Note: Please consult a professional if you are embarking on an expedition.

Acknowledgements

My first thank you is to you. Thank you for taking the time and coming along for the ride. If something resonated, please let me know as I'd love to hear about your own journey through life.

The biggest thank you (and subsequent apology) has to go to Charlie – one of the world's shining lights and a hater of soppy, sentimental, public outpourings of love. Charlie, you're my best friend, rock and sounding board. Thank you for everything you've done to enable this book to happen. Life just wouldn't be the same without you.

To Willow, little "Sprout", you've changed our lives in the best way possible. You've shown us love like no other and inspire us every day to be better than we are. Turns out, you're the best adventure of all. Thanks for reminding me of this on days when writing a book seemed an impossible task.

To Mum and Dad, thank you for laying the foundations of wanderlust and giving me and Jo the confidence to shape our own paths. Mum, I really am sorry I put you through so many sleepless nights (although I promise you the baby caiman really was cute).

To Jo, my little (but wiser) sister, thank you for going through the book with a fine-tooth comb. You inspire me daily and I'm so lucky to be travelling through life with you.

To Laura Bingham, you're truly one of the funniest, most inspiring trailblazers I know. None of this would have been possible without you. To both you and Ness Knight, your friendship in the jungle, and subsequently, has meant so much. You are two of the kindest and strongest people I know in both mind and body. We started this journey as relative strangers and returned as friends, bonded by belly-laughs, near-death experiences and a rogue, smelly pair of hog-stained pants. Ladies, I'll always be here for you.

To the community of Masakenari, thank you for your warm welcome and help with the journey. Your kindness will never be forgotten.

To Cemci Suse, Nereus Chekema, Nigel Issacs, Jackson Marawanaru, Aaron Marawanaru, Ant Shushu, Romel Shoni, Fay James and Jon Williams, thank you for patience, guidance and knowledge. You guys made the trip what it was. Together we created memories that will last a lifetime.

To Ed Stafford, thank you for being so generous with your time and advice. You're a real-life superhero with a heart of gold.

To Sophia Hauch and Anders Andersen, thank you for your hard work in organizing the logistics of the expedition on the ground in Guyana – and your subsequent help with this book. Knowing you were on the other end of a sat phone was a huge relief. Also, thank you in memorandum to Ian Craddock who steered us in your direction.

To the adventure community, thank you for embracing this expedition and offering us support on the way. So many people have helped us with the expedition (you know who you are) but special thanks to Chris Murnin, Andy Oughton, David Bain, Gabi Ridge, Al Pace, Sandy Loder, Dave Connell. Thank you for spending so much of your time helping us before we set off.

To my friends, thank you for your support, advice and love. You wonderful lot are the glue of life.

To my agents, Jo Cantello and Jonathan Cantello of Wolfsong Media, thank you for both caring for and believing in me.

To Chris Hoare, thank you so much for organizing my unedited diary and the research you did around it. Your interest in the trip has been both wonderful and insightful.

To our sponsors, thank you for your support and getting this trip off the ground.

Finally, to the Summersdale team... Debbie Chapman, thank you for championing this book (and others in this space) in the first place.

Claire Berrisford, you are the most wonderful editor I could have wished for. Thank you for guiding me through a very different jungle. Your patience, kindness and support has been incredible.

Before I started this process I had very little idea of how many people are involved in getting a book out. To the team at Summersdale, you have been the backbone of the whole process, breathing life into and bringing eyeballs to these words. A sincere thank you to everyone involved.

Publishing Director: Claire Plimmer
Senior Commissioning Editor: Debbie Chapman
Editor: Claire Berrisford
Copyeditor: Daniela Nava
Proofreader: Ross Dickinson
Design: Rita Eccles, Faye Lewis and Marianne Thompson
Typesetter: Clint MacDonald
Marketing & Publicity: Jasmin Burkitt
Sales: Claire Bradley, Aerran Keller, Philippa Painter and Rachel Rees
Finance: Maria Ball and Helen Belton
Rights: Irina Bruneli and Amy Hunter
Production: Kenneth McKay
Printers: CPI Print

About the Author

Pip Stewart is a mum, partner and writer.

She has a degree in history and politics from Oxford and a master's in journalism from the University of Hong Kong.

Pip has cycled halfway around the world and completed a world-first paddle down Guyana's Essequibo River. On one of her adventures she got a bit too up close and personal with a sandfly and found a flesh-eating parasite munching through her neck as a result. After contracting leishmaniasis, Pip now campaigns to raise awareness of neglected tropical diseases.

When not writing, she can usually be found outside with her partner, Charlie, and daughter, Willow.

Connect and share your own adventures through life: @PipStewart.

Trademarks

Altberg is a registered trademark of Alt Berg Holdings Ltd.; Avalon Organics is a registered trademark of Avalon Natural Products, Inc.; Barmah Hats is a registered trademark of Desert Oak Trading Pty Ltd.; Canon is a registered trademark of Canon Inc.; Clipper is a registered trademark of Flamagas, SA; Craghoppers is a registered trademark of Craghoppers Ltd.; DD Hammocks is a registered trademark of DD Hammocks Ltd.; Dettol is a registered trademark of Reckitt Benckiser (UK) Ltd.; El Dorado is a trademark of Demerara Distillers Ltd.; Firepot is a registered trademark of Outdoorfood Ltd.; Haribo is a registered trademark of Holding GmbH & Co. KG; Inmarsat is a registered trademark of The International Mobile Satellite Organization; iPhone is a registered trademark of Apple Inc.; Kayak is a registered trademark of Kayak Software Corporation; Leatherman is a registered trademark of Leatherman Tool Group, Inc.; Light My Fire is a registered trademark of Light My Fire Sweden AB; LocknLock is a registered trademark of Lock & Lock Co., Ltd.; Lululemon is a registered trademark of Lululemon Athletica Canada Inc.; M&Ms is a registered trademark of Mars, Inc.; McVitie's Jaffa Cakes is a registered trademark of United Biscuits (UK) Limited; Milky Way is a registered trademark of Mars, Inc.; Mooncup is a registered trademark of Mooncup Ltd.; Nalgene is a registered trademark of Thermo Fisher Scientific Inc.; NRS is a registered trademark of Northwest River Supplies, Inc.; Nuzest is a registered trademark of Nuzest IP Pty Ltd.; Petzl is a registered trademark of BIG BANG; Powertraveller is a registered trademark of Powertraveller International Ltd.; Rab is a registered trademark of Equip Outdoor Technologies UK Ltd.; Sealey is a registered trademark of Jack Sealey Ltd.; The Natural Confectionary Company is a registered trademark of Mondelez International AMEA Pte. Ltd.; THERMOCafé by Thermos is a registered trademark of Thermos LLC; Vaseline is a registered trademark of Unilever Global IP Ltd.; Vivobarefoot is a registered trademark of Vivobarefoot Ltd.; WhatsApp is a registered trademark of WhatsApp LLC

Inside cover images

1. Umana in Masakenari
2. Ness, Cemci and Pip pushing upstream on the way to the source
3. Cemci preparing fish on the blade of his wooden paddle
4. (From left to right) Aaron, Nereus, Jackson and Nigel in the dugout canoes
5. (From left to right) Nigel, Nereus, Jackson and Aaron preparing turu fruit
6. Nereus taking an axe to a fallen tree on the way to the source
7. Jackson happy we found a creek
8. (From left to right) Jackson, Cemci and Aaron on the way to the source
9. The hammock – our refuge for the expedition
10. Sheer exhaustion during the hike; (from left to right) Laura, Pip, Ness
11. Making our way to the source
12. Drone shot of the Essequibo
13. Ness passes out
14. Taking on the rapids
15. The river crew pose for a photo at Sloth Island Nature Resort; (from left to right) Ant, Pip, Ness, Laura, Fay, Romel
16. A happy day messing around in the water; (from left to right) Laura, Ant, Romel, Ness, Pip
17. Rice and fish cooking over the campfire
18. A full and double rainbow at Fay's resort, King William Adventures
19. Reunion – the joy of seeing Charlie again
20. Ant and Romel pose by rapids
21. Laura, Ed and Ran at Fay's Lodge, King William Adventures
22. Trench foot, a.k.a. my career as a foot-model is over
23. Fay helping us plan a route through the forks in the river; (from left to right) Ness, Pip, Fay, Laura
24. A hummingbird pops up to say hello
25. Pulling up to a dredger to ask for water
26. Cameraman Jon ready for action
27. The joy at approaching the finish; (from left to right) Romel, Ant, Laura, Pip, Ness, Fay
28. Pulling up for a quick rest as we hit the Atlantic Ocean
29. Fay and Laura battling a strong headwind
30. Celebration as we finish the expedition; (from left to right) Romel, Pip, Ant, Laura, Ness, Fay
31. In hospital undergoing treatment for leishmaniasis

Images 1, 3, 4, 5, 6, 7, 11, 17, 18, 20, 22, 23, 25, 26 and 31 © Pip Stewart
Images 2, 8, 10 and 16 © Laura Bingham
Images 9, 12, 13, 14, 15, 19, 21, 24, 27, 28, 29 and 30 © Jon Williams; www.jon-w.com

Have you enjoyed this book?

If so, why not write a review on your favourite website?

If you're interested in finding out more about our books,
find us on Facebook at **Summersdale Publishers**,
on Twitter at **@Summersdale** and on Instagram at
@summersdalebooks. We'd love to hear from you!

Thanks very much for buying this Summersdale book.

www.summersdale.com